Memoirs from a Prison Cell Trilogy: The Missteps of a Southern Boy

by

Terry Hill Sr.

Printed in the United States of America

First Printing, 2017

ISBN 13: 9781542766333
ISBN 10: 1542766338

Terry Hill Sr. Company
114 129th St S UNIT 19
Parkland, WA 98444
(360) 842-4286

FB.ME/Terrywaynehillsr.com

Authors Notes

I would like to extend this special thanks to my family, friends, editors, and readers who have endured this entire arduous and intimidating process with me.

For the sake of my mental and physical health, I injected a healthy dose of hilarity into these memoirs. Because now that my God-given conscious reemerged, depression started to engulf me. Nine prison stints, cracked-filled decades, womanizing, and negligence had driven me to the brink of insanity.

As you embark on this odyssey through my mind, I hope you remain open minded. Believe it or not, this fertile ground took nine prison stints and twenty plus drug-plagued years. Therefore, I ask that you take care in mining this fertile ground.

To respect the anonymity of others, I paraphrased some dialogue, especially for those who asked.

For those with skewed views (like I once had), I have purposely omitted the violence and the detailing of contrivance.

I, again, thank you for reading my memoirs. I wholeheartedly hope you have gleaned something that might lighten your families, friends, and neighbor's cumbersome load.

Remember: Never give up on anyone. Not for any reason. If a wretch like me can claw my way out of my self-imposed abyss – so can the next person.

Terry Wayne Hill Sr.

Acknowledgments

A great number of people have effected positive change in my life; some of you for my entire life. It is only fair that I pay homage to you all.

The Hill family: John Willy Hill: I love you, Dad. I have stepped up as the Patriarch. I am on a mission to snuff out some of the dysfunctionalism that's been plaguing our family. I'm going to make you proud.

Leola Hill: Mama, I profoundly appreciate your gallant attempts at corralling the family. Your knee-baby has thrust himself into the position of Patriarch. Promise to make you proud.

Thank you, sis, Patricia Hill-Hall, for your willingness to put in the work that will give our family a sense of normalcy. I love you forevermore.

Jimmy Hill: We haven't spoken since '91, I love ya bro. Do I have to dragnet Dallas, Texas to find you?

Jimmy William Hill: Although you are not around, I know you would be proud of me, proud that at last, I made it out of the Life.

Robert Hill: You have always been there for me, especially back in the days. Now, I plan to be there for you. I could never thank you enough.

Ronald Hill: It warms my heart that we are recapturing our long lost brotherly love. Let's never lose it again.

Mark Hill: You were/are a motivating force in my life. I am, more so than ever, vicariously using your positive qualities to propel me forward.

Renata Gant: My lovely daughter, all your life, for me, you have been a tough nut to crack, and that being within good reason. However, I am a firm believer it is never too late to claim birthrights. Thank you for your love. The best of our union is yet to come.

Lekrisha Lee: God bless you, my beautiful daughter, I am overjoyed that you have always welcomed me into your life with open arms, even when I had fallen short as a father. Given you are a God-fearing lady, you know that He will strengthen our bond.

Terrell Hill: You have a heart of gold, my son. Your forgiving nature has always confounded me. I am privileged to share your DNA.

Terry Hill Jr.: I am overjoyed that you have welcomed me into your life and we have had the time to bask in some quality time together, which has been a long time coming. Thanks for assisting me in becoming the Patriarch of the family.

My Fresno family: Aunt Betty, Aunt Loretta, Uncle Ernest, and Uncle James (J.J.), Thank you for always being there for me, especially during the 90's when I was in and out of prison and running rampant on drugs. Your being there played an integral part in my evolution. Love you all.

The Russell family: Unbeknownst to you, you have played a pivotal part in my making a turnabout. In a subtle manner, you taught me that it is never too late to build a sound character.

Chaplin Shannon O'Donald: I love and respect you for all the benevolence you have displayed to those of us in prison. I equally thank you for founding the Writers Group in which you helped foster a slew of talent.

Robert Miller: Your editorial prowess will forever be in demand. You were there for me when I couldn't place a comma, and couldn't transition from one paragraph to another. However, what I found to be of the utmost importance was when you told me my writing was garbage, but in the same breath, you told me I was a hell of a storyteller. That I needed to hear.

5

Kristine Schwartz: Your editorial skills truly complemented my memoirs. You help me get from the homestretch to the finish line. Your professionalism is impeccable, and I cannot wait to work with you in the future. Thanks a million.

Washington Corrections Officers: Those of you who took the time to read and talk to me about my memoirs for all those years, I am grateful. You were my launchpad.

Oran Jones (O.J.): You are my hero. After being incarcerated for over 45 years, you are still the most positive person I know. People in Washington State are still clamoring for your release. We hope that one day justice will be served and you will walk out of there a free man.

Terry Washington (Seattle T.): Your friendship transcends time, even prison time. I don't know how you did it, but you are the only person who got me summoned to the phone behind prison walls (on many occasions). You have a great mother, Joyce Hall; she has been there for you through thick and thin. Today, thankfully, she is like a mother to me.

Donald Thomas: You kept it real! You did so at a time when I was experiencing a haze from being a newly released prisoner. Aiding in my transition from prison to work release so that it was not too bumpy. From one author to another, thank you.

Jeff and Judy Du Guay: Transitioning back to society after being gone for thirteen years is unfathomable to most. Nevertheless, the fact remains that once a month, year after year, you came inside to see about me. Our love *still* stands tall.

Trugena Hardin: I love you, you need to know that. Although we are a bit detached these days, you are forever engraved upon my heart. If you ever need me, I will be around.

Armond Haydel (A.J.): I couldn't say enough about you if I wanted to. Like Donald, you assisted in my transition, back to society and still are through your moral support. I couldn't ask for a better friend.

The Horns: Jackie, John, Jamila, Regina, and Felicia, you will always be my extended family. I love all of you.

Tinamarie Ames: Thanks for bringing an array of talent and IT knowledge to the table. I especially thank you for your genuine friendship. I look forward to you being in my life for years to come. Thanks immensely.

Angle Cooper: You know me better than most. That said your support and belief in what I am doing means the world to me. Thank you, my friend. I will always have a special place in my heart for you.

Octavia: I cannot thank you enough for the finance, the time, and most importantly the mental energy you invested in Memoirs from a Prison Cell, and our friendship.

Aro Williams-Walker (T.J.): We adopted one another. You started calling me Pops; I started calling you son. Thanks for being an integral part of my commitment to change.

John Carlisle: Nephew. For me, it was a good day when a young brother of your caliber commenced to calling me Unc. Over the years, I too have eyed your positive change. And will continue to do so as long as you allow me to.

Steve Johnson: You are a true friend. I remember that you used to get goose-bumps when you talked about the success of my Memoirs. Guess what? Today is publication day.

Karlton Daniels (Knowledge): You are the brother that first tapped into my artsy nature. You invited me to the Writers Group, where you composed a poem in five minutes. Since then, I have become a fledgling writer. Thanks, Bro.

Dennis Trout: God bless you. You were there from the beginning. I deeply appreciate all of your input, even the first speech you helped me write. I love you brother.

Dan Maughan: I am forever indebted to you, my friend. You were my loyal typist and proofreader during the early stages of the Memoirs. Thank you. You were most helpful. I love you big fellow.

Joe Goree (JoJo): Thank you for being a good friend way-back-when I was on my last leg because of the cocaine. Thank you even more for being a friend to me in prison when I was finding my way. Thank you for believing in me as a writer. Now, what are we going to do about moving these books? LOL!

Vicki Bomsta: Thanks for all of the correspondence since 2000. I am still a man of my word, I will be visiting you in Puyallup.

Loretta Cardenas: Thank you for being a true friend for the past fifteen years. Looking forward to the next ...

Jalloreyann Meacham: You entered my life when I needed a friend. I was new in town and you offered unconditional support. Thank you.

Introduction

Memoirs from a Prison Cell Trilogy:
Missteps of a Southern Boy

What is the measure of life? Many standards have measured success, but throughout history people who achieve the most extraordinary feats offer the following advice: No matter what, never give up! And so it seems, those who have endured the greatest hardships and challenges rise from the ashes. Though they are often alone and without resource and comfort, they rise and meet the challenge, becoming more than they ever would have been without the journey. Terry Hill is, in my opinion, such an individual. He has lived for most of his life in the war zone, yet through self-discipline, study, and commitment, he has grown into a man of integrity, respect, and sincere empathy.

Through his writing, he healed the wounds of the past. It has provided cathartic release and healing for what was, for years, the life of a crack addict. But his primary purpose and motivation have always been to serve as a lesson for those who would follow after him. This memoir is his contribution. It is his song.

The culture of the life or the underbelly as Terry describes it was ingrained in him from childhood. And so it was into the life that he vested his considerable intelligence, charm, and desire. As with many addicts, he expected to outgrow the need for the flash and seduction of the life. Unfortunately, time ran on, and as the years grew to span decades, he vacillated between prison and the life until he transforms.

He has been given a second chance at life and afforded the opportunity to make amends for what was lost while his addiction raged. As any recovering addict knows, the process of healing involves making amends for past behavior and lost opportunities.

As a father, who holds his four adult children close to his heart, this memoir is his legacy to them; he hopes it will illuminate the man he has become while allowing them to understand the cost and the pain of his journey. Although Terry Hill cannot go back to change time, he hopes his children will one day understand he didn't fail them due to any fault in them, but because he was plagued by the illness and insanity of a drug addiction.

Now in his fifties, Terry Hill has spent years of his life in prison. Many who survive the terror and isolation of prison are forever changed. Tragically the trauma of such an experience often leaves men crippled by the conditioning of that harsh environment; they become a haunted shadow of who they once were—institutionalized. This term is a sterile representation of what is, in truth, the devastation of the human spirit. Those who survive are so haunted by the harsh experience they often resemble prisoners of war. Traumatized and abused, they are no longer capable of autonomy—they have retreated so deeply they cannot find their way back.

Men who can take the horrific reality of decades of trauma and use it to transform themselves into strong, mature, compassionate men, are exceptional, and rare. Terry Hill is such a man. After a lifetime of the hardest lessons, he has become a man full grown; known by many as a wise elder, willing to extend himself to men floundering in prison. He offers hope and strength to all who are privileged to call him a friend. I count myself privileged indeed to know him.

As he recounts his life, his voice is warm and compassionate, and though many moments strike at the heart, his tale is full of humor, personal insight, and humility. He wrote his story for you, hoping it would reach those who might take comfort and hope from his journey. Perhaps his life will stand, as he hopes, as a warning for those who think to choose the life.

Octavia Braman, Psy. D.

Consciousness
By Doyle Watters

Like most old friends, we enjoyed one another's company.

Talked about the past and the changes we'd been through.

In matter-of-fact language, up came the topic of birth.

He was born in sixty-three, the year of I Have a Dream.

Black and proud had not arrived, nor the clenched fist-salute.

Despite the struggle of so many, poverty continued its scourge.

As he stared at the razor wire, tell-me-more were my thoughts.

With head bowed, abused and forgotten, he described childhood.

"Moving home to home, life seemed worthless," he paused.

"I felt alone and ashamed," his statements caught me off guard.

As tears slowly filled his eyes, I refrained from saying a word.

Lifting his head, he sighed and began to smile.

Not sure what he was thinking, I knew time would tell.

Questions put on hold, while moving our process forward.

Respect was mutual, but our thoughts remained guarded.

Approaching the past, often difficult, we tread with respect.

Boundaries crossed, broken, rebuilt and redeemed.

A thin line walked regardless of nationality, is generational.

Then one day he mentioned the desire to become an author.

To articulate a book so his sires would know him.

My response, "Only you can hold you back." He grinned.

A manuscript in hand, he asked for honest feedback.

As I read, I admired his strength, and even saw some of myself.

The flow captured my desire for more; it was very profound.

Forgiveness fueled his urge to go beyond mediocrity.

With the stroke of a pen, he transformed anger into life.

Bloodline once deserted, was chased into the quiet of night.

12

He realized the love he thought betrayed him, was his own.
With the nightmares of youth subdued, he's finally become free.
Devotion will decide the distance and success of his journey.

Chapter One

IT'S STILL HARD FOR ME TO imagine how different times were in the early fifties. At twelve years old, my mother, Leola, was smitten by a six-foot-three, bowlegged, gap-toothed, twenty-year-old boy named John Willie Hill. Society must have been blind, simply looked the other way, or perhaps those were the arrangements back then.

On April 29, 1963, I came into the world, the seventh of eight children born to a poor black family in rural Louisiana. Leola was only thirteen when she started bearing children. By the time I came along, she had little time or attention to give me.

My father, John, was an abusive, alcoholic womanizer who drank away his paycheck before ever setting foot in the house.

During my childhood, our family rented a small shack from a farmer in Gibsland, Louisiana. Our house was a small, second residence on the back of the owner's farm. My family was poor, with little to wear and less to eat. On holidays and birthdays, we never, not once, received presents of any kind.

Our family survived on a minimal diet of pancakes with sugar-water syrup. The rest of the time we only had old, leftover biscuits that a nearby aunt periodically brought by. There was never any meat. *Ever.* On blessed but rare occasions, a pot of beans supplemented our biscuit and pancake diet.

We'd cook over an open fire because our father never paid for the oil needed to power the stove, let alone heat the house. With no electricity or heat, we suffered in the cold of winter and sweltered in the heat of summer. My mother tried to sustain her children by working odd jobs, but uneducated and unskilled, she was unable to improve our situation.

Even as a child, my sister, Patricia, who was only ten, worked by feeding the farmer's cows. With both parents gone most of the time, Patricia raised her seven little brothers. She did most of the cooking, especially after Mark, the last baby, was born.

When I was three, the landlord evicted my family from the little house on the farm for failure to pay rent. To stay off the streets, we moved into a tiny one-bedroom shack in Winnfield, a nearby town in Winn Parish. With nine of us crammed into the one-bedroom house, the living conditions were awful, but at the time, there were no other options.

Although Dad was a logger, he never brought his earnings home. Instead, he would hang out at the bars and get drunk after work. He would spend his money on other women instead of his family. It was known not only by our Mom, but all of us, that Dad was having relationships with other women. If that wasn't enough, family stress was compounded following the death of an older sibling.

Dad's behavior was a continuing source of contention in our household, the cause of many altercations, verbal and physical, between him and Mom. Even though Mom had eight children, being in her twenties, she was still very young. It was obvious to me, even at my tender age, our situation and living conditions disturbed her.

Despite the destruction of our family, Dad continued to disrespect Mom. He continued to drink away what little money he earned, and he continued to womanize right in Mom's face, and all this despite, during this time, having sired seven surviving children out of wedlock. When he did come home, there was always arguing, yelling, and fighting. Though I was young, I still remember the noise, the chaos, and the drinking that occurred when he was around.

My sister recalls times my father was physically abusive, not only to Mom but to us. When in a rage, he would swear and beat us whenever he could reach us. Dad would not only use his fists to hit Mom and us but would also grab any other item nearby to strike us. Those beatings included blows to our heads.

In '67, when I was only four, my parents separated due to father's alcoholism, abuse, womanizing, and financial abandonment. However, my parents did not just go their separate ways. This separation involved the complete and total dissolution of our family. My mother decided to go to Seattle where her mother lived, but she was unable to take us all with her, and Dad wasn't about to take responsibility for any of us. Thus, we were split up among the neighbors. I was so young that I believed the neighbors adopted me, even though my last name remained unchanged and there were never any adoption papers. These arrangements were not formal adoptions, and no state office or child protection agency handled the fostering. Instead, we were just given away to the neighbors, abandoned by our parents.

This transition happened to us with no forewarning or preparation. Mom just awoke one morning and announced she was leaving us to go to Seattle and that we would be separated and sent away to live with the neighbors. By nightfall, separate residences housed each of us. We were isolated from each other. This occurrence was very traumatic, and we all cried inconsolably. The accepting families, to make matters worse, were not close friends of Mom's, nor even people who were known to us, but were merely elderly couples living nearby who had somehow made Mom's acquaintance. These couples were apparently familiar with our family struggles from having seen us out and about on the streets of the neighborhood, looking poor, grubby, and uncared for, runny-nosed and hungry-eyed, wearing poorly fitted, and inadequate clothing. None of the elderly couples that took us in had children of their own.

Our grandmother, who lived in Seattle, came to Louisiana and took Mom back to Washington State, where she remained until she died in 1999.

My sister, Patricia, was the only sibling unable to escape father, as a neighbor didn't take her in as they did the rest of us. It wasn't until 1969, two years later, that Mom sent for her to come to Seattle.

When Mom finally sent for her only daughter, she also arranged for the baby of the family, Mark, to come to Seattle as well. Over the next decade, Mom slowly gathered her children back to her in Seattle, one by one. She sent for me last. For years, I questioned that. Why was I the last one? I stayed in Louisiana for another decade before I made the transition.

After Mom had left, Dad did not provide any care for, or keep in contact with, any of us children. In 1969, Dad moved to Houston, Texas, to take advantage of the construction boom, and that's where he remained until he passed in 2006, still estranged to the family he left behind.

Chapter Two

WHEN MY FAMILY WAS SPLIT UP, John and Inez Williams took me in. Inez was a licensed kindergarten teacher. John lived on his pension and worked odd jobs as a carpenter's helper. There were also extracurricular activities that I would come to know oh-too-well.

John was a nice guy, reserved, who stood about five-foot-seven. On the other hand, Inez was quite the opposite in stature and temperament. She stood about five-foot-eleven and weighed one hundred and ninety pounds. Because she didn't believe in sparing-the-rod-and-spoiling-the-child, she strictly enforced a no-nonsense policy. Many felt her wrath, including adults. I consider this period in my life to be the calm before the storm.

Although I was isolated from my family and terribly lonely, my life was still better because at least they were able to meet my basic needs. Inez was a great cook and John was no slouch, either. Whenever she was too busy, John's cooking more than sufficed. Every chance Inez got, she preserved fruit, vegetables, or whatever, always keeping the cupboards and pantry full.

Inez baked some of the best cakes and pies one could fathom, but her specialty was chicken and dumplings. They were the epitome of what chicken and dumplings should be. I loved them until an unfortunate incident occurred, which I will elaborate on later.

For a while, I had other children to play with, which helped my loneliness. Some of us shared a friendship that evolved into high school. That same friendship afforded me the chance to attend several grand birthday parties.

I remember one party vividly. I was misbehaving and running through the house. It just so happened that my big nose came into full contact with a lamp stand. Blood gushed out from my nose onto my clothing and the floor. I thought Inez would comfort me, but to my astonishment, she delivered my first public butt-whipping. It was humiliating. It blistered my bottom for days, and my little heckling friends would never let me live it down.

The Williams lived in an old house with a tin roof and a big front porch. The old tin roof always seemed to leak whenever it rained, even if it was a mere sprinkle. John and Inez were adroit at placing jars and buckets under the leaky spots; it wasn't unusual to see them running around the house.

Thinking of the front porch brings remembrance to watermelons and flies. Many times, I sat on that front stoop eating watermelon and fighting flies. There wouldn't be a fly in sight until I brought out the watermelon. Then they would try to muscle me out of my piece. It was a wonder that I even got half.

There was also a shotgun shack (a tiny house that one could see straight through from the front door to the back) adjacent to the house. Inez used it as a kindergarten classroom. The kids addressed her by the nickname, "Miss Missy." They called John, "Uncle Buddy."

The property, which we resided on, was spacious. Inez had at least three gardens full of collard, mustard, and turnip greens, along with tomatoes and various other vegetables. Pecans, fig, and plum trees also populated the property. When the weather permitted, I played underneath them.

I remember those stormy nights when the rain and pecans would fall on the tin roof, impeding any form of sleep. By the same token, some nights the light rain against the tin roof served as a sedative.

There were ditches all over the place, some big and some small. They separated our property from the neighbors' like boundaries. Maybe that's where I developed my phobia of snakes. Back then, the drainage systems were poor. When it rained, the water rose and overflowed the ditches. Along with the water would come the snakes. They would seek refuge under anything they could find, including the house.

For some strange reason, every summer these snakes — called King snakes — would come crawling out from under our tin-roofed house. John would chop their heads off. In amazement, I would watch them flop around in their dismembered state. He told me they wouldn't die until the sun went down. Being young and naive, I believed him. Even today, I can't stand snakes.

Many of our neighbors grew plum trees and vegetables. The Sneeds come to mind. They kept their property immaculate, with a beautiful lawn, and perfectly trimmed hedges that served as a fence. I once thought the Sneeds were noisy as hell, but years later, I would come to find out they had reason to be.

Many butt-whippings were dispensed because of the Sneed's watchfulness. Whether it was my terrorizing their cats and kittens, or throwing objects too close to their windows, the Sneeds would always report my actions back to Inez, and I'd receive another butt-whipping.

To me, Mr. Sneed seemed like an old troll. He had built a bridge in front of his property, and I would play on it from time to time, but anyone who rode a bike across it or hung out too long on this bridge would witness the ugly side of Mr. Sneed. Like clockwork, he would mysteriously appear from behind a screened-in porch with his face contorted, arms flailing, yelling, loud and belligerent until the intruders disappeared.

The Sneeds had an adopted daughter named Betty. (Quite a few of the elderly couples in Winnfield had adopted children.) For some reason, Betty took a special interest in me. I often went to Sunday school and church with her. There were many Sundays when Inez took me too. For some reason, John never once came along.

Gradually, Betty and I spent more and more time together. I took it that she was just as lonely as I was. Besides, I think she looked at me as the little brother she never had. She was a prolific storyteller. To this very day, the Old Testament tales she shared still have a profound effect on me.

Betty was a very attractive young teenage tomboy with jet-black hair, a smooth caramel complexion, and a radiant smile that she'd flash at a moment's notice. We played together often. I think she was a gymnast of some sort, because, like one of her ragdolls, she would toss me every which way possible. I didn't have enough sense back then to be afraid, but a bad landing could have been fatal.

Abruptly, the kindergarten closed. I wanted to believe it was because I was starting the first grade. Inez enrolled me in Pinecrest, a segregated, all black school. Elementary, middle, and high school all fused into one.

The environment at Pinecrest unnerved me because it was a dog-eat-dog atmosphere. Most of the time I was there I was apprehensive in one way or another. Whether I was getting pushed out of line for the restroom or the typical old bully tactics, I felt constant anxiety.

As days came and went, I started looking around for my other siblings. The only one who surfaced at school was my brother Robert. I discovered he lived only a quarter of a mile away. Robert was tall for his age, so he became his brother's keeper. He was a brazen young lad and avenged the unwarranted cruelty that befell me.

Only coming in perhaps a couple of days a week, his school attendance was quite poor. Sadie, the elderly lady he lived with, was also John's aunt. She was sterner than Inez, so his many chores came before his schooling. By far, Sadie's property was larger than ours was, with bigger gardens and plenty of chickens. There was even a café and a boarding house on its grounds. There was always plenty for Robert to do.

I also knew that my brother Ronald, who was two years older than I was, lived directly behind me. He lived with Ms. Nan, a woman declining in years. What separated our two properties were wild trees and brushes. Later, Ron and I developed a signal to beckon one another. One of us would climb the tallest tree in our backyard and emit a Tarzan holler until the other would come forth.

Ronald never came to school; it seemed like he was under lock and key. Ms. Nan rarely allowed him to come over and play with me. There were times when I would go over and play with him, but even when playing with Ronald, the work always came first. There'd be a ton of firewood to stack before we could even think of playing. With the task completed, however, she would treat us to freshly baked cookies. Scrumptious as they were, this quickly became old, but it was tolerable because I knew I was helping to relieve my brother of his despair.

Robert's plight was similar, except Sadie was more abusive. She felt as though she couldn't get through to Robert unless she beat it into him. It was the same scenario whenever I visited Robert, work-before-play. But even then, most of the time — no play.

Sadie was a snuff-dipping, devout Christian, and the best cook I've ever encountered, even better than Inez (which is something I would never have told the woman). I would purposely visit Robert on the days Sadie was making donuts and churning ice cream. Sadie regularly cooked because of the clientele at her boarding house, and from the workers at the lumber mill. They all dined at her cafe.

My tenure at Pinecrest endured for two more years. At that time, Inez placed me in Eastside Elementary, an integrated school. Eastside was a mile and a half from where I lived. Inez would take me to school until she felt I wouldn't get hit by a car or get lost. After that, she would only walk me to the highway and go back home. I would continue on my way with other children who had been going to Eastside for years.

While passing, I watched as squirrels ran up and down the trees. (The thought continuously came to mind that these were the same ugly little rodents I'd been eating at home.) Birds also sang a sweet little morning melody that I cherished as I walked along.

During the latter part of the '60s, my daily journey to Eastside was always eventful. People peered out of their windows at me. Some expressed contempt, not wanting me walking through their neighborhoods. Dogs barked and chased me. I was fortunate enough to make it out unbitten, but I did get a few pant legs ripped in the process. Inez would become irate and punish me. Being a seamstress, she made most of my clothes.

Eastside provided me with a well-balanced diet for breakfast and lunch. While drinking milk for breakfast, I discovered I was lactose intolerant. A bubbling feeling in my stomach and frequent trips to the restroom were the telltale signs.

(On a camping trip, Inez and I were having a fish fry with several other families when suddenly my stomach commenced to boiling. Silly me, the growling in my stomach served me right.

How could I expect donuts, milk, and fish grease to sit well on a lactose intolerant stomach?

Faced with such an untimely conundrum, with no restroom in sight, I quickly summoned Inez. At this point in my life, I was dependent on her whenever I got myself in a bind. She always had a good presence of mind—the fixer upper.

"Follow me," she said.

As we walked 30-feet into a patch of thickets, I began scanning the area, who knows what for, a restroom out in the middle of the woods? Yeah, right!

"Now what?" I asked, earnestly.

"You see that clearing over there," she pointed, "between those trees?"

"Yes, why?"

"Well ... what are you waiting for? Go over and cop a squat."

"Inez, if it comes down to this, I will hold it."

"Boy ... now listen here, get your narrow behind over there and handle your business! I will not have you embarrassing yourself or me. Besides, if you could have held it in the first place, why do you have that awful, strained look on your face?"

In a rudimentary sense, I wouldn't have ever imagined being stuck out in the woods searching for accommodations under which normal circumstances I'd taken for granted. *Sure hope this doesn't get back to my heckling friends*, I thought.

"Inez, where are you going?"

"Away from here. I'm not going to stand here and watch you nor ... smell you. Try less talking and more..."

A minute had not yet passed before I snipped it off like a dog taking a dump startled by an assailant.

"Inez, I called out, I'm finished." Within seconds, I heard rustling and crackling.

My legs were starting to go numb. The position was awkward. Looking up in the nick of time, I caught sight of Inez reaching up into a tree collecting a handful of moss.

"Here boy, take this and clean yourself."

"What am I supposed to do with that ...?"

Chances were, that was the first time I'd ever muttered an expletive within earshot of Inez.

"Either figure it out or use your hands."

Because of that abrasive experience, the remainder of the trip was a total fiasco.)

After breakfast, we had a short interval before the bell rang for the first period. While making new friends, I would frolic on the sizable playground and meander from one piece of equipment to another. Nevertheless, once again, bullies — new ones — reared their ugly heads. Robert remained at Pinecrest, so having an Avenger was a thing of the past.

Scarface, the name of one bully, must have been a man-child. He possessed the strength of an ox. What I could lift with two hands, he could lift with one. His name alone instilled fear. No one took him lightly.

Despite having a lion's heart, I soon learned there were times it doesn't matter how much heart an individual has; if one's out-matched in skill, then half the battle's already lost.

Scarface lived only two country blocks from me; I ran into him everywhere. For some reason, he felt that he had to put me constantly out of my misery. And I felt that I had to let him constantly know that I was a formidable opponent. We continued to wage war until I departed for Seattle.

After I had acquired several black eyes and countless bruises, Inez would physically force me to battle this raging bull, or else I'd suffer her wrath. She wanted to make sure she wasn't raising a punk or a coward that couldn't protect himself. Just to spare my narrow backside from being scorched, I'd sometimes fib to her that someone had held me while Scarface took some cheap shots.

He also had two of the finest sisters in our neighborhood. Because of our animosity, I never introduced myself to them. He was always the "guard dog" standing between them and me.

Other than Scarface, going to school at Eastside wasn't too bad. The teachers seemed to care genuinely. I didn't apply myself to the fullest. I did just enough to keep Inez's savagery in check.

During every semester, and in every class, the first mistake I'd make would be to take a seat in the back of the class, right next to a window. I often heard the squirrels and the birds better than I heard my teachers. I daydreamed and gazed out the window so much that my teacher would bang on the chalkboard to get my attention, or they would put me on the spot by saying, "Terry, would you repeat what I just said?" To my classmates' delight, I always seemed to make a spectacle of myself.

The school had a paddle policy strictly enforced by the principal. There were times the teachers would send me to the principal's office for a paddling. On one occasion, I observed that this shiny, thick paddle had suction holes in it. To me, it seemed that the principal took way too much enjoyment administering this form of punishment. He also had a nervous condition that caused him to shake uncontrollably, so you didn't know if he would always hit the target. From my desk in the rear of the classroom, I could see directly across the yard into the principal's office. I saw many students come out of the office disheveled. Black, white ... whatever, it didn't matter; no one was exempt from that infamous board-of-education hanging on the principal's wall like a prized plaque.

Chapter Three

MY MISCONDUCT AT EASTSIDE ELEMENTARY always made it back to the ol' tyrant, Inez. We didn't own a telephone, so whenever the Sneeds would summon her to the phone, I knew it concerned me, and most of the time it wasn't a favorable outcome.

Even though Inez was tough on me, I grew to love her, and even started calling her Mom, but the whippings I never grew fond of. In retrospect, I understood that I probably would have been in worse shape if not for her tough love. Those values and morals embedded in me still resonate today. They are priceless. I hold them dear. At times, they are all I have. And when times become unbearable, a person should have something to hold onto.

Despite my calling her Mom, we still had a love-hate relationship. I'd love that woman one minute, but in no time flat, I could hate her.

Bringing home my report card was always dreadful. I never knew if I had met Inez's expectations or not. When I didn't, it would be another fall from grace.

Inez and Betty helped me with my homework. Betty was thorough. She would walk me through my assignments step-by-step. Inez, quick to lose her patience, would often just do my homework for me. At test time, I'd be perplexed. Sometimes I wondered how I made it from one grade to the next. Were the teachers trying to get rid of me by passing me on to the next grade? I never knew.

At home, I found myself playing alone more and more. A soldier boy named Slick was courting Betty — I never took an interest in learning his real name — especially with him stealing Betty away from me. So, our quality time became practically non-existent. I hadn't realized how fond I had become of Betty until Slick came along.

Whenever I frequented the Sneed's residence, Betty would be so into Slick that she'd hardly notice me. They'd often wrestle, with Betty always getting pinned. The Betty I knew was a tenacious tomboy, so she shouldn't have been easily subdued. These sessions always resulted in them sharing a passionate kiss. Standing there watching, I found myself tormented to no end. The only choice left for me was to take my dilemma to Mr. and Mrs. Sneed. So, I conjured up some tale that Slick was somehow harming Betty with this form of wrestling. Mrs. Sneed, however, gave me a subtle smile; she understood my childhood anguish.

Amid all this, Betty was graduating from high school. Shortly afterward, the Sneeds gave Slick their blessing, and he and Betty were married. Betty volunteered me to be the ring bearer, which I dutifully declined. Inez, however, had the final say. Reminding me of all the years Betty had been there for me, she escorted me to the wedding by my ears. No one seemed to see, nor care about the dagger sinking deeper and deeper into my tender little heart. I endured the ceremony, but my wet eyes wouldn't allow me to bask in the pure beauty and true essence of the wedding. Shortly after, Slick whisked Betty off to Alaska.

Understanding the loneliness that was creeping back into me, Inez considered allowing me a pet. Most of the neighbors were hunters, and most of them had hound dogs (Little did I know one of those big floppy-eared creatures would become my best friend). She wouldn't let me have a dog or a cat, but she did allow me to receive a little chicken from one of the neighbors. Strangely, Inez named him Terry Jr. She let me keep him in the house. I kept him in a box in the closet by the back door. The noise Terry Jr. made almost got him given back to the neighbor. Somehow, the little fellow grew into a big, pretty, white rooster. Now it was time for him to make his home in the backyard.

Terry Jr. had a habit of frequenting Inez's gardens to eat insects, as well as the various vegetables. He would also leave his droppings on the back porch. To keep Inez from getting upset, I had to keep the porch hosed down.

Whenever I was at school, he would be at Inez's mercy. When I came home from school and saw feathers scattered across the backyard, I knew Inez had taken a broom to him. Whenever he wasn't beat half to death, he would faithfully greet me at the front gate when I arrived.

One day, I came home from school, and my little-feathered friend was nowhere in sight. After endless searching, I finally stormed into the house and confronted Inez about Terry Jr.'s whereabouts. She said, "Boy, I don't know, maybe the dogs got a hold of him, or he flew over the fence." I thought flying over the fence to be very unlikely because we were constantly clipping his wings.

With his being the man of the house, I decided to take my dilemma to John. That was a grave mistake. I should have known he wasn't going to oppose Inez. The look he gave me when I asked about Terry Jr. told me that he did sympathize with me, but that this was exclusively between Inez and me. I still remember that valuable lesson today, how anger can cloud one's reasoning.

It took a while for my senses to come into play. My sense of smell, that is. We had chicken and dumplings for dinner, and the whole house reeked of it. Terry Jr. simmered in the pot and no matter how much I seethed, it was useless. Just like the abandonment concerning my biological parents, and now, my feathered friend, this was merely the beginning of a lifetime of betrayal, including my continuously betraying myself.

Inez forced me to eat my dinner until I spewed it all over the dining table and floor. John sat there nonchalantly and ate his food. He then proceeded to watch the evening news. For once, I was hoping he would come to my aid, but he didn't. From that moment on, chicken and dumplings have never sat well on my stomach. Inez eventually stopped cooking them altogether.

Now, after school, I took to crawfish hunting, playing in condemned houses, collecting pecans, and dutifully helping Inez in the gardens. Crawfishing grew on me. I went on to enjoy it for many years. Hanging a little piece of bacon tied to a string and dropping it in a water-filled ditch, or a crawfish hole, became a great pastime for me. If I retrieved a nice batch, I could take them to Inez, and she would cook them for me. I'd watch them turn bright red in the pot. Cracking the shells open, pulling the waste out of the tail, and sucking the meat out of the claw was more than worth the trouble.

Playing in those condemned houses caught up with me in the worst way. One evening, I was playing inside of one, and I didn't notice a nail protruding from a piece of plywood. My left foot landed directly on the sharp point of the rusty nail. I thrashed around on the floor until I could endure the agony. I then hobbled home, bleeding profusely, to contend with Inez. To my disappointment, she was standing at the screen door waiting for me. She had always forewarned me to make it home before the sun went down. Not only had I let the sun set, but added to that, I had just injured myself playing in a forbidden house. To my surprise, she pounded my little behind until John finally intervened by saying, "The boy looks like he is about to pass out from the loss of blood." Finally, she composed herself long enough to clean my foot, patching it up with some old rags that she kept around the house.

For some reason, Inez didn't believe in consulting physicians. But she was big on home remedies. It damn near cost me my foot. After a week of my foot turning funny colors, swelling as large as my head, and causing my toenails on that foot to fall off, we finally made it to the doctor —and right in the nick of time. My foot was saved, but the toenails never were quite the same. They grew back thicker and brown, the color of the rusty nail on which I'd stepped. To this day, I've never gotten over being shy about my foot. It's quite embarrassing to me to unveil my foot for the first time in front of someone. I can't remember ever wearing sandals in the summertime, nor walking the beach barefooted.

I never had to worry about playing in those dilapidated houses again. The city tore them down and constructed new ones.

That was when the Johnson family moved in. There were six or seven of them, and they were a reminder of my humble origins. The father of that family had abandoned them as well, leaving the mother with the sole burden of raising those children. They were crammed into a shotgun shack. I don't think their father took them through the physical abuse that I suffered from my own. The mental pressure was still too much for their mother to bear.

With all this transpiring, I found myself several new playmates. Charles was a year younger than I was. He ended up being my best friend. His big brother, Joseph was five years older than I was, and we became friends as well.

Joseph taught himself karate by reading books, studying illustrations, and watching Bruce Lee movies. He was such an avid fan of martial arts and big-time wrestling that we began calling him Karate Joe.

Years later, I had to stop him from killing a man. The man knew karate and challenged Joseph to a spar. Somehow, he put the man in one of those TV wrestling holds and choked him, panicking the man enough to prevent his defensive techniques from kicking in. Joseph was choking foam out of him and wouldn't stop for anything until I started yelling and threatening to get his mother. The threats brought him to his senses, and he released his challenger, who slowly recovered.

The episode was the first of two trances that I witnessed Joseph experience. He also was homophobic. An older gentleman made the mistake of touching him on the shoulder the wrong way. The occupants of the house came running to see what had happened because they thought someone fired a gun. Joseph had slapped the shit out of the man because he thought it was a homosexual gesture. The man was rendered speechless. Maybe he was justified in doing what he did, but no one ever rubbed him that way again.

*****

Mrs. Johnson came in handy for a few of Inez's home remedies. When I would suffer an eye infection, Mrs. Johnson would provide the tit milk, the cure that was squeezed into my eyes. Inez would send me over to get this form of milk. It was unbelievable how the milk would be waiting for me, and how Inez involved me in the process.

Looking back, I find it rather funny. I would go over to get this milk, bring it back, and Inez would practically have to tie me down to squeeze it into my eyes. I quickly learned to tell Inez that Mrs. Johnson was out of milk. But Inez would just march me over and see for herself.

These home remedies just about killed me. Whenever I had a fever blister on my mouth, Inez would apply earwax to it. If her earwax were running low, she would summon Betty, and ironically, Betty always had a blog of earwax ready to apply.

*****

One evening after school, Charles and I were playing under the pecan trees in the front yard when I happened to glance over in the direction of the Sneed's house. I saw a new shiny black car pull up. Lo and behold, it was Betty and Slick. They got out, went around to the back door of the car, and opened it to get something from the back seat. Moving to get a closer look, I noticed it was a baby. Betty and Slick had started a family, and I was all but happy for them. I knew that none of this was bridging the gap between Betty and me. In any case, I greeted Betty and her new arrival with a pretense of cheer.

Between Mr. and Mrs. Sneed expressing their joy, Betty glowing, and Slick standing erect as if Betty were his conquest, my heart just sank and sank and sank. Finally, I'd had enough and went back home. The thirty yards back to my house felt more like a hundred-mile journey.

Betty and her family stayed for three more weeks before setting off again to Alaska. I never set foot in the Sneed's house again while Betty, Slick, and the baby were there. I didn't want the void in my heart to turn into an abyss. Before her departure, Betty came over to placate me. I knew all she said was heartfelt, but my fractured heart wasn't mendable. I vowed that with our next conversation, I would be grown up. Inez made me go out and help the Sneeds send Betty and her family off with a farewell. Little did I know it would be the last time that I would ever again lay my eyes on my "beloved Betty."

33

Chapter Four

AS I HEADED TO EASTSIDE ELEMENTARY during spring and summer, I always walked at a brisk pace. I felt a sense of urgency. To get there right away. Especially after being introduced to a kid's form of gambling, "shooting marbles.

I pocketed the marbles I won; those I lost my opponents pocketed. I tried to keep this new avocation from Inez; the times I didn't—my hind parts paid-in-full for my disobedience.

Inez unknowingly contributed to my habit by buying marbles for me. And boy, were they *pretty*! I cared for them like a girl would care for diamonds. The fellows and I called the exquisite ones, "toys." My toy was typically yellow and black, which I referred to as my *bumblebee*.

Though our property was expansive, shooting marbles alone was no fun; there was no one against which to measure my skill. Or, to partake in the excitement when several got knocked out of the circle or triangle, from let's say, 10 feet away.

When Inez apportioned my marbles, she warned against two things: gambling and getting my clothes dirty. Though I nodded in agreement, her admonishment was like expecting a hog not to wallow in slop. Far back as I can remember, marbles and dirt were synonymous. And, any "real shooter" knows, to have any proficiency, at a bare minimum, it was a prerequisite to get down on your knees.

Then there was Mother Nature's interventions: rain and hurricanes. By the time the flood receded and the ground had hardened—we marble shooters were on the farther side of desperation. We focused on our games so intently; it was as if the bell for the first period was ringing miles away.

Although I had one of the keenest eyes on the playground, there were those dreadful days I headed home long-faced. Of course, to face Inez with knee stains and an empty marble sack after having lost them all, including my prized bumblebee, was just adding salt to an already blistering wound.

Given her disposition that day, or whether she was otherwise occupied, chastisement could be on the spot, such as a slap-up-side the head in passing, or parceled out over time, which was the worst! Quickly, getting it over with would've better suited me, rather than have it dragged out. Anticipation often filled me, waiting for the rigmarole to play out: "Terry, when I finish with dinner, I'm tearing your little butt up. If I've told you once ... I've told you a thousand times ... Don't be messing up your school clothes. Bad back and all, I have spent countless hours hovering over that sewing machine making sure you have something decent to wear. Is this the thanks I get? As for that gambling—"

"Mom! It ain't gambling. It's playing for keeps."

"Well, you need to start playing for fun. When you're old enough to foot the bill, you can do as you well please."

I had hoped that her wrath would pass over, but it never did. Each stroke punctuated the *whuppin*. "Boy ... you made ... me ... do this ... you gon ... learn to mind ... even if ... I have to ... beat it ... in you ... till you're grown ... and out my house."

A torrent of tears poured onto me. Crying in unison *frightened me*.

My introverted nature didn't assist matters any; had I shown more outward emotion, promising not to do it again, perhaps the buffeting may have subsided sooner. Instead, I thrashed as if bare-skinned in a bed of fire ants. Her heavy-handed method was so unbearable that I endeavored to defy gravity's normal pull. Trapped on my cot by Inez's large, obstructive frame, feet first, I commenced to scaling the wall. Anything to escape the itchy,

35

green sap that was seeping into my welted skin from the braided twigs.

Even today, I still chuckle about how often I found myself capsized, with my feet bracing the wall, attempting to evade Inez's *scorching*.

Later, after calm had descended on her, my inherent, forgiving nature led me to ask, "Mom, why do you *whup* me for every little screw-up?"

"Come here boy!" she said, patting the couch, motioning me to sit down. "I love you, that's why. One day, boy, you're going to thank me!" *Although you've "gone on" Inez, I thank you always!*

Those palpable moments softened Inez and me; I perpetuated the mood by requesting my favorite story: How our union had come about, and why she chose me over my siblings.

"Well ... John L. (when times were endearing, she'd always emphasize John's middle initials, which stood for Lee) and I were walking to the store when we noticed several straggly looking, yet attractive, kids playing in the front yard, by the side of the house, on a plank lying across a ditch, and even in the road. During the evening strolls, I told John L., 'Look how cute they are.' John L., being John L., never said much. I couldn't take my eyes off the bunch of you."

"Mom, how did you know about our situation?"

"The entire parish knew. Mind you, your Dad wasn't much of a home-body. Often John would see him about town trying to be a "Big Shot" throwing his money away on ..." Stopping in mid-sentence, she must've assumed it a bit much for my tender ears.

Re-living the pain, milking the moment, I asked (although I sometimes felt like my siblings and I were a litter at a kennel), "What made you choose me? And don' t tell me cause you were so cute."

Each time she told this poignant story, it *moved* me.

"You were the only one who'd stop playing long enough to notice us. One incident you ran out on the road chasing your ball as John L. and I were passing. You were inches from me. And I must tell you, you were more interested in getting your ball than in two old folks passing through the neighborhood. You came so close I couldn't help myself, 'Hey little fellow! What's your name?' With terribly ashy knees, you looked up at me with tight, dark brown eyes and a gap-toothed smiled, then in that soft voice I've come to know, you answered, 'Terry', then you grabbed your ball and—"

"With the anticipatory impatience of a child, I asked, "Mom! Mom! You aren't saying I had beaver teeth, are you?"

"Boy interrupt me again, and I am finished. You hear?"

"Yes, Momma."

"Besides, you aren't fooling me; you should have all these make-up sessions memorized."

Influenced by emotion and melancholy, I whispered, "You and John are the best thing that happened to me, Momma!"

For a moment in time Inez would be touched, then donning her impenetrable exterior, she would carry on. "As I was saying, you quickly ran back across those two logs (make-to-do bridge) back into the yard, and off you and your brothers went. From that day forward, you seemed to have felt my presence; we connected. Afterward, every time I came around you looked at me and smiled. Feeling like I did about you and knowing the plight your family was in, caused my heart to spasm."

This part numbed me: The story carved from the gloom we lived in fed my child-like eagerness, with a big need to feel loved. Much to my liking, she persisted, "I wouldn't lay off John L. until he assured me we could welcome you into our home. And besides, you were cute ... Snotty nose and all."

37

Chapter Five

MONTHLY, SOMETIMES WEEKLY, a noted, ten-gallon hat wearing, insurance salesman, one Mr. Jenkins, frequented the Williamses. Granted, this hefty cast iron-black brother, in his loud-colored, double-knit three-piece suit, was my first encounter with a Big Shot (By my definition: an affluent hustler).

In Winn Parish, the man set the benchmark for having it going-on; he was the only brother driving an all-white convertible caddy with a red interior. If that wasn't show-stopping enough, his *fly* ride, for those times (the 70s), featured yet another attraction: a set of Texas Longhorns emblazoned across the front hood, and a bullhorn lever that rested beneath the steering wheel.

Each time Mr. Jenkins's "steel hog" rounded the corner, my legs didn't fail to get me there in time to yank the lever. I sometimes even blind-sided him by running up to the door and startling him. "Whoa, little man! Let me open the door first," he cautioned.

This perk Mr. Jenkins afforded me, made me the envy of my contemporaries. The bullhorn's loud bellowing had 'em drawing near as if it were a mating call.

Then, naturally, there were times Mr. Jenkins was short with me. He, Inez, and John had other business that didn't include a lonely kid striving for attention. Like most people who are engaged in shady dealings —sometimes sooner than later—it all comes out in the wash: Mr. Jenkins donned more than the hat of an insurance salesman, he also distributed unlicensed liquor to the Williamses and others who sought to make ends meet through underhandedness.

As time progressed, I remained awestricken by Mr. Jenkins. Winn Parish was tiny, with subdivisions called Quarters. The Williamses and I lived in the T&G Quarters. To this day, I still don't know why it's called T&G. Many times, the kids teased that it was named after the cartoon Tom and Jerry.

In a neighboring Quarter, Mr. Jenkins owned a Dance Hall with an attached greasy-spoon cafe. I became a patron of his greasy-spoon establishment, especially while trekking home from the public swimming pool. However, my devotion was not to the greasy burger; it had to do with the waitress, Mr. Jenkins' daughter.

For a time, I had been eyeballing her at school. I wanted to get to know her badly, but being an underclassman landed me in a poor position to do so. During recesses, she smiled at me and exhibited cordiality, but that was as far as it went. The inducement of a smile led me to spend many a summer afternoons sitting on those hard-counter stools.

Chapter Six

STRAIGHT OUT OF HER KITCHEN, Inez launched a locally famous Kool-Aid cup business. Kool-Aid cups were equivalent in taste to popsicles; the distinction was that they were frozen in Styrofoam cups. The Kool-Aid cups frozen, syrupy content attracted kids and adults alike.

Although I witnessed the manufacturing of these frozen refreshments, Inez would often deny my access to them. Inez had me on tight rations. I suppose it had to do with the sugar content; she didn't want me bouncing off walls or maybe, she was looking out for my ivory. At any rate, years later, I never developed much of a sweet tooth.

At the time, I craved Kool-Aid cups—badly. To the point of blatantly exhibiting impudence; I'd lie in ambush and prey on Inez's friendly, young patrons. They soon caught on to my "Begging Benny" ploy. As you may remember, "Begging Benny" was the infamous cousin of two of the characters (Russell and his big brother) from the cartoon series "Fat Albert." He'd blow into town often enough and was widely known for his begging, borrowing, and lying.

Inez's customers would barely have their little mitts fastened to their cups before I'd waylay them. My joyful friends didn't even make it off the porch before I started my shameless attempts to badger them for a lick, scoop, or whatever amount they were willing to render.

"Go get your own," some vehemently cried out.

However, there were those who deferred. "Just one scoop," some offered, "That spoon's too big," others complained.

From the perspective of my being a gluttonous kid, my teaspoon was more like a shovel. I can still see their young, cringing faces as my top and bottom choppers crunched down on their delectable Kool-Aid treats.

Then again, that was the thing about Cousin Benny; he always demanded the lion's share. Strangely, my likeness to this "sponge" came before having ever watched an episode of "Fat Albert."

Inez never let on about her secret recipe, so, one time I spied on John mixing up a batch in the kitchen. He was using a plastic gallon-sized jug, emptying two Kool-Aid packs and adding four cups of sugar, which gave it that syrupy effect.

Another sugar-fix that comes to mind of which I was deprived: leftover cake mix. I loved the stuff. On any given holiday, one could have sworn Inez's kitchen was a bakery. Rotating six to ten cakes, in an old-fashioned oven, was nothing for her.

Nonetheless, she was forever running me out of the kitchen. "Boy, you're just in the way," she shouted, "Find something on TV. I'll call you when I'm good 'n' ready."

An old, ugly, rabbit-eared, black and white television showed fuzzy at best. *What did she expect me to find?* For us, cable wasn't yet on the scene; we were lucky with four channels. Further, considering Inez baked late at night, there wasn't much to find on the "tube" at such a time. For the most part, I sat with the TV watching me, dozing off and listening to the repulsive drone of critters scurrying behind weatherworn wallpaper. Only to be awakened by the clacking of spoons scraping the inside of bowls.

Inez, at last, summoned me into the kitchen, where I attacked the rim of bowls with tongue, nose, and fingers (a messy affair indeed), only to come up short each time. Taste buds were not yet whetted; I desired more: "You didn't leave anything in the bowls."

"Boy, I know what I left in those bowls. Either enjoy what's left or put them in the sink."

Years later, however, I realized she had done me a favor, shielding me due to first-hand experience. Not taking from Inez's pristine beauty—mahogany-hued, high cheek boned, strong jaw line, and a decent grade of hair—but it was apparent she, herself, needed a dentist.

Chapter Seven

CARMEN, AN OLD WIDOW, was championed the meanest elder in the neighborhood. Though in her fifties, there were still remnants of her having once been attractive. She looked to be of native descent, with curly, salt and pepper hair, high cheekbones, and a reddish complexion. Her scowl didn't detract from her beauty either.

Many times, while retrieving overthrown balls from her property, circumstances provided us with the displeasure of coming face-to-face. Like a parody of a soldier running through a field of land mines, I would dart in and out. By chance she spotted me, after regaining my ball, I'd run back quickly.

If caught, I was collared and at her mercy. She was, by no means, the tell-the-parents-type. She was of the belief that it takes a village to raise a child. Then she'd wait for the recipient of the whuppin to report the altercation back to their parents.

On Halloween, the prospect of free candy served to stiffen my back, and I would brave my fears. Halloween was the only time I dared to go near her morbid shotgun shack. On those nights, it didn't matter what the signs indicated: no trespassing, beware of dogs, or no soliciting. It didn't matter; there were treats to be had. And, from behind my Batman mask, I yelled deafeningly, "TRICK OR TREAT," in Carmen's face. That would be my get-back for her spooking me all year long.

Halloween was my night... And my custom would ward off evil. Carmen appeared annoyed that I came calling. So, she would drop two or three miniature sized Tootsie rolls into my bag and shout, "Get out of here!"

That night her being a cheapskate nearly gave birth to my first illicit act: Snatch and Grab.

Months on end, as we kids played in the alley next to Carmen's, a young boy peered out her window. I never saw much of the boy except for the silhouette of his blockhead. However, his favorite pastime seemed to be watching us frolic. But as time eventually reveals, one day as we played, she called out to me. "Hey boy, over here!"

I shuffled over—with circumspection—to where she and the boy were sitting on the front stoop. I also did not know she was an alcoholic and devoid of tact. "Meet your little brother Michael," she said listlessly.

You done lost your friggin' mind, I uttered privately.

Nevertheless, with politeness Inez had taught and beat into me, I responded, "How is that so?"

"Boy, you both got the same Dad," spraying me with a pungent odor stemming from whiskey breath.

What was I to say or to do? I didn't remember much about my father. Now ten, I hadn't seen the man since four.

Getting a good look at the boy, I saw likeness: that old square head. *Apparent* in all Hill boys.

Anxious to get back to my stickball, I offered, "Miss Carmen, I don't know much about my father, so you might want to take this up with Inez," before she could further extend the conversation, I jetted back to rejoin the fellows.

She screamed, "He's your brother."

One of my playmates asked, "What did that old witch want?"

Not wanting the whole neighborhood in the family's business, I answered, "She wanted us to hold the noise down." I did not want to tell 'em I had just come across one of my Dad's displaced seeds.

Upon divulging the matter to Inez, it seemed to be of more interest to her than to me, and of course, Inez thought the kinship to be true.

After school the next day, Inez patted our worn couch, signifying me to take a seat. She then proceeded to tell me that Carmen's younger sister had birthed my father's child. She then remarked that I should go over and properly introduce myself. I couldn't wait; it was nice to have another playmate who was family.

Two things, however, put me off about Carmen right away.

First, the place was a furnace, and she was against turning down the heat. Second, whatever the ungodly creature that was slow cooking in her pot, the smell just about killed me.

Another couple of things I found disturbing: Michael appeared afraid of his own shadow. Whenever I tried to sit next to him, he'd dash into the next room. Second, and most importantly, he had autism. A kid myself, I lacked the know-how to communicate with him. The too few times he did elect to speak, it sounded muffled.

Mike and I made a conscientious go at Brotherhood, and he would egg me on as I played. He even started trusting me a little, yet he never left the front porch.

Carmen's visage was always contorted as if she didn't think I made a good enough effort as a brother to bring him around. A kid myself, I didn't have a clue. I was clearly in over my head. Inez tended to have all the answers to life's conundrums. Thus, I always headed home frustrated and unnerved looking for answers.

Chapter Eight

ONE MORNING, BEFORE INEZ SENT ME OFF TO SCHOOL, the captivating sound of Michael Jackson's voice cemented me in my tracks.

John's old wooden radio was rife with static and roaches, but for the first time, it served a far greater purpose than *just* for Dodgers baseball.

Until then, I hadn't heard much music. *Least not R&B.*

The Williamses lived off memories—Big Band era, Waltzing, and such. They weren't current, nor did they own anything current. The old, shabby TV positioned on a plywood stand was reserved for Hee Haw, Green Acres, and Lawrence Welk. Therefore, when my classmates spoke of up-to-date sitcoms, I listened angrily, intently.

However, I now had a voice in the matter: through Michael Jackson I had (sort of) gained entrance into their Tinsel Town gossip.

Having revealed my hunger for blab, I at once realized I should have remained mute. Some kids know nothing of contriteness; they quickly exposed how archaic conditions were within my household.

The Duncan's lived a short distance away. I remember them clearly. They were among the scant few (whom I knew) who didn't reside in a shotgun shack. Not only did they live in a rambler, but they also owned a color TV, a turntable, and their kids had enviable toys...

The Duncan's were comprised of old man Duncan—the patriarch, his wife, their son, Sammy, and daughter, Gaynelle, her three sons, and two daughters.

To my good fortunate, both Cynthia and Lisa were around my age, but I didn't have a rat's chance with either. Cynthia had been on my radar since kindergarten. She also possessed a disarming smile. (Rumor has it that she is still in possession of that 1000-watt smile.) She was the Homie Lover Friend-type: we could talk about anything and everything, play dodgeball and then some—straight tomboy—we even attended church. For me, one of the highlights of attending church was taking in Cynthia's melodious voice.

That aside, I took delight in how proud they were of their appearance: in their ruffled and pleated dresses, ballet stockings, and pilgrim shoes. On some visits, I even smelled hair burning from hot curling irons. *Young and primping.*

In respect to providing for her children, Ms. Gaynelle was in an elite class. There were times when I was around, and her motherly instincts led her to ask, "Terry, have you heard from your mother? Is she taking you back to Seattle when she comes?" Though she meant well, my young mind sensed underlying pity; the uncomfortable exchange sometimes left me feeling like a waif.

Weeklong tedium drove me to the Duncans for recreation and entertainment. So much so, that on this Saturday, I was welcomed by something novel. Entering, I thought I had heard music blasting from their turntable. Instead, it was the TV on full tilt: my first dose of Soul Train.

Fluid, fast dancing, intimate slow dancing, pantsuits, suspenders (not yet fashion conscious, I thought suspenders were for farmers and blue-collar types), felt-brims, and giant afros all had me enthralled. Soul Train was my kind of party, and my kind of affair. In my young mind, I had not yet been elevated to the ranks (but OH would I someday arrive!) of the hipsters, who had flair.

It all started coming together; Soul Train was where Rogerick had honed his dance moves. Most of the time, before my arrival, the living room furniture had already been pushed against the wall, giving the setting an appearance of a makeshift dance floor.

That being the case, Rogerick had room enough to mimic the Soul Train dancers' prolific moves, with his siblings serving as contestants. Feeling like a fossil, I self-assigned myself to a familiar role: wallflower.

Rogerick repeatedly brought the house down with renditions of the Robot, silky spins like Michael Jackson, and Michael's proud strut, snapping his head back.

Although I was content holding up the wall, I still wasn't impervious to the amusement happening before me. Looking on with envy, I thought how cool it would be to dance like Rogerick, to have showmanship and be center stage. Caught in reverie, I feigned an offbeat rhythm, which Ms. Gaynelle caught out of her peripheral vision. "Terry," she said, "why don't you show us what you got?"

Again, if my memory serves me correctly, on that day, I donned my first clown suit. Plus, due to Ms. Gaynelle's coaxing, that day it was determined that I had two left feet.

Seeking applaud equal to that of what Rogerick had so rightfully earned, I sauntered onto the substitute dance floor with the affected coolness of the Soul Train hipsters. That was the best part of it. As to what happened on the floor—from then until now, the debacle remains a blur—I do recall, however, that it was not a "Soul Train Affair."

Gladly exiting the floor, I extended a half-hearted wave to Ms. Duncan, and said, "See ya next Saturday. Couldn't seem to find my rhythm."

My trip back home was far from triumphant. Along the way, I uttered every imaginable expletive. And who did I encounter along the way? Carmen and her prying eyes. The humiliation I'd heaped on myself had me ready to rub noses with the woman. I even spat a few curse words at Inez and John for their reprehensible acts of conservatism: A quiet evening of viewing the Smothers Brothers, square dancing and listening to a raucous banjo weren't enough anymore. I, like Rogerick, had an affinity for soul music.

Chapter Nine

IN THE EARLY SEVENTIES, LIFE CONTINUED TO BE A
CONSTANT UPHEAVAL. One Saturday afternoon, I climbed a
tree in our backyard to fetch my brother Ronald. He hadn't come
out for several days and I was becoming anxious about his
absence. Finally, overcome by curiosity and concern, and
without Inez's consent, I paid him and Ms. Nan an unannounced
visit. And what I encountered was much, much more than I
bargained for.

Entering their front yard, I looked around for Ronald. I could
not find him. Glancing around, I noticed the firewood lying there
unchopped.

My only choice was to knock on the door, which I had rarely
done. Ms. Nan already had the door open with the screen door
closed to keep the mosquitoes out.

She told me to come in, which I did. I immediately inquired
about my brother. Instantly, a dejected look came upon this
elderly lady's face. Seeing Ms. Nan in distress made me want to
turn and flee. The dismal atmosphere in her home and the
emptiness in her eyes were almost too much to stand. She kept
saying, "They came and took my boy. They came and took my
boy. They came and took my boy." At that very moment, I felt the
love she had for my brother.

All this time I thought he was just a workhorse, a hired hand
or something.

Most of the time I would only see Ronald stacking firewood
and tending to the many chores required of him. None of this was
indicative of the love Ms. Nan had for him.

Ms. Nan proceeded to tell me that my mother, Leola, had sent for him to come to Seattle. My mother's boyfriend, Leonard, had driven down to get Ronald and had taken him back to Seattle. Hearing this took my focus off Ms. Nan. What I had just heard was incredulous to my young mind. Why did no one inform me of my brother's departure? Why hadn't Ronald come to say goodbye before he left? I was next in age to the baby, Mark. Why hadn't Mom come down from Seattle with her boyfriend to see about me? What a quandary for my young soul. For weeks, I would sneak over to see if Ronald had come back from Seattle.

One thing I did consider was how this guy, Leonard, must have had a lot of love for my mother to drive across all those state lines to get a child that wasn't even his. Shortly after, I heard that Mom had taken Leonard's life because of his physical abuse and infidelity and that she was in a prison called Purdy for manslaughter. Hearing this made my spirit sink even lower. I began to wonder if I would ever make it back to my mother. My question was how Mom could go and get involved in another abusive relationship after all that Dad had inflicted on her? Later, I would learn that this isn't an uncommon practice among abused women.

Once again, my sister, Patricia, had the tall order of raising two of her siblings, Ronald and Mark. Only this time she had some assistance because she was married. Oddly, her husband's name was Ronald, too, and later, he and I developed quite a meaningful relationship.

Ronald's departure shortened Ms. Nan's life, and not long after that, she passed. Rumor had it she was grief stricken. It wasn't hard to envision after seeing her in such a state of mind.

For years after, I walked—no, ran,—past Ms. Nan's desolate old tin house consumed with her grief. I could have sworn she was standing behind those dingy windows, staring at me with those sad eyes. Never again do I want to look into a pair of eyes such as hers.

After this misfortune, things began to be a little different at the Williams' residence. John started to show interest in me. He started embracing me, and even started calling me his "boy." All the attention and love was heartwarming.

Sometimes on those very hot, humid summer days, he'd allow me to join him at his friends' homes. We would sit under shady pine trees and I would listen as they swapped stories and drank cold beer. Every time John wanted a fresh beer he sent me to the ice chest to get it, and I'd pop the top and take a swig. Most of his friends would say, "Buddy, why you giving that boy alcohol?"

He'd answer, "I'm just killing the worms in his belly!" I honestly believed this was when I started acquiring my taste for alcohol. When he wouldn't give it to me, I'd throw a tantrum until he gave in.

Inez didn't drink much, except maybe on holidays. Whenever she stumbled across those occurrences of John giving me a drink of beer, she'd curse him out and slap the beer out of my hand. John would then have to sneak me a swallow from time to time.

Besides this inappropriate behavior, John's love for me unfurled in different ways. One day after school, I punched a big bully in the face and took off running at full speed, the bully in hot pursuit. We ran for blocks and he was gaining.

John was doing carpentry work on a house near the school. He saw me blazing by with this guy on my heels. Seeing me running for dear life, he came to my rescue. To see this sixty-something-year-old man running and yelling to save me touched me and made me feel that his love for me was genuine.

By the time he finally arrived at the scene, the bully and I were so tired we were holding one another so we could catch our breath. Obviously, John broke it up, but he would tease me about this incident for years to come.

*****

It was rainy, windy, and snowy that year, so I was reduced to entertaining myself inside. Occasionally, I would see people come and go. At first, I thought nothing of it because I thought these were acquaintances of the Williams. After further observation, I could see that these visitors never stayed very long and that they were always leaving with brown paper bags under their arms. Inez and John were selling unlicensed liquor from their house. It now was plain to see why the Sneeds were so nosy. The traffic had aroused their suspicions.

Fortunately, it was during this time I met my biological father's brother, Uncle Otis. He would later become my favorite uncle. When he'd periodically come over, I thought he was coming by to check on me, but no, he was coming over to get whatever was in those brown paper bags.

Every time he came through, he'd give me some pocket change to put into my piggy bank. Having gotten used to this, whenever he showed up dry, I'd have to pat him down just to make sure. Even though he was my uncle, Inez saw this as a form of begging and quickly put an end to it.

Even though Inez didn't want to, I would badger her until she would sometimes let me visit Uncle Otis at his house. I soon discovered that he, too, was selling liquor out of his house. The difference between him and the Williams was he allowed his customers to hang out and drink while listening to music.

I was hanging out at Uncle Otis's when I uncovered the fact that his house was the storage place for my Christmas gifts. On Christmas Eve, I was playing inside his house with his grandchildren when I came across a makeshift closet that hadn't been there previously. Later that evening, I came back to the room by myself and pulled the curtain back. There was a blue bicycle and train set that Inez had promised me for Christmas. The only disappointment was the bicycle was a girl's bike. Inez had gotten a girl's bicycle to protect me from injuring my genitals. Her reasoning was that a boy's bike had the straight bar running from under the seat to the handlebars, and that could be dangerous if I fell. After that, Christmas took on a whole different meaning. There wasn't any need for me to wait up for Santa anymore.

Uncle Otis had a lovely wife by the name of Aunt Willie. She was a character. She was the first person that I'd seen eat red clay dirt. She craved the stuff. She even shared some with me a time or two. But no matter what, I just couldn't acquire a taste for it.

Another interesting thing that took place at Uncle Otis's house was the food they cooked. They feasted on bullfrog legs, raccoons, possums (which were extremely greasy), and squirrels, which came in a nice thick gravy.

Chapter Ten

APPARENTLY, SELLING UNLICENSED liquor in Winn Parish back in the '70's was quite lucrative. Everyone seemed to indulge in it, whether for profit or personal use.

The Williamses were given the opportunity to sell liquor on a much larger scale. A Caucasian gentleman, who owned a gas station, became their new sponsor. That's when a plan hatched to relocate. We moved from the old tin house to a larger place mostly constructed of plywood. Roaches, rats, and termites soon moved in as well. For years, they attempted to take over. And maybe they did. For despite the fogs, bombs, and the exterminators used, the roaches wouldn't die. They multiplied.

The new house consisted of three bedrooms and a large living room, with the living room converted into a miniature dance floor. I was happy to have my bedroom. For years, Inez and I had shared a room, with me sleeping on an undersized cot. John had his room, which was puzzling. They called one another "honey" and "baby," but there was not much intimacy between them. I concluded that the thrill was gone.

We were only six blocks from where we had previously lived. One disturbing thing was that we were only fifty feet in front of a railroad track, with a lumber mill directly on the other side. The train ran through at all times of the day and night, its noise always deafening. Other than that, those tracks were a boon, serving me well whenever I'd get enraged. I'd walk them for miles until a sense of tranquility would start to descend.

It was during these refreshing moments that I began to come to terms with the fact that issues and drama are a part of life. During those troubled times, I learned the necessity of preserving my psyche. Everyone has this innate ability if they'd only tap into it. Those tracks also led to a truss bridge where I did my best crawfishing. Along with that, I'd pick the wild blackberries that grew alongside and turn them over to Inez, who'd then make blackberry pie.

Within weeks of the move, the house was transformed into a cafe/juke joint. Many of the people in Winnfield, people I didn't know, started frequenting the place, with Inez's cooking expertise immediately coming into play. It wasn't long before the workers at the mill were dining there for breakfast, lunch, and dinner. Even Sadie's customers started trickling down to Inez's place.

Sadie and Inez attended the same church. Sadie, being a true elder of the church, didn't believe in illegal activities. Where Sadie went to church every time there was a service, Inez's attendance suffered once she started running the Juke Joint. She did, however, make me go every Sunday. From time-to-time, usually every fourth Sunday, Inez would go with me. All this sanctified hollerin' and faintin' didn't sit well, though, because it seemed so phony. How could Inez be cracking heads and poisoning souls one minute and serving her Maker in the next? Inez always blew me away with that.

We had neighbors on all sides except the back of our house, which was where I played and climbed trees. The neighbors on the left were the Hunters. Mr. Hunter's wife, Catherine, was the only woman I've ever seen willing to stand up to Inez, even if it meant fighting. Everyone else cowered before her.

On the right side of our house was an old concert hall that used to be called the Sing Swing. Rumor had it that back in the '50's and '60's it was the place to be. The owner of the Sing Swing was an eccentric old lady prone to sickness, so she couldn't keep the place up and running. She did sometimes rent it out, but the shows paled in comparison to its heyday when it used to be filled with standing room only. That was when the likes of B.B. King and Muddy Waters performed there. But even in the '70's, I'd hear that loud music blaring through the Sing Swing's walls, and the transcendental feeling of being in that bygone era would momentarily engulf me.

Catching John in one of his reminiscent moods, he shared that it was at this very place he'd met Inez. It had been love at first sight. He mentioned asking her out to the floor, and later, while they danced the night away, how he'd proposed to her. She accepted and their storybook romance began.

For an illegal establishment, the Juke Joint ran smooth. Two individuals came by daily, K.C. and Luther — the town drunks. K.C. was a war vet. Sometimes, he'd awake from an alcoholic stupor, having flashbacks of Vietnam. That's when Inez would escort him to the door and tell him to come back the next day. K.C. and I became good friends. We'd play checkers and various other table games because he didn't have a life, or a girlfriend. Before the war, he was debonair and known for being the best dancer in town.

What I remember most was how K.C. always kept a fresh Playboy magazine in his back pocket, carried as though it were his wallet. He never left home without it. Sometimes he'd show it to me, but when he didn't, I'd snatch it and run until he threatened to tell Inez. K.C.'s preference of alcohol was this cheap sweet wine called "White Port." Due to his government check, Inez allowed him to have a tab.

Luther was, by far, more of a drunk than K.C. He'd get so wasted that several times we found him under the front porch or off in some ditch. Unlike K.C., he was always angry unless he was intoxicated. He seldom talked to me, but whenever he did, it was him boasting about his hometown of Mobile, Alabama.

Luther was the best handyman in town. He built my doghouses and Inez's chicken coops. He also assisted with the garden. His handiwork impressed Inez, but I wasn't impressed because most everything he built was out of cheap plywood. It would look good for a while, but once the heavy rain and hurricanes came, it turned to crap.

Being directly in front of the lumber mill, wood of any kind was never a problem, even sawdust. The workers would steal it and bring it over to trade for alcohol.

Life took on a whole different meaning with the opening of the Juke Joint. Inez built a patio, installed lawn chairs, a couple of barbecue pits, and whatever else she could think of. She never had a chance to enjoy any of it, but my friend Charles and I did.

Inez pretty much ran everything around the house, including the books, which would later come back to haunt John. His passiveness was a weakness. One wild weekend, about three in the morning, a loud primitive scream awakened me. Having an altercation with a male customer, John had run to his bedroom to get a pistol, and then returned, brandishing his gun. But he allowed the customer to walk up to him and get too close. The customer stabbed him in the chest with a pocketknife. He was getting ready for another stab when one of the customers wedged a chair between John and his protagonist, preventing the fatal blow.

I stood there, half asleep, watching John with a pistol in his hand, not firing it, and bleeding like a stuck pig. In this case, Inez was the real Avenger, coming out of nowhere with a leaded bat and pulverizing the guy's head, saving her husband's life. The stab wound came within a fraction of an inch from John's heart. From that point on, I had an eerie feeling around some of the customers, sensing impending danger once they became intoxicated. It also killed me to think of John — especially with a gun — as a coward.

After this had taken place, the nightmares began. There were nightmares of John getting killed, nightmares of Inez killing someone, or nightmares of the guy Inez had battered returning with a vengeance. The violence seemed to escalate. Inez was the bouncer of this tiny establishment, and she ruled with an iron fist. Inez would nick, cut, or shoot. Even during those days and times, Inez could easily have faced incarceration. Despite all her terrorizing, she never once set foot in a cell.

Once, right in front of Uncle Otis, she slapped me in the mouth with him just sitting there watching the blood trickle down to my chin, not saying or doing anything. I gave him a glare that stated, "Even you, my flesh and blood, is just going to sit there and watch this *ol' tyrant* terrorize me!"

*****

By now, I was in middle school and growing like a beanstalk. Being that I wasn't far from eye-to-eye contact with Inez, she felt the need to drive her point home, making me get several twigs she could twist into a switch whenever I needed disciplining.

Middle school wasn't all that bad. I clearly remember this one African American teacher, Mr. Ely. Now here came the paddle-policy all over again. Almost everything peeved Mr. Ely. I'd thought all this was gone once I'd left Eastside Elementary. I was sadly mistaken.

My favorite teacher, and not mine alone, was one Ms. Paine, a woman pleasing to the eyes with a figure to do Thelma from that '70's sitcom, *Good Times*, quite proud. Despite there always being a sternness about her, I felt she was a kitten on the inside.

Sports in middle school weren't that bad. Although I never got the opportunity to showcase my talent. All those years of playing basketball on an old bicycle rim as a hoop, playing football in horse fields and pastures, and even the streets, counted for naught. When things finally moved to my favor, Inez wouldn't let me attend practice because of my many chores. Someone had to dispose of all those alcohol boxes. It became my duty to burn all the boxes and evidence. I could use gasoline to start the fires. Inez caught me during a rebellious moment, and I purposely started a fire a few feet away from the house. The back of the house caught fire. John happened to be looking out the back window when he noticed the flames. Fortunately, I could put the blaze out with a garden hose. Once again, I had to contend with Inez, and once again, she triumphed — triumphed over my ass.

After that stabbing incident, John never recaptured his spirit. Physically, he recovered fine. But as fate would prevail, he started having these tremendous headaches night after night. Everyone pleaded with him to go to the doctor. But for some unknown reason, he wouldn't, and it cost him dearly.

Inez and I woke one morning and noticed that John was bedridden, staring at the ceiling with his face contorted. He'd also suffered the loss of vision in one of his eyes. Now he didn't have a say in the matter. Inez hurried him to the local general hospital. Further diagnosis revealed that he had suffered a major stroke. He remained in the hospital, where I visited him every day after school. He regained most of his eyesight, but his left side was completely paralyzed.

Somehow, Inez convinced the therapist, who gave John his daily session, to teach me how to assist John in his exercises. That way, once he came home, we wouldn't have to bring him back and forth to the hospital every day. The added chore I didn't mind, because I wanted to see John walk again. Unfortunately, he never did. There was, however, a little progress with John taking baby steps with his walker. Shortly after that, though, he just gave up. Something inside *died*. He sought refuge in drinking a half case of beer and smoking two to three packs of those harsh Camel non-filtered cigarettes each day.

Under these extreme conditions, my grades plummeted. There were days I was so fatigued that I'd almost pass out during the two-mile journey to school. Inez's way of compensating for this was letting me have my first dog -- another responsibility for me to assume.

The neighbors gave me a pretty, dark, floppy-eared hound dog that I called Midnight. He evolved into a real nice dog, as well as my friend. He would walk me almost all the way to school until I made him turn back. And sometimes he'd be halfway to my school to greet me once it let out.

One day, hearing Midnight hollering, I went to the backyard to see what was going on. Inez was chasing him all over the backyard, beating him with a 2x4. It was while chasing him she stumbled on an old tree root, fell, and broke her arm in two places. From what she said, Midnight had started hanging out in the henhouse and was sucking down eggs. Since Inez had a broken arm and she could no longer work, I helped in the kitchen. We wanted to keep our clientele. But even with an arm broken in two places, Inez was still a force to be reckoned with.

One day I came home from school, Inez told me she'd caught the dog sucking eggs and had shot him. He had then run under the house and bled to death.

She had one of her customers haul him to the city dump to drop him off like a piece of trash.

Chapter Eleven

THE TURMOIL BETWEEN INEZ AND I CONTINUED TO RISE. Feeling I was of an age that required a form of discipline besides getting my backside beat when she'd send me to the backyard to gather twigs for a chastising, I'd just keep going. If her duties at the cafe permitted, she'd hunt me down. Whenever I'd see her coming, I'd take off running, but there were times when she'd creep up on me. I often wondered why my playmates let her sneak up in the middle of a football or basketball game without warning me. Maybe they enjoyed the show of her collaring and dragging me off. There were times she'd wait for me to come home. Once there, she'd be patient, waiting for me to be tucked in for the night before literally giving me a rude awakening.

I wasn't a runner like my brother Robert who'd run away from home for days at a time until Sadie would find one of his hiding spots, usually inside of a boxcar. Robert told me he didn't know how she continually found him, that he'd come to the conclusion that Sadie must've been possessed. She'd found him all times of the night, regardless of where he was at, and most of the time he couldn't outrun her either. She never stopped coming. She'd walk and walk until she collared him until once more he was in tow and headed back to their residence.

Robert wasn't permitted to visit me often. Sadie frowned on the environment in which we lived. Plus, Robert had an image as a church usher to uphold.

Whenever I was free of my duties, I'd visit him. Sadie had a dog named "Killer" that would always lie under a shade tree in the front yard facing the gate. Robert would yell from the porch, "Open the gate and come in. He's not going to bother you."

The thought would rush through me that this same salivating dog had bitten Robert a few times for running from Sadie, so I'd yell back, "If you want me to come play with you, put a leash on that dog."

As always, as soon as we made it to the playground, Sadie would have a chore for him, or she would send him to the store for something. None of this worked in my favor because Inez would have me on a time limit. By the time Robert finished his chores, my time would be up and I'd have to return home.

Because Robert didn't want to stop playing, he'd end up saying something smart to Sadie and she'd knock him down with a fist. Sadie, though a little woman, was muscle-bound. From years of hard labor, she had Popeye forearms and huge biceps. From what I'd seen, Robert feared her more than I feared Inez, and perhaps with good reason. Robert continued to run away from home over and over until he was eventually placed in the Louisiana Training Institute (L.T.I.), a reform school.

Back at home, Inez allowed Charles to stay over, which was convenient for everyone. It helped shoulder some of my workload while relieving him from a destitute situation at home. His father, Charles Sr., was one of Inez's customers who loved Inez's chitlins, pig's feet, and smothered pork chops, not to mention the ice-cold beer.

I couldn't see it, but Charles and I were at a pivotal point in our friendship. Inez had me wound so tight I started directing my anger towards him. By the time I realized I was using my friend as an outlet for my rage, it was too late for us to salvage our relationship. It hurt that the beautiful friendship we once had as kids was slipping beyond our grasp. He endured as much of my infliction as he could, but eventually he stayed home.

When I wasn't swamped with one thing or another, I enjoyed the refreshing elevation of the trees. Another purpose for those trees was evading Inez. There were times she'd be searching, calling out for me, but she never once thought to look up. It was in those trees that I had found a place of peace for my troubled spirit. But whenever I returned from one of my little excursions, Inez was more than ready to deal with me.

Things were different when we weren't in the midst of our love/hate relationship. I'd get the essentials I required, as well as whatever else the seasons might bring.

One Christmas, I convinced her to get me a speed-bag. I nailed it to the side of the house. Later, she regretted purchasing it. Whenever I felt the weight of the world on my shoulders, or whenever I was mad at her, I'd pound it without mercy. The noise would have a resounding effect throughout the house that would make Inez livid.

One weekend during this period, I had a bit of a windfall. My father emerged out of nowhere with his new family. It consisted of his fiancée and her five children. Inez's little Juke Joint was just his type of place. Having the atmosphere he liked, he fit right in. These type of establishments were where he had hung out while our family went through living hell.

Our father/son relationship was ill-fated from the start. His being there, drinking and calling me son nauseated me. I thought to myself, *"Eight years later, he surfaced from nowhere as if he'd never left."*

The highlight of his presence was his stepson Russell, a boy around my age; we instantly jelled. Dad blew in and blew out like a tumbleweed. He'd stay the weekend; then be gone before I even knew he'd arrived.

As a twelve-year-old, my outlook toward my father was different. There weren't too many fond memories so his rapid departure didn't make me too unraveled. Life began to teach me the harsh lessons of accepting things for what they truly were.

His presence, however, unsettled Inez and during these times, she'd be even nicer to me. Loving every minute of it, I basked in the ambiance every time the opportunity presented itself.

Another good thing was Robert's return from reform school. He had grown taller and bigger with an attitude changed for the worse. The Louisiana Training Institute had failed at reforming him. He was now more defiant and Sadie knew it. Upon their first altercation, she had his probation revoked and him sent back to reform school.

I bemoaned his departure. Robert was my only remaining sibling in Winnfield. Plus, Robert was promiscuous, expounding with graphic detail about the female anatomy and other splendors I had yet to encounter. Sex 101 taught by Robert.

Before Robert's departure, our older brother, Jimmy, paid us a visit from a neighboring parish. Being a farmhand, Jimmy wasn't afforded as many chances to interact with other children as regularly as Robert and I. Most of his days were filled with attending to crops, chickens, hogs, and cattle.

While in Winnfield, he lived with Uncle Otis. For some reason, he never visited me at Inez's place. I initiated most of our bonding by seeking him out. Usually, I'd catch him on the field playing sports. Robert, being the consummate troublemaker, wanted me to involve Jimmy in some of my battles with bullies. Not having seen my older brother since I was four, it would have been unwarranted to get him involved in this frivolous drama. After watching his unorthodox style of playing sports, I wasn't sure if he'd be up to the challenge anyway.

Jimmy's stay in Winnfield was short lived. It wasn't long before he was en route to Houston, Texas to live with our father.

Being more diligent in his work than Robert or me, Dad welcomed him with open arms. With Dad's tiny construction business in full bloom, Jimmy would fit right in.

Jimmy remained in Houston, employed by our father, until he realized he was only spinning his wheels, with Dad getting richer and him no better off than when he'd first arrived a year before. Jimmy soon boarded a Greyhound bus and embarked on a journey to the great Pacific Northwest to be with our mother.

Seemingly, Robert would take the same path as Jimmy. Once again, Robert returned from reform school, only this time he was more undisciplined than ever. Sadie didn't stand a chance at corralling him now that he was well over six-feet tall and just under two hundred pounds. However, he lost the accommodations of Sadie's home. She banished him to one of her boarding houses.

Soon overcome by his unruliness, he'd climb the fence once Sadie retired for the night. Upon his return, Sadie's dog, Killer, would be there to sink in his teeth, simultaneously alarming Sadie that there was an intruder encroaching. Any woman with a boarding house, let alone one who'd been running her business alone for years, owned a gun. And any intruder who'd been to reform school several times should have been lying there with dog bites and bullet wounds all over him because he had infringed on this elderly lady's property. If she had shot him, it would have been justifiable, but Sadie, being a God-fearing woman, didn't want to take Robert's life. She, however, did the next best thing. Since his probation at L.T.I. had expired, she placed a call to Dad in Houston, letting him know it was urgent that he come and get his son or he'd be getting him later in a body bag.

With my favorite brother whisked off to Houston, I was now officially alone and the last sibling left behind in Winn Parish. At every opportunity, I would check with Uncle Otis to see how my brother was doing in Houston. The things I heard weren't too pleasant, what with Dad having turned Robert into a workhorse and only periodically giving him an allowance.

When Robert's rebellious nature surfaced once again, Dad wasn't going to stand for it. But his heavy-handed form of discipline was too much for Robert to bear. One evening Dad was beating Robert from one end of the backyard to the other when the fence broke from Robert's impact against it. Picking up a broken two-by-four, Robert turned the tide, striking Dad on the back a couple of times before running away from home, leaving him running rampant in the fourth largest city in the United States, too afraid to return.

Houston was a far cry from Robert's Winn Parish and boxcar days. From what I heard, Dad's fiancée pleaded with him to let Robert return, but Robert refused, opting rather to journey to Seattle, Washington.

Chapter Twelve

AFTER ROBERT'S DEPARTURE, I was in a tailspin. The thought of being the only child left behind wouldn't stop haunting me. No matter how much I immersed myself into whatever was taking place in my life, the thought of no one caring, the thought of how nice it must be for Jimmy and Robert to have reunited with our other siblings, the thought of how nice it had to be in Mom's care, would not let go of me.

The only way to bridge the gap between Robert and me was to open a line of communication with Sadie. Attending church made it possible to speak with her after the services. Or, when Inez didn't have her claws sunk in too deep, I would visit Sadie at home and do a little handy work or run a few errands.

One benefit of visiting Sadie was that she would take me fishing. Like me, when fishing she was more at peace. These were perfect times to ask about my brother. With her simply using me to vent, and rarely giving me the answers I desired, I quickly grew tired of being her sounding board. That and I didn't want to be consumed by her grief like I had with Ms. Nan's.

I used the money I received from helping Sadie around the café to get my Afro Sheen and other hair products. I felt content about how my afro looked before I left for school. Inez felt that I hadn't shown the "kitchen" (the very back of my head) enough attention. She'd say, "Boy, give me that comb." Then she'd rake my head from the back to the front until she felt it was presentable. I didn't like my afro being combed in that manner, preferring to start from the front. Plus, being twelve, I felt that I could manage my hairstyle.

Other times, she would braid it for me, with my parts squared off as evenly as possible. But with her so heavy handed during these sessions, my scalp felt as if it were being pulled off. Eventually, we tried another option. She'd use a hot comb to straighten my hair. That was a grave mistake because the heat from the burning comb would have me jumping in the chair until I'd eventually get burned. When I'd finally get released from the torture chamber, my hair would be sticking up like a porcupine's quills. I wish I would have known back then that all I had to do was duck my head under the nearest water faucet and I'd instantly have my nappy afro back.

During one of these sessions, Aunt Willie came by to hang out and indulge in a little drinking. She also wanted to keep an eye on Uncle Otis. There were always a few single women hanging around for a free drink or two. Aunt Willie noticed my hair looking as though I had stuck my finger in an electrical socket. She told me that she could possibly give me some French braids. Now I was stuck with convincing Inez to go along, and that the time she'd spent on my hair hadn't been in vain. By some stroke of fortune she agreed. Over the years, Aunt Willie had had plenty of practice doing her daughter's and granddaughters' hair, so my French braids turned out nice. For some blessed reason, and despite having a mean streak from hell, Aunt Willie took to me. Maybe she empathized with my situation.

*****

Our church, in preparation for an upcoming renovation, put some older pews up for sale. Buying five for the Juke Joint, Inez placed the longest two inside for the customers' convenience, two out on the patio, and the best one in the backyard under one of the shade trees. For the most part, I used this last one. It felt kind of weird having these church pews around the Juke Joint knowing they'd been prayed and worshiped on for years. Inez's customers didn't seem to mind having them around, especially K.C. He staked a claim on a corner seat. Soon, the novelty of having them around wore off, with the pews becoming nothing more than another fixture in the Juke Joint.

*****

Something occurred to Inez and me, a turnabout in our relationship. It might have had something to do with the fact I was turning thirteen. Or, maybe, she took into consideration what had happened to Robert, and that I was probably headed in the same direction — towards reform school.

She started talking to me more and trusting me more. When she let me take the three-and-half-mile walk to the public swimming pool alone, I knew things between us were getting better. If I made it back at the designated time to tend to the chores, things would remain harmonious between us.

Having been an introvert up to this point, I finally started to open up to Inez, sharing with her the contents of my heart. Telling her I forgave her for the heinous acts she had wreaked over the years; I noticed a tear escape from beneath the lens of her eyeglasses, and we started to hug. At that moment, I felt as though I was wrapped in a cocoon of love that would never be reproduced.

Inez had started letting me cook my breakfast, but she still rose early and would stir around the house before I'd leave for school. So, when it had been more than a week of her staying in bed, I knew that her lethargy wasn't something that fit into the normal scheme of things. When I asked about her health, she assured me all was well. But the thought kept coming, where's the woman who's always been there to galvanize John and me?

Inez's energy continued to wane. Then came the migraines and severe arthritis. Inez was so unyielding that she never considered consulting a physician. Sadly, we woke one morning and, just like John, we found her helpless. Her helplessness was the saddest sight I had seen up to this point in my life. My terrorizer, my protector, was being carried nearly lifeless from my home. And, just like John, when the results came back, we found she had suffered a major stroke.

Bewilderment had set in. Would I, too, suffer this fate one day? What would John and I do now that we had to run the Juke Joint alone? John carried a pistol on the side of his wheelchair, but I wondered if he'd use it?

My trips to the hospital were extremely bleak. Seeing Inez lying there with tubes in her nostrils, IVs in her arms, and a nearby bedpan, caused my heart to ache to no end.

Even though he'd never admit it, the ebb and flow at the Juke Joint were too much for John and me. Knowing it would be unfair to talk to Inez about the state of our home while she was in her condition, I kept my mouth shut when I visited; Deciding instead to enjoy what little respite there was, together with Inez, in the serene atmosphere of the hospital.

Uncle Otis and I would take John to visit Inez twice a week. He'd sit there with trembling lips, teary-eyed, staring at the love of his life. It was too much for Uncle Otis and me, so most of the time we'd walk to the concession stand to give John some alone-time with her. We'd come back an hour or so later, and John would be sitting there in solitude with Inez staring at the ceiling.

I made a solemn attempt to coerce John into keeping the "Closed" sign on the door of the Juke Joint, but that was totally out of the question. John felt as though he had to keep the place

71

up and running until Inez returned. With the woman having always exuded so much strength in the past, there was nothing less than a full recovery expected of her.

With the place not the same without her, the situation was taking a huge toll on me, mentally and physically. One small comfort was John teaching me how to cook a few meals so that our customers didn't slip beyond our grasp to go back to Sadie's Cafe.

Learning to cook pig's feet and various fried foods came easy, but when it came to gumbo, I couldn't get the swing of it. When it came to gumbo and other Creole dishes, Inez was untouchable.

Another area I was having difficulty with was wringing the necks of the chickens. Even catching them before this process began wasn't easy. Seeming to sense something amiss, they'd run amok whenever I approached. I used to watch Inez; a quick jerk of her wrist would send the body of a chicken one direction while the head would remain limply in her hand. I did more torturing than wringing. It took me minutes to do what Inez did in seconds. Neither was I too fond of soaking them in hot water and plucking the feathers off. The smell emanating from the hot, wet feathers never sat well with my nostrils.

Since falling ill, Inez hadn't said a word to me, but I still felt the need to be close to her and tell her how overburdened I felt at the house. One day, I caught her slightly batting her eyes and murmuring something. I leaned over the bed to hear what she was saying. "You guys have worked me to death. You guys have worked me to death." Baffled by her statement, I didn't have an immediate response. After waiting weeks for her to speak, this is what she uttered.

My shoulders slumped on my long, empty walk home. The thought of Inez, the backbone of the Williams family, the woman/man of the house succumbing to self-pity was unfathomable. I wasn't ready for it. Once at home, I shared what had taken place with John, but he didn't provide me with the answers I was hoping for. John could seek refuge in his drink, but for me, *thirteen* now, the trees, the train tracks, and the crawfishing had become obsolete. Without a cushion, I was being forced to deal with the mighty blows of life.

The next morning we received a knock at the door from Catherine, telling us we needed to get to the hospital immediately. I ran to get Uncle Otis so he could give us a lift. Once I got to his house and explained the circumstances, Aunt Willie also decided to come. Uncle Otis, Aunt Willie, and John all piled into the cab of the truck while I rode in the back with John's wheelchair.

Excited, I thought the hospital was calling us to inform us of Inez's release.

We made it there as fast as the speed limit would allow. John entered the room first, then we followed. Rigid, Inez lay there, her eyes open. All of us were in a state of alarm. It was hard to believe that the hospital would call us to view a corpse. The doctor came and apologized, explaining that sometime before dawn she had suffered a brain stroke; he had thought she might pull through, but her condition had worsened until death resulted.

That was a very, very sad day for us. It was unbelievable. It seemed that one minute Inez had been the picture of health, and in the next, her health had failed unimaginably. The "silent killer"—high blood pressure— had seized her.

High blood pressure is prevalent amongst Blacks. In my early 20's, I would learn that this same disease existed in me. Later, high blood pressure would also claim my biological mother's life. It's hard for me to imagine that it never occurred to Inez to get her blood pressure checked, especially on the trips when we took John in for his monthly check-ups.

This same lethal disease intervened in my brother, Robert's, life. His condition was like John's. But, fighting back tooth and nail through vigorous exercise, proper diet, medication, and an unwavering will to live, he reclaimed eighty percent of his health.

Local customers continued to patronize our small establishment, but things weren't even close to being the same as during Inez's reign. For years, I entertained sinister thoughts concerning Inez. Now with her departure, the love I felt for her, that I had repressed, inundated me. When Inez died, a part of me died, too. She had been there with me during my impoverished days as an uncared for, snotty-nosed kid when I was lost and distracted. How could she leave when the chasm between us was just starting to close? How could John and I possibly shoulder the load without her? I was only thirteen. Why did my little world have to implode? With Inez being there, I was pure, innocent, obedient, and untarnished. Without her, I was not sure if I was ready for what lurked ahead.

I felt like the chickens when they'd take their roost in the middle of the day because of a coming storm. I just didn't know mine would be a tsunami.

Going to Inez's funeral, seeing her lying there in the casket and, later, seeing her lowered into a six-foot hole, crumbled me. I wasn't ready to say good-bye. My final words to Inez were, "I'll forever love you, and I truly wish you could have been here as I turned into a man."

Aunt Willie consoled me to the best of her ability. She couldn't understand why there wasn't any outpouring of tears. She didn't even know that I was an introvert. John pretty much did me a favor by staying out of my way, or maybe, being an introvert himself, he understood.

For weeks after school, I'd retire to the pew in the backyard under the shade tree. One day I was just lying there when something inside burst and the tears began to flow like a river. It appears Inez had caressed my soul, assuring me that our souls would unite again someday.

Ironically, it was with my return to the Juke Joint that my character forever altered. Still, I would go on unfailingly thinking of Inez, holding her within my heart — at least until the day that drugs started to permeate the essence of my being.

Chapter Thirteen

SHORTLY AFTER THE MID-SEVENTIES, sultry singer Millie Jackson made a big splash with a song that many women sang along to with fervor. What little I did decipher from the lyrics, Millie repeatedly used the word Par-tay (or something of that nature).

Sister Childs, a divorcee for whom I often ran errands, was stuck on the song like a needle on a scratched record. I surmise, it's safe to assume, that the devil must've gotten into Sister Childs (around this time, comedian Flip Wilson said it best when he said, "The Devil made me do it").

All I knew was that Sister Childs had changed. She was no longer that pious member of the choir who had once belted out angelic-like hymns. Now, with a marriage gone awry, gospel albums were sprawled across the living room floor, with Millie's worn-out record perpetually spinning on the turntable, and if it wasn't playing—Sister Childs was humming it.

I loved the song, too. I loved the energy in which Millie exerted while singing it. I also loved Sister Childs's rejuvenation. In part, because I thought Ms. Jackson was singing about partying, having a down-home-righteous good time.

As Sister Childs continued to exhibit an abundance of renewed vigor, a cigar smoking, middle-aged gentleman with wolfish features started hanging around, which gave me insight into the happenings with Sister Childs, and with him there, my errand services were requested less and less.

Can't say that I much liked the fellow, his being a drifter and all; neither did I know much about his background, generally supposing, like many, he'd hopped off a boxcar. What I did know, though, was that he was impeding my mannishness.

To add more clarity, those days one would say that Sister Childs had weight back there – or "junk in the trunk" – in other words, an enormous posterior. Her endowment would shut down operations while she'd take her mid-morning stroll into town as she'd pass by the mill (just another glorious view the Juke Joint afforded me). Cat-calls would come from mill workers operating caterpillars, forklifts, and dump truck ... all bewitched by Sister Childs' divine gift.

If I weren't making brief trips to the store for Sister Childs, or taking pleasure in other plausible amenities, her phone was growing out of my ear. Then there were Saturdays when her niece visited. Hours on end, she and I sat on the porch playing Jacks or Pity Pat. I admittingly had more interest in the man on the moon than such girlish games. I endured. There's much to be said about a testosterone drove teen. And luckily, for the niece, something came up, and she stopped coming around. The way I saw it, she was a Pity Pat game away from becoming a woman. To my shame even as a teen, I was a *pup* on the prowl.

Talking 'bout dogs on the prowl, K.C. kept me in the know by providing me with teasing glances at porn mags. If not voluntarily, *again*, when he'd nod off from over-indulgence, I'd lift it from his back pocket. Dead drunk, he'd awake and pat his back pocket or the inside pocket of his sports coat. If his prize possession were missing, he'd wail like a banshee.

K.C. and I manipulated one another to a science. And with time moving forward, K.C. fell deeper into porn.

As the Juke Joint jumped with gaiety and inebriated lovers clung, K.C., to my satisfaction and others, piled up more porn mags. One of note: *Hustler*. From a quick examination, I discovered it to be more hardcore than the glossed over Playboy.

Men, even with their wives close by, buried their faces into K.C.'s *Hustlers*. Especially, pictorials of John Holmes.

Even today, I hate to think that the Juke Joint's patrons were enthralled by this white man's equipment. Nonetheless, John Holmes' widely celebrated 14 inches had those brothers in shock—a white man wasn't supposed to be hung like that. Least in the eyes of brothers, who professed to represent the *legend*.

Inez was no longer around to check my behavior, to slap me in the mouth. I, thus, felt like the Juke Joint was "my joint." On weekends when customers impatiently banged on the door, I often opened it and served the impatient customer in my fruit-of-the-looms, sporting an early morning "boner." Why not? The place had already given me the vantage point to view a myriad of stark naked bodies.

There at the Juke Joint, sex seemed airborne, and the hairy membranes inside my nose stayed frosted with it.

Moreover, subtle talks with Robert about the facts of life had readied me for puberty. At least I thought. He even lectured on (as he called it), "the art of masturbation." I strongly dissented; the idea held no appeal. Furthermore, the Juke Joint's environment already was the launchpad for my sexual throes.

Even with unjustifiable disdain towards Mr. Walker, begrudgingly, I had to admit the man had flair: sporting reptile cowboy boots with matching belts, and the latest double-knit, three-piece suits that were purchased from a Flagg Brothers' catalog. Flagg Brothers' catalog; hip threads for a town that shopped at the Dollar Store and Thrift Shop.

Mr. Walker, in an inscrutable manner, blew into town and within three months assembled a make-do Juke Joint. Simply for the sake of knowing that "Juke Joints" inundated Winn Parish, with distinctions merely being name and function. One could, I suppose, call me a Juke Joint connoisseur: A connoisseur in that I was in awe of dance halls, dusty floors, blood stained walls, and hanging around grown folks.

Among the gore, there was history: aged flyers of legendary musicians, Blues singers, and well-known guitarists.

Blues never sat well with me; though, primarily it was all folks listened to at the Juke Joint. I found it too oppressive, but for a short time, it did grab hold of me. Especially, B.B. King's unique guitar plucking and his singing something about a "Lucille." For years, I suspected the love affair of which he sang to be some fine woman; however, as it turned out, Lucille was a guitar.

As we know—with black folks—Blues have deep roots; however, in my case, I shied away from Blues for two reasons: sad and drunk folks would listen to it, then drum-up all their problems—especially, that of long lost lovers.

As a kid, I remember asking myself, *why would folks sing along to this music*; or *for that matter, even listen to it if it elicits such sadness?*

Many years would pass before I would come close to answering that question:

As with other emotions, sadness becomes addictive.

In no time at all, Mr. Walker's place was jumping, and that made me mad. Why? Because the Juke Joint was becoming emptier by the weekend. Left with no other course of action, I snuck into his place every chance I got.

Wasn't long at all before Mr. Walkers' knack for attracting and sustaining customers explained itself. I had to give it to the man; a shrewd businessman he was. Underage or not, if my quarters fed the Jukebox and pool table, he pretended to be oblivious to my being there. In fact, much of my pocket change was squandered, even gambled away there; there were customers who felt my money wasn't exempt, either.

Each time I burst through Mr. Walker's saloon-like doors, it was plain to see that his place had more to offer than the Juke Joint, such as the notorious Boom-Boom-rooms.

The mere opening of a Boom-Boom-room door resulted in many a miscue; numerous pool games were lost because patrons were trying to catch a glimpse.

Chewing on the butt of a cigar like a horse chewing hay, Mr. Walker would cock an eye whenever I went too close to one of those rooms.

On many occasions, a sister with creamy brown skin was the object of our attention. She occupied more rooms than any of the other women, I've now termed what she must've had— "that red-snapper"—the kind of stuff that once *it* gets a hold of you, there's no getting enough. And the foot traffic suggested she had just *that*.

It still brings me great pleasure to recall the first weekend this temptress sashayed into the Juke Joint. She provided the place with an up close and personal view of a pair of crimson colored painted-on Daisy Dukes. With much respect to the *Dukes of Hazard's* Daisy, that evening, this woman took cutoff jeans to new *heights*. She was stacked. Serena Williams stacked! And it was as if she waved a magic wand over the Juke Joint, causing men to salivate.

Winnfield, a town full of mills with its loggers partying virtually every day was motivation enough for her to move into a boarding house two blocks from the Juke Joint, one block from Mr. Walker's, and open her own shop. Let's just say, she had no need to reserve the Boom-Boom-rooms anymore.

Mr. Walker still remained a true character. He established himself as the Gene Simmons of that time; he had a *thing* going on with his tongue that kept his place at full capacity, with debauched women. I thought nothing of it as he teased women in popular fashion by licking the length of his cigars. Further, his popularity gave rise to plenty envy (although Sister Childs and other women saw it differently, understanding Mr. Walker's talents); K.C. even got himself a new subscription catering to that esoteric group of men....

Earlier on, though the message shot over my head, Ms. Millie Jackson had been spelling it out in her song; she had been singing about a guy, like Mr. Walker, one whose tongue defied the conventions of sex.

*****

Nightly, I crept in and out of my bedroom window. Wasn't long before I recognized that I didn't own the night; there was another night owl: Old lady Ms. Esther. She lived in the alley behind the Juke Joint. And she would see me passing at all times of the night.

Creepy that Ms. Esther was, known for dousing folks with urine that was slung out her back door. I tried hard to make it my business to be vigilant when passing her place; although, there were times she'd surprise me and splash that greenish yellow urine a few feet in front of me. If I were to describe the smell, I'd have to say a skunk's acrid odor had nothing on Ms. Esther's piss!

In an old maid's uniform, she sometimes surfaced at the Juke Joint. Always buying a couple of beers to go. One thing I can give her credit for is not blabbing about my comings and goings. Perhaps it had to do with what little I knew of her business: From time to time, she played hostess to a couple of the Juke Joint's patrons. Many times, as she ushered the visitor out the back door, my timing was impeccable; we locked eyes as if to say, "I won't tell if you don't."

The next time our paths intersected was at church. My being there was strictly perfunctory; Ms. Esther's being repentance.

As she sat in a front pew, the Holy Ghost seized her as soon as Pastor Williams got into the meat of his sermon. She—a stout, big-boned woman, all 200-plus lbs.—could've easily suffered her convulsions alone. Although she got the customary fanning, the aid of tentative ushers was slow to arrive. Boy! Could she act out––a whirlwind of elbows, knees, and feet, always resulted in fainting.

I continued blazing my trail pass her shotgun shack, and she persisted in giving me a searing gaze with ten or so off-grey alley cats running in and out her back door.

Out of nowhere, an owl scare threatened to interrupt my forays into the night. The gossip was—an old hoot owl had assailed two children. As far as I was concerned, no owl was going to quell my fun. Besides, at that time, I was attempting to get next to an older girl named Patty.

On one night, I came face-to-face with what might have been this alleged owl. And I lost the staredown. The creature had a more fervent look in its eyes than I; I opted not to do battle. I'm uncertain as to whether it was the owl that was spooking the neighborhood or not; however, the owl had more relevance when it did a 360-degree turn of the head, eyeing me from every angle. Of course, I chose to skedaddle on home.

That night the owl did me a favor in breaking the spell of Patty, a teenage mother, who had been turning me into a young sucker. She was a consummate teaser. She knew what I wanted and dangled it before me like a carrot, had me delirious. She'd reel me in with porn-like numbers, swirling her tongue around popsicles and ice cream cones. Or saying, "Terry can you fasten my bra," all the while getting ready for her real suitor. If that wasn't enough, "I'm hungry," she'd gripe. And off I'd go to fetch burgers and fries at the truck stop at 1:00 A.M. like a good lap dog.

As if I hadn't been slapped hard enough yet, there were times the baby's father would come around and she'd leave me inside to sit with the child while she and he tried to rekindle a dying relationship. Thanks to Patty, that would be my first and last stint at being a sucker of that sort. My being reserved got me nowhere.

To her and the owl, I was grateful for the lesson...

Chapter Fourteen

FOR YEARS, the "Field" functioned as an old plot of land for football and basketball games, and church-sponsored Easter egg hunts. Finally, to every kids' delight, the Parish furnished swings, seesaws, and a shed that gave us cover from the rain. However, they failed to replace our old hoop. Nevertheless, we made do with the net-less, rusty rim. It didn't' matter. Dr. J. inspired us. He was our Michael Jordan. Basketball was a big part of our lives, and we played in most weather, only thunderstorms and lightning scared us inside.

The Field also made a good scrapping spot to settle our differences. Whenever anyone got mad about a foul, or too rough of a tackle, it was on. Some of this was okay, but in my view, a lot of it was mindless carrying on.

One fellow, named Horace, would run home to get his Dad's shotgun at the slightest altercation. Most of us had good enough sense to scatter whenever Horace went into his fits of retaliation. I never waited around to see if he was bluffing or not. I'd get back to the Juke Joint as quickly as possible. Strange as it seems, Horace always resurfaced at school as if nothing had happened. We often questioned our sanity for letting him back into our games.

That aside, Horace and I had an ongoing conflict. I had no regard for the fact that he was older than I was, and I had never forgiven him for an insidious act. One Halloween night, he had made me the butt of a prank by chasing me down and smashing a rotten egg against my head. Thankfully, not long after, I experienced a growing spurt, which rendered Horace and I equal in size. And I leaped at every opportunity to punish him for his insolence.

On the other end of the spectrum, Horace had three Brick House sisters (of the sort, the Commodores sang about). Two of them were tomboys and played boisterously with the fellows and me on the Field.

The eldest of the three often assisted me in abusing the swings. Rather than swinging side-by-side, we stood facing one another other on the same swing, alternately using our legs to pump the swing higher and higher, nearly touching the power lines and elevated branches. From across the Field, cantankerous, old folks would yell:

"You bad ass kids stop that before you kill yourselves."

"I'm telling your parents."

"You're tearing up the equipment before others get a chance to play on it."

Other times on the Field, Derrick, a lefty, and I got into formidable battles. Besides being a lefty, he had another oddity––during our bouts he would shed tears. *Strange emotions.* I was uncertain of which option to take: fleeing from the lunacy or picking up the nearest inanimate object and go a little crazy too.

Despite the scraps and scars incurred, we somehow sustained a friendship.

Ironically, it was at Derrick's house where I discovered an odd recipe: his brother adding sugar to beans. At first, I admonished him for wasting such a good helping of beans. Why? Beans ... I love 'em!

Tiring of my odious comments, he set out a saucer of sugary beans. After sampling what I had thought to be wasted beans saturated with sugar, I conceded—not bad. In fact, they were good. As most would do, he gave me that I-told-you-so smile.

Another time while on the Field we spotted a cutie pie, a red-skinned sister. She sat watching us from old man Chris's front porch. Now... we had a history with old man Chris, who with good reason held us in contempt for robbing his plum trees. The most succulent plums in the T&G Quarters. We had a strong desire for them and shook the old man's trees down whether they were green or ripe. Our taste buds *forever* watered for Mr. Chris' fat, juicy plums.

Our excursions into his backyard didn't come without risks. You see, if old man Chris could've gotten his gun out and had been able to hit the broad side of a barn, that alone would've compelled us to take our plum raiding elsewhere. Often as we raided his trees, I pictured him like a startled bat taking flight in daylight, which characterizes old man Chris' actions and state of mind. If I were to supply a mental picture of Mr. Chris, I'd say he was identical to Grady on "Sanford and Son."

The plum trees were in plain view from his kitchen window, and the rustling of leaves and crackling of branches always alerted him. Often when he had spotted us, we would hear him skidding in the hallway infuriatingly slamming into walls, heading for his hunting rifle. We continued to fill our caps and pockets with plums while old man Chris steadily fumbled and bumbled in his kitchen. By the time he had focused his coke bottle glasses, we had had our quota and were ready to roll. I always wondered how he hunted coons and rabbits with such poor vision. Cryptic indeed!

Before digressing, the subject was the girl on the porch. She would come out and watch whenever we played football, for the porch afforded her a panoramic view of the Field. She never set foot on the Field, though. Being new in town, I'm sure she thought it better to sit and watch, sort of check things out.

Being the boys, we had interpreted her action of watching us as a sign of interest. As most vain youngsters would do, we dared one another to accost the out-of-towner. Forever partial to a reasonable dare, with little difficulty they persuaded me to engage her in conversation.

The porch was only a stone's throw from the Field. A bad pass thrown intentionally landed near Mr. Chris's mailbox. As she stepped down from the porch, I guesstimated her to be around 17. Leaning forward to get the ball, she looked me square in the face and asked, "What's your name, boy?"

Now that was not a good start to any conversation with me. I responded with, "Hold up with the boy stuff; you don't look to be much older than I am." You see, hanging with grown folks daily, made me feel grown, not 14; therefore, I took her comment as an affront to my ego.

"Seeing that you have an age complex, let's try this again. My name is Shelia. What's yours?"

"My name is Terry," I responded. For even at 14, I had an exaggerated sense of self-significance. Glancing back to the Field, I observed my good-ol' friends beckoning me. I continued, "I'm pleased to meet you, Shelia. You should try coming out on the Field sometime. In the T&G Quarters, the Field is as good as it gets since there's no other form of recreation around here. If you're interested, most of the girls around here play a *mean* game of tetherball."

"Thanks, I might just take you up on that offer."

She never made it out onto the Field, although my involvement in activities on the Field brought Sheila and me into regular contact. However, I lacked a certain proficiency in football, though I made up for it with asinine, attention seeking behavior. However, Shelia also found me to be personable and we began talking more. Though, she still acted a little coy.

In the passing weeks, I looked to extend my contact with her and noticed an attractive, older woman. I thought, *"Um! Mr. Chris done scored himself an old lady."* Then I remembered he had a boarding house (like much of Winnfield) and figured she was probably a tenant.

Thanks to Uncle Otis, I didn't have to linger in a state of curiosity about the older woman for too long. Catching him a little inebriated at the Juke Joint, he chided, "Nephew, I see you're getting paid to turn off the lights on the Field, these days." I looked at him puzzlingly. He then added, "You're spending an awful lot of time there. Hope it has nothing to do with the fresh face in town." He couldn't have been more right. "If so, wouldn't be right to set your sights on your sister!"

Another of life's curve balls.

"My Sister?! Thought I only had one."

"Naw Nephew, Shelia's another of your Dad's offsprings."

When the opportunity presented itself, I marched right up to the front porch. The woman who I thought to be the mother asked, "Your name's Terry, right?"

"Yes, Ma'am."

"J.W.'s your Dad?"

"Yes, Ma'am."

Another woman from Dad's checkered past.

She looked at me with disgust. I wanted to lash out and inject a little venom of my own. However, I thought it wiser to keep my comments to myself.

"Don't just stand there looking like J.W. Take your gapped-tooth ass on over there and give your sister a hug. It seems you two have already met."

It felt as if I were in quicksand; my feet were immovable. I was ashamed of the thoughts that had been swirling in my head.

How was I supposed to hug this girl like my sister when I'd attempted to put moves on her?

There's no denying that which is true. Shelia was dead on Dad; she had those pronounced Hill features—thick eyebrows, big nose, and a Grand Canyon smile.

A mere three years my senior, she adopted the protective sister role. Though she still wouldn't come out on the Field, nor darken the door of the Juke Joint. During other friendly encounters, she would proudly claim me a little bro; showing pure kindred love which I, in return, relished and reciprocated.

A step-sister, half-sister, out-of-wedlock-sister, it didn't matter, she was a Hill all right; like the birds, like the rest of kin——she had migrated. *Up and moved.*

Then there was my little brother Michael with whom I seldom had contact. With certainty, I knew where he stayed, yet I wasn't about to enter Carmen's orbit. The woman was out there *emotionally*, and not wanting to get wrapped up in that caused my relationship with Michael to suffer.

On perhaps two occasions, Carmen showed up at the Juke Joint. And she brought Michael. She could guzzle beers with the best of 'em—but alcohol didn't assuage her evilness. During those brief visits, Michael and I made an earnest try at bonding. I wanted so badly to gel with my little brother; however, the egregious mistake of rough handling him, resulted in his retreating deeper into a shell. Plus, Carmen appeared ready to butcher me for making him cry. She didn't understand—my true aim was in getting him to interact with other children.

In short order, someone else became of interest: Michael's biological mother, Felonia, a regular patron of the Juke Joint. Though she kept hush about it, she looked upon me with favor because of Michael. And because of the cumulative nature of my mannishness, I, too, looked upon her with special regard due to her having a blessed figure — a figure that was the envy of most women at the Juke Joint.

Weekends belonged to Felonia; she lived to strut her divine endowment at the Juke Joint. She in a pair of seamless slacks left an indelible imprint on my memory. Moreover, watching her taught me another thing—when some women get drunk, please let there not be a super-fine woman in the midst; the "bad" one always gets accused of trying to steal the other's man. Felonia was fine as she wanted to be, but incapable of fighting off a gnat.

It was bound to happen, so when the cat-fighting began, unsurprisingly, I would grapple with the patrons for a ringside seat. I even had the pleasure of retrieving several collector's items...

*****

That summer, following my weekly dip in the public pool, I noticed white scaly spots on my arms, neck, and shoulder areas. All summer long, I fought off the miserable itch of tinea versicolor (a skin fungus). I thought it a symptom from chlorine. I couldn't quite put my finger on it; it felt like a thousand maggots leeching off my skin.

Another time while leaving the pool, I spotted Shelia on the porch of a shotgun shack. She was in repose, taking in the sun's rays. Seeing her brought me immediate unadulterated elation. I rushed to her. She invited me to take a squat, and I expressed my deepest concern regarding her disappearing act. In turn, she tried pawning some whack tale off on me, her little brother. Her confession was that she had taken off and gotten into a relationship. Like many before her, she had been swooped up by a mill worker who promised a life outside of Winn Parish, including marriage, the white picket fence, a family—the typical dreams that are salable to virtually any seventeen-year-old.

I now, in turn, played the protective sibling. Supported by mannishness--I was better suited for the role, anyway. It displeased me to see my sister performing duties of a housewife, slaving over a stove and pinning clothes on a clothing line when she should've been working on getting her diploma. *Corny*, though. I determined the easiest way to get back at her boyfriend—for wasting her life—was eating up his food. Something essential for which he labored. So, at every turn, I invited myself to dinner, especially at the slightest whiff of beans and ham hocks. As I've mentioned, I had a strong liking for beans. So much so, my brother Robert had previously named me "bean" and the nickname stayed attached for some time.

As the story continued—Shelia, again, disappeared from my radar. Shelia, another family migrant....

*****

Crazy. One morning before school, a neatly dressed elementary student ran up to me short of breath. (The two schools—elementary and middle—were only a stone's throw apart.) He wanted to know if I was Terry, to which I replied, "Yes, I am."

He then introduced himself as Kenneth. Then dropped the boulder: "You're my brother!" Little Kenneth provided me with an interesting way to begin my day. And I had seven periods to mull over another of my father's misdeeds.

I didn't dare doubt Kenneth's disclosure. A song had long supported what I believed to be true about Dad: The Temptations', "Papa was a Rolling Stone." In my sometimes dreamy state at the Juke Joint, I would relate many of life's enigmas through songs. "Papa was a Rolling Stone" was a definite standout. Whenever Melvin's (of the Temptations) baritone chimed in about Papa's markings at different homes, I clearly envisioned it to be my father.

That weekend Kenneth invited me over to meet his mother. After seeing her, in this case, I nearly upheld my father in his infidelity. To me, Lucille was the black version of Dolly Parton. While there, she set the record straight about her and my father's brief union. Providing everything short of a blood test, she professed that little "Kenny" was indeed my brother. At that point in my life, I was as gullible as the character Gomer Pile on "The Andy Griffin Show."

I was glad to be big bro; Kenneth made sure that I abided in the role, too. He now had a big brother who was tasked with backing off bullies. Later, he'd point out at least a dozen. Damn! Many of them were attempting to bully me.

Age didn't seem to factor in this level of madness; if you had pocket change or anything worth seizing you were a target. Kenneth gave me more of a reason besides my own to rail against them. It touched me witnessing little Kenneth convulsing because some middle school kid had emptied his pockets.

Weekends were now reserved for Kenneth. We spent a lot of time playing on his pinball machine, and up until that point, I hadn't seen one. Not only that, he had quite an array of modern toys sprawled across his mother's decked out pad. I wasn't used to seeing plush carpet and drywall; linoleum was all my eyes had beheld. To me, Lucille's pad had the makings of a penthouse. Like the Jefferson's, I thought she had "moved on up to the Eastside." "Moved on up," she did! Like many, she was enjoying the synthetic fruits of the housing development boom—the projects.

One morning before the first period, Kenneth had crossed over to visit me behind the gym, where all the black kids hung out before class to play basketball or football. That same morning, he came within seconds of seeing big bro lying prone eating dirt.

(Mary was an eighth-grade classmate with whom I thought to be sharing a crush. We had been passing notes for weeks. And silly me had carved our names inside hearts on desks, trees, and whatnot.

Well Keith, Mary's boyfriend, decided to teach me a lesson. As I was not paying attention, he casually walked up to me, and like Bruce Lee dropped down on one knee and slammed the heel of his palm into my very private parts. The acute pain suggested he was trying to shove them up into my throat.

Had he not just rendered me speechless and inert, I would have threatened to kill the fool. With my family jewels aflame, I fell like a sack of rocks. And right before my world blackened, he promised, "If you ever mess with Mary again, you'll get more than just a taste." It would be next to impossible for me to recount his threat/promise in its entirety, because for that brief period, my world wasn't as I had previously known it to be. However, I still can picture that bearded, gritty smile, possibly because I never saw him again.)

As little Kenneth extended a good morning to me, my voice had not yet returned. When I did utter something, it raised concern within Kenny.

It's crazy how in the end it all played out. Though I'm unable to remember what happened following that period, for some inexplicable reason I perpetuated the hereditary pattern ... I abandoned little Kenny.

Chapter Fifteen

CHAOS ENSUED AFTER INEZ'S DEATH, with John sleeping less and drinking even more. I began skipping school, and when I did go, it was only to play sports. Topping things off, the Juke Joint was now more lawless than ever.

Me on the other hand, a mere sip of beer now and then no longer sufficed. I had graduated to 16-ounce cans with so much of the stuff lying around, and with John not being remotely accurate with the inventory (let alone customer's tabs) as Inez had been, no one was going to notice a few missing cans.

During a trip to the restroom, I caught one of our customers climbing through Inez's bedroom window, the room where we now stored the alcohol. The man even had the gumption to put a finger to his lips for me to be quiet as if I were a five-year-old kid. When I brought this to John's attention, he not only shrugged it off but he continued allowing the guy to patronize our business. Customers continued coming through Inez's window to raid the alcohol as if our untrustworthy customers were heralding news that the booze was free for the taking to their equally deplorable friends.

An old, cheap pile of plywood, previously swapped for drinks, now finally came in handy. I nailed a large slab of it over Inez's window to foil the plans of any future theft by any of our so-called customers. With the theft of our liquor putting us in the po' house, there was no confusion as to why the Caucasian gentleman was sponsoring our place less and less.

Sometimes John's bizarre behavior would throw me for a loop. He even allowed the guy that had stabbed him to start hanging around again. His head is the one Inez had beat into mincemeat. He'd gone straight from the hospital to jail. Who's to say he still wasn't harboring animosity towards us? Whenever I had to serve him drinks, that ugly, horrific scar running down the side of his head seized my attention, its presence hypnotizing. It reminded me of Inez's violence, and served as a warning that this same man, at any time, could go ballistic. There were moments when we'd indulge in small talk, but he'd just grind his teeth and chew on his bottom lip. Wasn't long before I concluded it best to leave the angry fellow to himself.

With Inez no longer around, I was without harness or shackle. Those explicit things shared by Robert wouldn't stop entering my mind, and I couldn't wait to experience them for myself. During that time, my hormones were screaming so loud I saw things that weren't there. Of the female customers, one was a woman named Anita who gave what I thought were inviting smiles and glances. I took it a step too far by boring my eyes into her cleavage and other pleasurable places.

With Anita enjoying the drink, I bided my time. Her boyfriend received a monthly check. But with them drinking it up, there was always a shortage of money. Most of the time, when the liquor was depleted, he would either remain in a stupor or stumble off home. No matter the outcome, Anita always found it hard accepting that the party was over.

She was a lightweight moocher, with an old man who only partially took care of her insatiable desire for alcohol. Which, for her, meant she didn't have to mooch full time. When her man's pockets became barren, she'd have the look of a sick puppy and either John or one of the customers would buy her a drink.

Living wrong, one's conscience has a way of gnawing.

Outlandish things started taking place, or things I perceived to be outlandish. During nightly trips to the bathroom, I saw

Inez's door open, and that is when I knew it hadn't been open when I had first walked by. It was hard for me to fathom my mind playing such blatant tricks. Making matters worse, I would hear the front door open ... then creaking, as if someone had walked across the living room floor before stirring in the kitchen. Whenever trains ran through in the early morning, they would shake the house and drown out the creaking and the noises that had me enthralled. But this only added to my fright.

I asked John his theory concerning folks who were no longer with us. This question turned out to be a ghastly mistake. He told me that he'd been born with a veil over his eyes enabling him to see dead folks and dead animals all his life. It was why he wasn't afraid of dying. I believed him. After all, he did allow a guy to knife him while he stood there with a pistol in his hand.

Skeptically, my next question was, "Do you have any knowledge of Inez visiting this house since she passed?"

"Seen her tucking you in last night."

With him not smiling, I had no alternative but to take him seriously. I also knew I didn't need to be hearing this. Now, there wouldn't be any sleep. I stood there in front of John doing my best to pretend I was the brave fellow. Despite thinking highly of Inez, the thought of her ghostly remains tucking me in gave me the *heebies*. If she was going to be immortal, let her do it up in heaven. As though it were the topic of the day, John continued with the subject, dooming me to a day of heavy contemplation.

In crisis situations, however, my young mind served me well. I needed an outlet, a reprieve of sorts. I needed a friend like Charles, someone to help me ward off the things driving me crazy. It wasn't easy convincing Mrs. Johnson to let him come stay with me for a time, and he wasn't sure if he even wanted to come because of the sour note things had ended on between us.

He kept saying, "You know, your problem is you be tripping too much."

I assured him that wouldn't be happening anymore. And then, needing all the backup I could get, lured him with promises of all the ice cream he could eat and all the cold soda he could drink. I spoke of us frequenting the public swimming pool, and the benefit of seeing his father regularly.

Finally, he agreed.

As days passed, we recaptured our old friendship, but things were still questionable. Charles did most of the nighttime chores. I didn't like going into Inez's room, especially now that it was darker because of the plywood nailed over the window. The room was too damn creepy for me now and, rational or not, I felt as if I could sense her lurking in the shadows. At least part of these feelings were due to guilt. I knew I wasn't living right. The drinking, the lusting, and all the rest of my mischievous behavior was beginning to weigh on my conscience.

*****

With summer rolling in, Uncle Otis had begun nudging my father about me visiting him, so Dad sent me a bus ticket. My first ride on a Greyhound was quite enjoyable, the scenery and cordial people fascinating. Due to several layovers, I didn't arrive in Houston until late in the night.

For one reason or another, Dad wasn't at the station to greet me. Instead, he sent his fiancée and two of her children to pick me up.

Dad's fiancée was extremely nice, with a kindness that would be unwavering throughout my stay. Dad wasn't good at expressing affection. All I got from him was a lukewarm hug.

Except for normal kid stuff, the children and I got along great. Esther, Raymond, and D.D. were older than I was. Robin was two years younger, while Russell and I were the same age. He and I spent more time together than anyone, with him serving as my tour guide throughout the different areas of Houston.

Raymond was the heckler and comedian of the bunch. He always made funny cracks about me, my clothing, my being a virgin, and whatever else he could get a laugh from at my expense.

Esther was dating, so she didn't have much time for anything except her boyfriend and her teenage issues. Whenever we did interact, it was always positive. She'd pinch my chubby cheeks and call me cute, all quite the boost to my feeble self-esteem.

Robin was a cute little chocolate specimen. A tomboy, most of the time she just smiled and stared at me.

At six-foot-eight, and with a giant afro topping him more than seven feet, D.D. was the family tree. He chilled in his room, talked on the phone, smoked some good-smelling reefer, and listened to the soul music of the '70's. He was the individual who introduced me to the "Funk Music" of Bootsy Collins, George Duke, and Parliament. Also, D.D. gave me my first real introduction to pranks, but on a much broader scale.

One day calling me into his bedroom, he told me there was a phone call for me. Placing the receiver to my ear, I heard the sweetest, softest voice ever. She began telling me how we could indulge in all kinds of erotic things. But whenever I'd ask for her name and number, D.D. would snatch the phone and say, "Don't be asking my girl that!"

I received these calls for two more weeks until one day there was a malfunction in the recording. Using my gullibility, D.D. had taken me for a ride. But those sweet recorded voices had taken me on a sexual odyssey. He told me that these girlfriends of his had been given permission to talk to his little, innocent step-brother from Louisiana. No question I was the laughingstock of the house. I had often wondered why everyone snickered at me. D.D. had told them to go along with the practical joke. But with my feelings altogether punctured, I didn't see the humor.

Russell and I started scouring D.D.'s room, looking for whatever we could find. I didn't feel so bad about it since D.D. had made such a spectacle of me. Russell and I would find condoms and different colored rolling papers—no doubt for smoking reefer. Though we did find matchboxes filled with seeds, we never did find his stash.

It was in Houston where I had my first run-in with a gang. Apollo was the leader. He'd sent one of his torpedoes (followers) to check out the new kid on the block. One night, while Russell and I went to the corner store for a Slurpee, this torpedo rode by on his bike, and for no apparent reason, tried to spit on me. Russell started laughing, but I grew madder by the second. Calling the guy a punk, I then hurled a few insults his mother's way. Russell didn't find that amusing at all. He knew I was flirting with danger. The torpedo, however, turned around and leaped off his bike ... a moment later, we were doing the dance.

Seeing he was going to be having one long evening with this old country boy, he pulled out his switchblade. Afraid of taking a knife in the back, I was unable to run and instead learned just how fast I could backpedal. Luckily, Russell had made it back to the house to get Raymond and D.D. Getting there just in time, D.D. yelled, "Germaine, what are you doing? That's my step-brother!"

Germaine yelled back, "Then teach him to watch his mouth."

I would go on to see Germaine everywhere: the gym, the swimming pool, and all the house parties. Eventually, Apollo sent

Germaine to recruit me for their gang. When I declined their offer, we got into another skirmish. (I've always been more inclined to be a loner.)

Later, I watched them extort a prominent businessman's son. His car was their car. His money theirs. And when that wasn't enough for them, they made the kid steal even more money from his Dad. All I knew was that I had no interest in this gang.

Raymond claimed that Bunny, the neighbor's daughter, was his girlfriend. Speaking with her about them being an item, she denied it. Being that she and Raymond's courtship wasn't official, I made designs on Bunny. Raymond warned me to keep my distance, but she was a little too exquisite for me to take the hint.

Bunny's house was the only place in the neighborhood with a ping-pong table. She loved the game. Having played for years on cheap plywood tables back in Winnfield, it just so happened to be a game that I excelled in.

Still hot at Russell for the incident with Daryl, I planned to terminate our friendship. He'd been bustin' a gut while I could've been seriously injured. Russell's Mom encouraged him to do something special, so we made up with him taking me sightseeing through the town. I was in awe of this big metropolitan city. The skyscrapers were nearly a hundred stories. In Winnfield, one was lucky to see a three or four-story building, the grandeur of it all was astounding. Houston had a beautiful skyline. That very day birthed my fascination for big city life. The idea of being around the movers and shakers, the hustle and bustle, had ensnared me.

Russell and I snuck into swank hotels and rode the elevators to where we'd stare down at the people on the ground. That far up, people looked small as ants. Security would either chase us out or escort us to the sidewalk. From there, we'd ride the transit buses all over the city and into the different wards. Russell even showed me the Fifth Ward.

Fifth Ward had the southern climate Dad loved. Russell showed me the *Hole in the Wall*—another Juke Joint—where Dad spent most of his time. Being that I was now in the big city, I couldn't help but think of Robert being a runaway in this vast place. I remembered Russell telling me how Robert once slept on these transit buses whenever he'd get tired.

Our last stop of the evening was the famous amusement park named *Astro World*. From quite a distance, one could hear people screaming on a roller coaster called "The Cyclone"· It was supposed to be one of the biggest and steepest roller coasters in the world.

Russell had an intricate scheme that would permit us free entrance. He explained that the fence was made of some rubberish kind of material, flexible enough that we could squeeze through. Once we made it to the small opening, I saw it was slightly larger than our heads. Because he was bigger than I was, Russell went first. With a little help, he managed to wiggle through. The plan, of course, was to pull me through from the other side. Half my body made it through when Russell just stopped. Looking up, I saw a big German shepherd 15-feet away headed directly for my defenseless self. Russell ran to a prohibited area and started scaling a fence. Quick, I abandoned the plan, and wiggled back to the safe side from which I had come. Everything was a mess, with Russell on the inside, and me on the outside. How were we going to explain this to our parents?

Anyway, the thought came to hang out at the exit doors. After an hour of waiting on Russell to come out, I decided to barge in when the next group exited. Once inside, I was chased through the maze by security. It felt like forever, but finally, I got away.

In passing, I happened to encounter an elaborate disco. I knew Russell was an excellent dancer. (And with a promise that I wouldn't get too close, he'd even tried to teach me how to two-step. We'd put black eyelash thickener on the peach fuzz of our mustaches and sneak into the local discos.) Sleuthing further, I noticed Russell and a lovely young lady dancing away. Immediately, I walked onto the dance floor and told him we needed to talk. He told me to let him finish his dance. Right then, I realized that in a heated, sticky situation, he would never be there for me. No matter how much I liked him, I could only take him at face value.

The following day he attempted to make it up to me by taking me to the house of a promiscuous girl that had shown a slight interest in me. I was in the midst of having my first sexual encounter when her Dad started keying the front door. He had come home early from work. Out the window I went, headfirst. Once again snickering, Russell was waiting outside. This time I wasn't so mad at him. The thought of what had almost taken place had my mind in a far loftier place. I savored those pleasant thoughts for a long time.

Russell had other grand plans. That day I was introduced to his roguish side. There was a large grocery store called Weingarten's. For days, we went into this store and stole whatever we wanted. I, being the novice, was the one who came close to getting caught. Store security had been watching me through the mirrors facing down the aisles. But Russell and I made it out before I was apprehended. We did, however, notice two of the security guards trailing us. They would give chase until they reached our gang-infested neighborhood.

The little time spent with my father isn't worth mentioning. I spoke with him maybe three times in the course of three weeks. There was an awkwardness we couldn't seem to get past. Dad would drink after work, come home, eat dinner, bathe, and go to bed. Then he'd wake the entire house with his chainsaw snoring. It was while Dad was asleep that I noticed Russell sneaking into Dad's room and rummaging through his pockets and wallet, retrieving whatever he felt would not be missed. It was wrong, but I didn't care; I even held out a hand for my cut.

My time in Houston had ended. A day before it was time to leave, Dad's fiancée told me not to tell Dad she was taking me shopping for school clothes. I didn't see what the big deal was, but I enjoyed the fair sum of money she was looking to spend. Once inside the department store, she told me to pick out whatever I wanted. I was so stunned by this good deed that she had to prod me to start shopping. I chose some of the apparel I had seen in the recently released Saturday Night Fever.

Morning came fast. Dad had already left for work, so his fiancée dropped me off at the bus depot. After we had embraced, she told me she would love to have me in her home anytime. I sat there, knowing that in only three weeks' time, I had outgrown Winnfield and that things would never again be the same in that small town.

*****

Arriving back home, I found more than I had anticipated. I would never have thought folks like Charles and John could have missed me so much. Not even sure if I was coming backing, John was more than happy to have me home.

Charles, of course, needed me to help lessen the workload. Still, I had to commend him for enduring the Juke Joint and all its drama.

What I enjoyed most, however, was the welcome back I got from the neighborhood kids. With most of them having never been out of the parish, they were inquisitive. Plus, they had found my new flair irresistible. The bell-bottom double-knit slacks and jeans, the fake silk shirts, and the platform shoes got me more attention than ever.

John and Charles, though, weren't ready for the scoundrel I had become. I had started stealing money from the cash box so Charles and I could afford more recreation. We started going to more events at school, hung out more at the parks, snuck out the window at night to take in the local fair, as well as patronizing the local Dairy Queen. Charles didn't like participating in my scandalous activities, so I left him behind a few times. After that, he started keeping stride.

Charles's Mom must have sensed me corrupting her baby boy, for on this one weekend, she made him go home. That left me alone to deal with the creaks and shadows of Inez, the presence of which I was starting to sense even during the day. My conscience was killing me. I wasn't living right, and Inez knew about it.

Charles's Mom must have been clairvoyant, for if she hadn't pulled him away, Charles would have been a witness to, or even a participant in, the contrived way I lost my virginity.

It happened that sometimes John would get so intoxicated he wouldn't know what was going on. One specific early morning, there was no one at the Juke Joint except Anita, her old man, and K.C. John was out of it, Anita's old man was slumped over from drinking too much, and K.C. only had a corner left in his wine bottle so he began stumbling towards the door. With the liquor now gone, Anita bore her commonplace sad look.

I had wheeled John to his room and helped him to bed. As usual, he was out before his head hit the pillow. When I returned to the front room where Anita was, she gave me an intense look like never before. By now, K.C. had gone, and her old man was still slumped over and slobbering. I asked myself what Robert would do with such an opportunity? I then went to Inez's room and got a pint of vodka. Coming back into view of Anita, I held the vodka aloft and then proceeded to my bedroom.

She followed.

That morning, any pretense of remaining purity was taken away by this thirty-plus-year-old woman.

Ten or so minutes after our getting started, her old man woke from his stupor and headed for the restroom. Looking down the hallway, he noticed two gyrating naked bodies. Coming into the room, he called out, "Anita, what on earth are you and that boy doing?"

Anita shamefully turned her head while I desperately continued screwing this other man's woman, knowing all the while I was running the risk of a physical attack while in quite a vulnerable position.

Though I was spared any wrath, Anita's old man remained disgruntled. And despite his continued patronage, every time our eyes happened to cross, he'd give me the stare, the one that told me that if only I had been a bit older... That, and the reality that Anita was no longer allowed to come by.

Not to be dissuaded, I would try to catch her next door at Catherine's. Catherine would come over to get alcohol for her. When she did, I'd make up an excuse to use her phone so I could be around Anita. I tried everything under the sun, but Anita just seemed too embarrassed to do it again.

I even thought about visiting Anita at her home while her old man was getting blitzed at the Juke Joint. But Anita and her old man lived in Ms. Nan's old haunted house, and I couldn't bring myself to brave the memories there. Unsurprisingly, John was informed of what had taken place, and quite surprisingly—at least to me—the man did everything but shake my hand and congratulate me. He even told me how he'd often wondered if I only just played sports when I was absent for all those hours. Being that it was my first time, I preferred just to let John entertain his thoughts concerning my virginity.

What I did know was that I had lost a sacred part of myself, and that I had lost it to a sad, alcoholic woman who had probably slept with half the town.

Chapter Sixteen

SADLY, FOLLOWING MY SEX SCENE WITH ANITA, my hormones continued to rage. Becoming outright obscene, I found it difficult keeping my scruples intact. Most of the single women at the Juke Joint were now under my heavy scrutiny. Some knew, and some were too intoxicated to concern themselves with what a teenager might be going through. Wasn't long before I realized that my efforts were futile.

Despite Charles and I having been close, our relationship had now turned impersonal. And, after giving the situation some thought, I knew why. Charles constantly watched me while I was in white heat, failing at attempts to seduce even his sister. With much displeasure, he moved back home. Our friendship never was restored. And even to this day, the division between us remains.

Even with Charles back at home, I'd sneak out of my bedroom window and visit his house. Karate Joe would be watching karate flicks until the early morning. And if not those, then it was shoot'em up, bang-bang westerns. Mrs. Johnson was always asleep. Charles would sometimes be up with his big brother watching television. Their sister, Doris, would be on the phone, courting. She was a year or two older than I was. With reason, however, age never prevented me from making an advance.

Doris was a tomboy, so whenever she grew tired of my pestering, she'd turn on me like a tiger. John would sometimes ask, "You been runnin' through sticker bushes, or did you get snagged in a barbed wire fence?"

Not able to say I'd been pestering Charles's sister, I received what I deserved. John and I both enjoyed the laughter at my expense.

Most of the teenage girls in my area preferred older guys, the older men having more to bring to the table than I did. I didn't have a car for the drive-in movies, not to mention the other activities that took place in the backseat, and the local in-door had been closed for years. Nevertheless, Charles's sister remained the hunted and I the hunter, until I departed for Seattle.

About that time, John's cousin from another parish, a female, came to live with us. Though she was supposed to do the cooking, she ended up doing a lot more of the drinking. In her sixties, with her wintry smile, she was at least good-looking. Unbeknownst to John, she had been waging war with hard liquor for years, and most the time, she was drunk before noon, often resulting in her passing out before dinner. Safe to say, with her tussle with the bottle, alcohol was the victor.

No surprise, and no doubt, quite convenient for her, she slept in Inez's room, where the alcohol was kept. During trips to get more booze, I often saw more than I should have. It was a quick lesson learned that with an over-indulgence of alcohol, there often follows a lack of modesty.

One late night en route to the restroom, I looked into John's bedroom ... and I couldn't believe my eyes. John, flat on his back, and her astraddle. With no one seeming to notice, I took in the view for several more minutes before carrying on with my business.

Charles Sr. had a thing for women in their sixties or seventies. If I remember correctly, he was in his early forties. One thing I do know, he was smitten by John's cousin. Charles Sr. had a smooth, charcoal-black complexion coupled with a nice personality that made him a favorite with the women of the Juke Joint. And there was instant chemistry between him and John's cousin. Not long after, he started crashing with her in Inez's room. Most of the time this was on the weekends which was when he could afford to get drunk and careless.

My little sexual event with Anita did nothing but increase my sexual hunger; I had to wait for an opportune time. One evening, as John's cousin was taking off her stockings, I entered Inez's bedroom and attempted to blackmail her. I told her what I had witnessed with her and John, and that if she didn't have sex with me, I would tell her boyfriend, Charles Sr. She laughed, "Boy, get the hell out of my room."

She then told me that I hadn't seen what I thought I had seen. I didn't tell Charles Sr. and she never mentioned my proposal to John.

For me, the kissin' cousin cliché was more than just a line.

*****

The winds of change brought more, unexpected, good fortune my way.

Patricia, my sister, her husband, Ronnie, and their daughter K.K. paid me a visit. While there, they lived in Sadie's place. Each day after school they would come over to the Juke Joint. The three of them showered me with much love. Ronnie and I developed a bond that still exists today. I can still remember Ronnie asking, "How can you focus in this place and do your homework?"

I smiled, "I've gotten used to it."

I hadn't seen Patricia in years, but all that nurturing love she'd once given me came flooding back. Perhaps from being the oldest sibling, she whole-heartedly did all she could for her brothers. I can't speak for the rest of the Hill clan, but I know she will always have a sacred place in my heart.

(Actually, "I'm disturbed that I haven't heard from her the last few years. Amid my current incarceration, loneliness creeps in no matter how hard one might work at warding it off. Longing for loved ones slithers in, too. From my many prison stints, I've come to realize the brutal truth, whether it's loved ones or whomever, some folks just don't have it in their hearts to extend affection to individuals who're imprisoned. The emotions that stem from loneliness can cause a man to fall prey to things that do not benefit him. Patricia once asked, "Brother, are you institutionalized? Is there something you enjoy about being incarcerated?"

I have constantly tried to convince her how much I hate being locked up. Being a part of the recidivism so often read about in the paper, I was not able to easily sway her with my protestations. She's even gone as far as spelling it out with a bit more simplicity. "Brother, you must like folks telling you when to go to bed, when to get up, and when to eat."

My beloved sister saw more in me than I ever saw myself. The hurtful look she'd get in her eyes because of my actions wore on me in the worst way. I knew she was telling the truth, but I was dealing with an unforeseen force, one that had me enslaved. No one can fully understand unless they've been in the clutches of this unanticipated bondage. There are times when a person gets in too deep, to where he or she can't make the changes for the better on his or her own. One day, I'll sit down with my sister and have a nice little chat about how prison saved my life.)

My emotions were unabashed when it came time for my sister to leave for Seattle. She felt the same way. Again, she was making the long trip home without me. I tried to look at the bright side of things. She had traveled far to see about her little brother.

And it was only right that I tuck that tender gesture away in my heart for safe keeping. I should have taken the day off from school to see her on her way, but I'd thought going to school would help soften the blow of the departure. I was wrong. Instead, I couldn't seem to focus on, or accomplish, anything. Nothing but thoughts of her and her little family invaded my mind.

*****

The combination of medication and alcohol started having an adverse effect on John, with his inevitable mental anguish directed towards me. But due to the rogue I'd become, much of the verbal aspect were warranted. He never caught me stealing, but with things disappearing at opportune times and me having the most access, it was understandable that I was the target he so often pointed a finger towards.

Eventually, moving beyond mere words, he started launching the closest objects he could get his hands on. My way of thinking was: why should I subject myself to this? So instead of being a target, I'd go hang out in the neighborhood, on the field, at someone's house ... anywhere until it turned nighttime and the mosquitoes ran me in. By then, he had cooled down.

But it wouldn't take long before the drama between us resumed.

After one of our episodes, I went to Sadie with a proposition she couldn't refuse. I said I'd tend to all her chores if she bought my school clothes and housed me in one of her boarding houses. She more than gladly accepted my offer. But it wasn't long before things went awry between us.

Sadie had trust issues, and from what I'd been told, "The only way to make a man trustworthy, is first to trust him." No way this was going to happen with her. She wasn't going to trust me. Her expectations of me were unrealistic. Just as I had gotten myself in with Sadie, I found a way out. Afterward, having gone through this brief experience with Sadie, I got to know what it must have been like to walk a few miles in Robert's shoes.

It was about this time that Aunt Willie passed. Everyone around the Juke Joint was shaken with the loss. The grim reaper had called upon my favorite aunt. Rumor had it that her demise might have been helped along by her consumption of red clay dirt. It troubled me to see Uncle Otis so discontented. It troubled me even more to attend another funeral. The thought of Inez in a casket for all time had me feeling powerless dealing with anyone's funeral. Aunt Willie had always extended her love to me, and it was my rightful duty to pay my final respects. But come funeral time, I was paralyzed.

Uncle Otis's had been one of my favorite retreats. But now that Aunt Willie had passed, I was reluctant to hang out there. And then there was my conscience, ready and fast to condemn me. I wasn't sure if I was ready to deal with yet another ghost, even if all this ghost crap was self-induced.

At the least, John and I had been conversing time-to-time during my stay at Sadie's. With our differences ironed out, I was more than happy to move back in, at least if he didn't become too unhinged again. Plus, it was nice not having to bathe out in the hallway like I had at Sadie's. My conscience reminded me that my behavior had contributed to John's attitude.

*****

One day, getting home from school, I found my mother waiting for me. Her presence at the Juke Joint had me completely dumbfounded. In prison, she had become chummy with this construction worker named Samuel. A long-time corresponding girlfriend had introduced them. She'd been spending her parole at his residence. Also, Samuel was the one looking after Mark and Ronald while she visited me. During her stay, Mom lived at Sadie's in Robert's old room.

We never conversed about the state of our family or any of the thoughts that may have been holding her captive. So, I based things on the positive aura coming from my mother. Now, though, I see why I'm so reserved, so introverted. It was inherited from her. This was the start of my learning how my mother couldn't express herself or show any affection. I've always taken under consideration that Mom started bearing children while she was young and immature, that she's always carried an enormous burden of pressure.

I couldn't help but inquire about Robert. She told me that Robert and Samuel didn't see eye-to-eye, that Robert's rebellious nature had flared up once again, and that he'd been ousted from the premises.

When we weren't talking about this or that, I would just stare at her, my mind beset by thoughts of her being out of my life all those years. At the same time, watching her smile at me illuminated my soul, let me know where I had acquired my own big, wide smile.

Though she didn't drink hard liquor at the Juke Joint, Mom would knock back a few cans of beer. Her favorite color must have been red. Daily, she'd don this thick, oily red lipstick and whenever she'd drink her beer, lip-prints would be left on the can.

Samuel started calling every day, several times a day, requesting Mom's return. Knowing she'd soon depart, I asked if she had brought me any souvenirs from Seattle. I wanted something to remember her by. She said she'd left so fast that she hadn't had the time. All I knew was that I needed a piece of my mother, something of value to her, so I started collecting the cans with her bright red lip prints on them and placing them in my closet.

The time finally arrived for Mom to leave. We exchanged hugs and good-byes, then she headed back to Seattle. With that, everything returned to the same old run-of-the-mill drudgery at the Juke Joint.

Whenever I felt the need to be close to Mom, I'd take the beer cans out of the closet. I kept them for months until John said I had to do away with them—something about the alcohol attracting rats and roaches. Might've been the barley in the beer, I don't know. Reluctantly, I disposed of them.

Mom's visit had unsettled me. I strongly felt I no longer belonged in Winnfield. Soon, John and I started getting into arguments over insignificant things again, with the final straw coming from him throwing a beer bottle.

Turning, I ran out the front door but before I could shut it behind me, John fired his pistol over the top of my head, missing the back of my skull by about a foot and leaving a gaping hole in the door. I couldn't believe that John had shot at me. The only thought that registered was that he'd had a pistol in his hand when he'd been stabbed. I had been thinking the medication and drinking were driving John crazy. Now I had the confirmation.

I often pondered about what was pushing John over the edge. Could it have been that when we'd gone to the bank to obtain his life savings it wasn't there? I remembered pushing his wheelchair into the vault where the safety deposit boxes were kept. The bank manager had opened the box, and John had reached in and pulled out three fifty-dollar bills and some Avon jewelry. He'd been so stunned he almost fell out of his wheelchair. His life savings had been squandered.

This ordeal had John mentally shaken for quite some time. I couldn't begin to imagine what Inez might have done with their finances. I surmise that when one relinquishes total control, as John had done, this could be one of the unfortunate results. Now he was stuck with regret, no finances, and no answers.

Uncle Otis was now my only cushion. I let him know what had happened with John, and the gun. Taking me in, he placed a call to my mother, letting her know that John had fired a bullet barely missing my head. It was months before she responded.

*****

One day out of the blue, my other brother, Jimmy, the oldest of us boys, came to see me. What had me mystified was why Mom had named two of her sons Jimmy? Over the years, Mom seemed to be battling so many issues from the past that I decided to let this one pass.

The first thing I noticed about my brother was that he was big, easily six-six. The second was that he owned a car. A gentle giant, he tried teaching me how to drive until he started smelling the brake shoes. I had been riding the gas and the brakes at the same time. Sadly, that would be our last encounter in the flesh.

I've spoken to him twice in 30 years. One time, I built the nerve to ask my father about Jimmy. Dad told me, "That's Mr. So-and-So's son." From that day on, I understood things concerning Jimmy a lot better. Jimmy was the outcast because we had different fathers. Maybe that explains the two Jimmy's.

Last time I spoke with Jimmy, he was in Dallas, Texas, working as a dietician. Unknowingly, I lied, saying I'd be by shortly to visit. I never made it. And that ended up being the last time I, or anyone in the family, ever heard from him. When he didn't show for Mom's funeral I felt he'd been lost forever. Another sad family episode.

*****

Always between jobs or selling unlicensed liquor, Uncle Otis, nonetheless, always made sure I had my needs met, and that I attended school—daily.

Coming in from school one day, I learned from Uncle Otis that I had a hundred dollars waiting for me at the Western Union station. It was to cover my trip to Seattle. Back in the '70's a hundred dollars could be stretched. He drove me to the shack that housed the Western Union office. There, I gave them my middle name. That was the code to use since I didn't have any identification.

This was the day I'd been waiting for since I was four-years-old, the time had finally come to rejoin my mother and siblings. Before departing, I treated Uncle Otis to Dairy Queen. Our favorite meal had always been fried chicken with fries and a large vanilla malt.

It was rough breaking the news to John. Even after all the turbulence, he hated to see me leave, and I hated looking into his moist eyes. His words still resonate today, "How can you do this to me after all I've done for you?"

For years, those words have vexed my soul.

The next day, Uncle Otis took me to the tiny Greyhound Depot where I purchased my one-way ticket and he hung out with me until my bus came. When it was time to leave, he gave me a manly embrace and did his best to keep his eyes dry until my bus was out of view.

Finally, I was on my way.

However, once the bus turned the corner and Uncle Otis was out of sight, I wept more than I had ever wept before. My soul was weeping because of what awaited me in Seattle. I was to be reunited with my mother and family. What opportunities would this mean?

If only I'd known how clueless I was.

Chapter Seventeen

NAIVETÉ ABOUT RUINED MY TRIP TO SEATTLE. It all started with a three-hour layover in Alexandria Parish. With nothing to do but wander in and out of the terminal, I soon grew bored and made the decision to check out some of the shops along the street.

Salt Lake City, Denver, and Los Angeles, amongst others, made it difficult for me to remain inside the depot. The lure of these big cities had already snared me back during the time I'd spent in Houston. Finally, I did reach the great Pacific Northwest, then the Evergreen State of Washington, and last but not least, Seattle, the city of rain.

The day I arrived it was raining and windy. I placed a call to Mom but since Samuel had taken the car to work, she had to wait for my sister, Patricia, to give her a lift to come and get me.

A bit irritable, I waited. I'd been hanging out in depots, and beyond, for three days and didn't understand what could be taking them so long. Finally, they arrived and the greet was all big smiles and hugs.

My mother's apartment wasn't far from the Greyhound bus station (unlike my sister who'd driven from the other side of town), and was on the second floor with a nice decor. What appealed to me was the Africa pictorials hanging on the walls. This two-bedroom apartment was cozy and was going to take some getting used to. Regrettably, one of these tiny rooms was going to have to be shared by me and my two brothers, Ronald and Mark. Looking out the window at Yesler Boulevard some two blocks away with its allure of pimps, whores, and dealers, I knew I could make the adjustment.

With Mark and Ronald still at school, Mom told me about a park three blocks away that had an outdoor basketball court. So deciding to take her up on the offer, I went to kill some time while waiting for my brothers to get home.

The park was far better than any in Winn Parish, but being a school day, was scarce of kids. The bit of youth that was present were the regular truants. Some of these later became my friends, the kind I didn't need, and more examples of the wrong kinds of choices I made as a kid.

One big fellow smiling with a full beard, headed my direction. To my amazement, it was my big brother Ronald matured beyond belief. We hugged and talked about everything two forlorn brothers could think of.

Then we played some ball.

It was wonderful being back together. No more climbing trees and no more Tarzan hollers. We were now under the same roof. Little did I know that the unbreakable bond once shared had been laid to rest in Louisiana.

Ronald looked at me and said, "That skinny guy coming our way is your brother, Mark."

This anorexic-looking fellow with that big, wide, trademark Hill smile came running to me with such exuberance that the collision almost knocked me down.

With the after-school crowd finally piling in, we could play some full-court games. What a joyous occasion to flaunt my Louisiana backwoods skills for my two citified brothers.

Mark was more outgoing than Ronald, and shortly, I would learn that he was also a master manipulator. Before we left the park, he whispered that tomorrow would come some fun that I'd really appreciate.

When we made it home from the park, Samuel was there watching the evening news from the couch in the living room.

119

Mom introduced us. Shaking hands, he gave me a gritty look, grinding his teeth, and showing the muscles in his jaws as if to say another one of them damn Hill boys. Later, Samuel would stress that all he ever wanted was to have my mother for himself.

After the newness of my presence had settled in, we cleaned up and took our places at the dinner table. I could tell from the vibes emitted that Mom was overjoyed by my long-awaited arrival. The fact she couldn't articulate her feelings verbally didn't matter; I was elated just the same from the care being transmitted back and forth. Whenever she'd stare and smile at me when she thought I wasn't looking conveyed an untold story of love.

Mom hadn't lost that good southern style of cooking. The food was quite delectable, but the glare received from Samuel made me feel like he was only thinking of me as another damn mouth to feed.

An old country boy himself, Samuel knew I could easily eat him out of house and home. And he wasn't far from the truth. I had a bottomless pit for a stomach. Where I had come from, folks loved to see you eat and the food was plentiful. Back in Louisiana, food that Mom had to go to the market for was grown right in a person's backyard; this new level of frugality-with-chow would take some getting used to.

Before I retired for the night, Mom told me I'd be enrolling in school the following week. The rest of the night entailed Mark and Ronald speaking disparagingly of one another. Listening to them bicker, I couldn't help but gaze out the window at the intriguing nightlife waiting outdoors.

Ronald spoke of Mark being in juvie for stealing bikes, motorcycles, and whatever else he could think of. Mark bashed Ronald about being a Momma's boy and not having had many girlfriends. The comedy roast lasted a few hours until Samuel finally sent Mom into quiet us down.

While the others slept, I spent most of the night fixated on the action taking place on the boulevard and dawn ended up rolling in quicker than my tired eyes had anticipated. Breakfast didn't consist of the grits, eggs, and pork chops to which I'd become accustomed, and it was with a heavy heart—and an empty stomach—that I realized cold cereal or instant waffles were now the norms.

Mark and Ronald devoured their breakfast and rushed off to school. With Samuel a foreman at a construction site, he made his hurried exit as well. This left Mom and me with plenty of needed quality time.

Unfortunately, before we could get too engrossed in conversation, several loud whistles from outside seized our attention. Looking out the window we discovered it was Robert. Why hadn't he just knocked on the door? Mom told me he wasn't allowed in the house. Nonetheless, having learned of my coming to Seattle, he'd come to greet me. There was a small grassy park right outside our complex, and I met Robert there.

With Robert speaking of the good-ol'-days, the morning slipped away. He said he wanted me to meet some of his friends. Naturally, I was more than pleased by the idea, but since Robert was such a renegade, I'd first have to get Mom's consent. "Fine," she said, "but come back as soon as possible."

Not really knowing what I was in for, Robert assured me I'd enjoy myself, that I might even find favor with his female friends. Robert's feet never failed him. He'd been a marathon walker/runner since those elusive days in Winnfield back when Sadie was always hot on his trail, as well as during his nomadic stint in Houston. I hadn't planned on walking two miles for the occasion, but it was well worth it once we arrived.

Robert introduced me as his favorite little brother. The two females present were attractive and cordial. The liquor was endless and the music rather soothing. They kindly told me a brother of Robert's was a friend of theirs and that if I were ever in the neighborhood, to feel free to call. Even though they appeared to be in their 40's, I quickly agreed.

With my head starting to spin a little, I figured it best to make it home. Before we parted ways, Robert promised he'd be whistling for me again soon. The breezy walk home cleared my head, hopefully enough that Mom wouldn't notice my drinking. In fact, I was glad to be off my smoking feet. I had yet to build the tolerance for walking up and down Seattle's steep city hills. Robert did own a car, but with him not keeping up on the maintenance, it was currently out of commission. Plus, he'd accrued several tickets for driving without a license. There'd be no driving around in Robert's nice green Nova anytime soon.

Mom and I shared a little small talk when I got back with her asking the typical questions: How did I feel being away from Louisiana? How'd I like the contrast between city and parish? I didn't dare tell her of my fascination with the city right outside my bedroom window, which so far had been the highlight. She inquired about the relations between my brothers and me. And on and on. Yes, with the many years of separation things were lukewarm between us, but the ice was slowly starting to melt.

Mark, the young master manipulator, finally made it home from school. True to his word, he took me by Sharon's. Sharon was a 28-year-old woman who lived in a luxurious apartment. Exchanging introductions and pleasantries, Mark persuaded her I was a virgin. Being more than ready to gladly accept the pleasures she'd bestow upon me, I didn't argue. Afterwards, I made a mental note to not forget the way back to Sharon's place.

Later, the knowledge would come in quite handy. On the way back home, Mark told me he'd been acquainted with her for a while and that he thought she liked me. He also told me not to mention it to Ronald, because then Mom would surely find out. Later, I'd discover that Sharon was a prostitute, had been for years. This was the first of many sexual escapades involving me and my little brother.

And let me say, the little fellow never rested. There was always something brewing. I've yet to encounter anyone with his vast reserves of mental and physical energy. It was unfortunate that Mark's boundless pools of vigor had been channeled in the wrong direction. Problems or not, he quickly became my bosom buddy. With him, there'd never be a dull moment. Little did I know, he was helping fuel my sexual addiction.

At home, I could see why Ronald was the healthiest in the family. While Mark and I were thin as rails, he had the physique of a professional linebacker. Ronald made sure his chore of washing dishes never changed. And while performing his chore, he made sure his hands helped themselves to whatever was left over.

The day finally came for me to enroll in school. Garfield High was the largest school I'd ever attended. In the late '70's, Garfield was predominately black. I found out later that Quincy Jones and Jimi Hendrix had also attended Garfield High. Because school had already been in session for several months, getting the classes I wanted to be in turned out to be difficult. Luck running strong, the classes I did end up with turned out all right. In between classes I'd see this girl named Donna. She had a locker in the same vicinity as mine.

Donna reminded me a lot of Betty so the attraction was instantaneous. And with my southern drawl, she found me irresistible. She also liked the way I stuttered and stumbled over my words. My moss-grown wardrobe brought about much hysteria also. Even my brothers, Mark and Ronald, got their fair share of chuckles from my antiquated clothing. Little did they know, the laughs at my expense would be ending sooner than they could've imagined.

Don't remember how I landed gymnastics, probably something to do with all the alternative class picks being filled. With the class coed, things worked out just fine. Including myself, there couldn't have been more than three other guys for the close to twenty females in the entire class. And with my southern accent, I was again happily the center of attention. By now, I was starting to acclimatize and already started using this to my advantage. More than that, I was ready to start fraternizing with girls my age.

This one Prince look-a-like, a fellow named Dana, wasn't enjoying the laughter and attention I was getting. The school's Casanova, and immediately taking a dislike to some potential competition, he barraged me with a string of profanity. Fuming at the oral assault there was still a side that admired the audacity of this five-foot-three-inch banty rooster. But before things could escalate into something physical, the instructor kicked us out of class.

Despite the rocky start, Dana and I developed into good friends. In fact, we remained friends for quite some time until a particularly unpleasant event took place between us.

Dana was one dapper individual, with a very distinguishable style of dress. He went on to show me how he'd attained his extensive wardrobe. Almost daily, he'd frequent some of Seattle's largest and well-known department stores. There, he'd shoplift whatever the occasion allowed. Being that I desired those fine garments as well, I started accompanying him on these little five-finger ventures.

Whenever she wasn't present, Ronald was Mom's eyes and ears. So it wasn't surprising when she looked at me reproachfully after discovering a closet full of new clothes. She'd been tipped off by my envious brother. Likewise, she knew that I was no longer wearing any of the clothing I had brought from Louisiana.

Dana and I became partners in crime in many ways. I quickly learned that his addiction to sex compared to mine. His mother was a school teacher so his pad was available five days a week for our sexual excursions.

The school had taken on a different meaning for us. We began attending only to get high or meet girls who were as promiscuous as we were. Just like us, they hung out in the hallways or in the school's parking lots smoking marijuana. Dana and I were on a quest for sex and more sex.

My voracious sexual appetite continuously led me to Sharon's door. I provided her with my youthful stamina and she, unfalteringly, provided me with her sexual prowess. Fortunately, Sharon only lived three blocks from my school. When things were uneventful, I'd split and call upon her. With her hooking mostly at night, she'd be there, for the most part, to answer my call. Mark didn't like the fact that Sharon and I were getting closer but what could he expect after introducing me to the woman?

Meanwhile, Donna and I were engaged in a courtship that was quickly maturing into a full-blown relationship, but not without its rough spots. Donna was getting thrown off balance by the rumors going around. In particular, the one of my having sex up on the school's third floor after classes let out. I was guilty, yes, but there was no way I was going to admit to it. After all, my glands had a mind of their own, and a will that would not be denied.

Donna had a secret she was keeping from me, too, stopping by her home one day, her teenage cousin answered with an infant in her arms. The baby was Donna's... a staggering blow. Despite being the very definition of infidelity, the idea of another man in Donna's life was frustrating; the reality was, my lady-love had a baby, and that baby had a daddy. Somewhere along the way, I knew it all was going to spell out drama and of the kind, that up to this point, I'd been free of. At some point I knew I'd be meeting this fellow, a reality I wasn't looking forward to.

She said she'd been unwilling to tell me because I probably wouldn't have understood and that she was afraid the revelation might end our relationship. But I loved her and was sure that I would've understood. Amid this friction, she went on to call me a cock-hound. Little did she know she'd hit the bulls-eye.

Everything she said rang true.

Having been on the receiving end of plenty of tutelage from older women, my sexual aggression was a bit too much for Donna. Whenever I visited, we'd spend most of our time in her bedroom. But she wanted more. She wanted to hold hands, take strolls through a park, and go to a movie... basically just do some of the things that lovers did. But it wasn't in me. I had it all wrong, and she didn't have that supernatural ability it would take to quench my thirst for sex.

*****

One weekend, my brother Robert came whistling for me. Mom understood our closeness and most of the time she didn't object to my spending a little quality time with him. He'd take me to the house where he was living with his mushroom eating Caucasian friends, Dan and Mary. Being swingers, the least one could say about them was that they had a very open relationship when it came to sex. Since I was under eighteen, I never got the chance to swing with them. But I did get to hear all the graphic

126

details Robert provided. Most of the time they'd drink beer, eat shrooms, and listen to the Beetles.

Truthfully speaking, the whole scene I was thrust into had me behaving badly from the start. This would be just one of the many holes I'd dig for myself, deep pits that would take several decades to climb out of.

The season changed and once again, summer found itself at the door. From Samuel's first glare from across the living room, I knew something was stirring. In reality, I thought it a possibility that he was thinking of a way to rid himself of the Hill clan. Without fail, his grand scheme came into view sooner than I thought. He'd somehow convinced Mom to send us away to live with our father, and before I knew it, my brothers and I were on a bus headed for Texas.

Chapter Eighteen

AS SOON AS THE BUS PULLED OUT of the station, Ronald began missing Mom. Mark, the adventurous one, marveled at the idea of seeing different faces and places. I wasn't all that thrilled with the idea of going back. Plus, thoughts of Donna and everything else getting left behind kept invading my thoughts.

Depot debutantes aside, the bus ride back to Houston wasn't as pleasant as the trip to Seattle. With the cramped quarters and the oppressive humidity, people were testy. Ronald's nerves were frayed to the edge—not a pretty sight with a man his size. But with Mark ... well, he couldn't have cared less.

After three days of bus-riding blues, we finally pulled into Houston. Like before, Dad didn't come to greet us. Instead, he sent his faithful fiancée again. Mark and Ronald took offense, but from my previous experience, I understood Dad—a little.

Being more of a homebody, Ronald was looking forward to some rough adjustments. Dad had the perfect remedy waiting for him and his dishwashing hands.

Arriving at the house, I found things the same except for Esther having moved out with her boyfriend. Mark and I didn't hang around the house as much as our homesick brother, instead we took pleasure in Russell's accommodations. With Ronald, Dad figured his hanging around the house for a willingness to work. Before Ronald knew it, under the scorching hot Texas sun, he was transformed into a construction worker. Week or two later, Dad forced Mark and me to try our hands at it as well. Fortunately, shoddy work saved us and a short time later we were released.

Things didn't work out as smoothly as they had with my first visit. First, Robin had started budding rather nicely and Dad's fiancée didn't feel too comfortable having my brothers around. She had cause. The young master manipulator was on the prowl, and it didn't help matters with Robin thinking Mark a cutie. It was only a matter of time before her defilement, because she wasn't ready for a player like my bro.

With Mark and me no longer employed by our father, Dad's great idea was to send us to Louisiana. Astonishingly, Dad drove us. Upon arrival, a strange thing occurred. Dad pulled in front of Uncle Otis's and told us to go and say hi, that he was in a hurry. As we did this, Dad drove off. The whole situation was uncomfortable for Mark and me, and Uncle Otis was caught completely off-guard. Explaining everything to the best of my ability, he just shook his head in disgust; knowing his brother, he was no longer amazed at the despicable things the man did. For the time being, he was stuck with two menacing nephews and two more mouths to feed.

Without delay, Mark surveyed the tiny town of Winnfield and almost immediately began wooing the girls I had grown up and gone to school with. Didn't take long for them to yield to his charms either. Neither did it take long for him to make some new enemies. Mark was oblivious to how fast talk traveled in this small community. Practically overnight, the brothers of these young women became quickly irked that some city-slicker had swooped into town with only one thing on his mind.

With John having grown haggard from the struggle of maintaining the Juke Joint, there was no warm reception when I brought Mark around. And Mark didn't like coming unless he got a chance to climb through my old bedroom window for a few cans of cold beer. It wasn't long before an end was put to that.

He had one bumpy entrance heard by John and after that, John banned Mark from the Juke Joint.

With me, the old folks in Winnfield were stand-offish. They could sense a change in me that wasn't for the better. Even Mrs. Johnson didn't welcome me with open arms anymore but she did, at least, allow Mark and me to visit. Charles was no longer around. He had gone to stay with some relatives in a nearby parish. Enjoying my brother's big-city stories, Karate Joe took to Mark fast.

With things pretty limited in Winnfield, Mark became restless. And it goes without saying that something was bound to happen. It did. One afternoon on our way home from the local grocery store, Mark spotted a motorcycle parked on the side of a mobile home. Wasn't but a moment before his adventurous spirit took hold. Being a big dirt bike, he (of course) needed my assistance in pushing it off the property just in case someone was home. We didn't need to sound an alarm. Once we got two blocks away, he kick-started it and we took off.

Everyone in Winnfield knew that when we came to town we didn't have a motorcycle, so seeing us blazing through the neighborhood for days at a time on a bike started causing some friction. Even Uncle Otis started to question us, but with no proof on-hand, he had to back off.

We kept the bike in an old unused barn.

Then things began to get even crazier. One day I went to the barn to check on the bike when I noticed there were three more. Ridiculous. Looked as if every bike he laid eyes on, Mark stole. Soon we even had the local law cruising by Uncle Otis's, checking us out from behind their suspicion-filled mirrored glasses.

Mark did his best to teach me how to ride, but all he achieved was helping me learn some new ways on how to kill myself. My timing with the clutch and throttle were uncoordinated. Though it wasn't a good idea, we let Karate Joe join in and I'd take him for long rides out in the back-ways. Seemed to be one of the most fun times of his life.

One day we stopped by the local grocery store to pick up some goodies. After we had what we wanted on the counter, the owner asked if we'd seen a bike fitting the description of the one we had in the barn. Of course we hadn't seen it. But the store owner had a little ingenuity of his own.

"Fellows, I don't know if you are aware of this, but we're offering a $500 reward for that bike. So, if you come across anything, you yell out a word. Could end up being half-a-grand richer."

Walking back to Uncle Otis's, we pondered what could be done with that kind of money. Didn't take too much ponderin' either. Not with that kind of bread on the line—plus, we'd still had three more bikes to boot.

Going out to the barn, we brought the bike to the grocery store. The owner asked us to push the bike around back while he went to get the reward money. To this day I've never seen police officers arrive on a scene so fast. Hoodwinked like the suckers we were, the whole town shook with laughter.

Arriving at the jail, I noticed Karate Joe crying in a cell. I felt terrible. I'd gotten my longtime friend into trouble. And there was no way out. On top of being caught red-handed with stolen property, several of Winnfield's upstanding citizens had filed complaints about our little band on bikes disturbing the peace throughout the neighborhood. Karate Joe had been brought in for questioning the same day. Considering he was over eighteen, and thinking him the bad influence, they let Mark and me go under the stipulation that we were considered to be under house-arrest—indefinitely.

We were just being escorted out of the jail when Mrs. Johnson and her two daughters arrived. Mrs. Johnson was so disappointed in me. All she could do was look at me and keep walking as her two daughters called us everything except a child of God.

Knowing house-arrest wasn't going to work, Uncle Otis sent Mark back to Houston. I got to stay around for another couple of weeks. I'd sneak away from the house to visit John. He had moved in the gentleman Karate Joe had slapped to help out around the place. John wasn't ready for no old folks' home—not yet. There was some more drinking to be done.

Still, things were now a lot more inconvenient for John. No longer being sponsored by the Caucasian gentleman, John's sole source of income came from the sporadic profit generated from the Juke Joint and his monthly pension. And as far as the Joint went, it was fading fast and had already turned into a repulsive pigsty hardly worthy of the roaches that had over-run the place.

John truly wanted to ask me to stay, but he'd seen the change in me. There was no more deep southern drawl. I had purposely worked to shed it. And from my short time in Seattle, I had adopted street-lingo as my tongue. No more the county-bumpkin, my role models now consisted of hustlers, procurers, thugs, and drug dealers. Winnfield would never again fit into my scheme of things.

Though I loved them, there was no one in my immediate family to hold my respect like my sister, Patricia, a woman I revered and the only positive influence out of the whole clan. Having said that, what John had sensed within me was true. I was out of control, spiraling down and I couldn't see it. And if I had ... I probably wouldn't have cared.

Not able to afford to keep me around, Uncle Otis sent me back to Houston. The first thing I noticed was Mark and Ronald weren't anywhere in sight. Ronald had become so homesick that Mom had sent for him. And Mark had been so disruptive, he'd soon followed. Dad's fiancée, while thinking that I belonged in Seattle too, really didn't mind my staying.

Odd, how fast I could run to slit my throat. Seattle was just a trap waiting to spring. My stay in Houston lasted for a mere three weeks. Then I was sent back to Seattle for the start of school. That would be the very last time I'd see my father alive.

Back in Seattle, things had changed drastically. Ronald was living with another elderly couple, and after getting into trouble, and having Mom and Samuel kick him out, Mark was in a group home. Samuel wanted Mom all to himself, so there'd be no exception made for me. Exhibiting a timely show of kindness, my brother Jimmy let me stay with him and his fiancée.
He was renting a nice three-bedroom house with two of the rooms unoccupied. Things were working out fine when growing restless I linked back up with my old crony, Dana. We began using my brother's house for our personal "projects." With Jimmy and his fiancée employed, we had the place to ourselves the whole day. School was secondary at best.

When Dana and I didn't have the luxury of a stolen car, we'd catch the transit system and take our revelry out on the downtown area. Occasionally, we'd stop to woo some of the beautiful ladies passing by. One instance will never escape my memory. Dana and I were walking down the sidewalk when three ebony beauties headed in our direction. I didn't know which one of these gazelles Dana might have set his sights on, but mine wouldn't deviate from the brown-skinned, bow-legged one that was just the slightest bit overly-dressed for her age. She wore a tight gray skirt with a matching blouse and stiletto heels.

Her name was Marline.

Unfortunately, Dana mesmerized her.

He had a reputation, and I had yet to establish mine. By any description I was a handsome brother, but he was light-skinned and so good-lookin', his features were almost feminine. All types of things went through young black females' minds concerning light-skinned brothers. They considered that having a baby by one of these men, or perhaps a man of another race, would ensure them a beautiful child. Or, at least, a child with good hair. I learned this by asking various women why they preferred brothers with lighter skin.

Though she was probably just being nice, Marline did give me her number. Later when I did place a call, she was rather dry, informing me that she was looking at taking off to Oakland, California, for the summer.

Shortly after, I saw her again downtown. Reminding her of Oakland, she said she'd come back early. Of course, she'd been brushing me off which was fine; what she didn't know was that this ol' southern boy wasn't going to be side-stepped that easily.

I made time to visit Mark, especially on Sundays. Every Sunday, one employee at the group home would cook the best pancakes that I had ever eaten. The environment there was strange, but I had to look in on my little brother. Possessing an incredible violent streak, I wasn't worried about Mark's safety, but rather quite the opposite. But my worries seemed to be misplaced. Mark appeared happy with his situation, and the people around him, staff included, seemed happy with him.

It was the other residents that I didn't know what to make of. They appeared to be robots, only going through the motions either from a lack of love, a lack of hope, or from having been stripped of something sacred. I didn't know. But it was a look I remembered, and one I'd see again years later, with fellow inmates.

After several weeks of visits, I became friends with the staff cook that made those delicious pancakes. A man quite reserved and seemingly depressed, and considering our growing rapport, I finally asked: "What's with the gloom?"

Some things are better left alone.

I wasn't close to being ready for the answer. He told me he was originally from Delaware, a free-spirited person since the '50's, and that he'd been hitchin' across the states when one day he thumbed a ride from a trucker. He told the man he didn't have any money. The driver pulled out a pistol and got his compensation. "What do you mean? What happened?"

"He got his comp-en-sation."

Traumatized, the man had never healed from this horrific experience, and since that time had been unable to be with a woman. While he cried in my arms, I tried my best to comfort and console, but the help he needed was well beyond anything I had to offer.

Though it might've been unfair, I was never again comfortable at the home. Not able to tell Mark why, I simply said we'd have to dine on our pancakes elsewhere. From the beginning, I'd sensed something troubling in the man's eyes, but then I had to open my mouth and ask. Now I needed to distance myself.

Mark went on to live in many different group homes and would never again make it back to Mom and home. He had changed too much. Mom wasn't allowing him back, and Samuel was well-pleased.

Knowing my schooling was suffering (an inevitable result from not attending), Jimmy convinced our mother to let me back home. This put a lot of tension between Samuel and me.

Now that I was back in the neighborhood, there'd be a lot more time for Robert and me to spend together. And there was.

On the other hand, everything started coming at me too fast: sex, booze, and pills. I perceived it to be fun. Somehow I even found myself participating in orgies with Robert and his friends. Seattle had turned into a smorgasbord of sex, booze, and drug-abuse. I knew my behavior was getting out of hand, but there was no way for me to stop.

Chapter Nineteen

WEEKENDS WERE EXCLUSIVELY FOR THE FUNK. I lived for the Funk. Something 'bout *that* Funk music of George Duke, George Clinton, and Bootsie Collins that moved me. I cannot explain it. I knew that the funky bass guitarist Bootsie Collins and the eccentric showman George Clinton transmitted an effusive vibe.

Rotary Boys Club served as a key component to my becoming one with the Funk. You just had to be there Friday nights. Even the squares and hip squares packed the joint, if for no other purpose than to decorate the walls or to witness the entrenched thugs "turn the joint out." I, too, was in that number, watching with keen eyes knowing full well that someday I'd be among the ranks of such thugs.

During that time, George Clinton's band, Parliament, was burning up the airways with two songs: "Flashlight" and "Aqua Boogie." The Funk blared from Rotary's gymnasium and rang out into the neighborhood.

A special thanks to Anthony Ray who was spinning the vinyl. A product of the same environment, but different as he excelled in school. Like many of us, he regularly frequented the Boys Club yet expressed no interest in converting to our waywardness.

Years later while incarcerated at Pine Lodge (a Pre-Release Facility), a youngster whom I had befriended could not seem to get his fill of "My Posse's on Broadway," by Sir-Mix-A-Lot. The young man played the cassette 'til the cassette player chewed it up. He then bandaged it with scotch tape. His obsession with the song raised my awareness to Sir-Mix-A-Lot's genius.

Then again while in Corcoran Correctional Facility, I watched as Sir-Mix- A-Lot was engaged in a television interview, instantly recognizing him as Anthony Ray. I smiled. I was happy that someone from around my way had kept it real and in doing so had done it his way—the right way.

On a Rotary's night, Dana, Mark, and I typically waited 'til midnight when the place was crowded, then performed our reconnaissance, casing the joint for hot babes who were inconspicuous to others.

Inside, we operated differently. Dana had no sense of urgency. Celebrity status had already claimed him. Mild pandemonium had erupted as word circulated that pretty boy Dana was in the club.

Mark was off doing his own thing. He had his own groove, a blend of cockiness and persuasiveness, which worked well for him.

It goes without mention that both Dana and Mark could out maneuver me on the dance floor. It didn't matter though. With the lights dimmed and the floor packed, I meshed with the crowd and therefore got sweaty in the musk filled gym with the rest of those who'd come to party.

If my roguish nature hadn't earned me favor among my peers, I'd have gotten laughed off the dance floor like *Carrie*, minus the blood. I still couldn't dance a lick; that sort of rhythm continued to fail me. The ability to act cool was my redeeming quality, which averted attention from my two left feet.

Otherwise, I would have been a prime candidate for ranking. Ranking was brutal during those times. Ranking was when mouthy fellows took the liberty amongst themselves to play the dozens, talk shit about one another's mother, disabled sister, one-eyed dog, and such.

It got ugly.

Of course, these razor-tongued individuals could've easily shredded me, though my coolness protected me from their onslaught.

At the height of any party, those dreaded words were always yelled: "I DON'T CARE WHERE Y'ALL GO, BUT YOU GOT TO GET THE HELL OUT OF HERE." For me, the timing was always bad, say, in the middle of my swapping phone numbers, getting my grind on (slow dancing closer than close), or even better yet, trying to extend the evening in a more intimate manner.

Those of us without regard for curfews joined the "after party" in the parking lot. We got tilted and out came matchboxes of weed, beers, and pints of liquor. Now ... the real party was *launched*.

Girls who had a strong liking for bad boys hung out against their parents' wishes. I, too, blew past my 1:00 A.M. curfew.

Strangely, the car show (stolen cars) was most appealing to me. With the club now secured, cars raced up and down the street doing donuts in the intersection.

Later, this same craziness nearly earned me a bullet in the back. Hard and fast, I strived to earn my stripes. As this foolishness gained momentum, it raised me to an elevated status amongst my peers, serving as helium for an already enlarged ego. I learned quickly that I'd be looked upon with favor for doing what others had not the courage, or stupidity, to do yet wanted *so* badly to do.

On a Saturday night as the party let out, I was determined to be the one who would "turn the party out." Turning the party out these days takes on an entirely different meaning, as in, someone getting shot or killed. Back in the day, however, a fight or some disruption that alerted the law was considered "turning the party out."

Driving a motor vehicle without the owner's permission, I raced up and down the block with reckless abandon. A police car appeared out of nowhere and got on his bullhorn, ordering me to pull over. Which I had no intention of doing as I wasn't yet ready for the extended stay in the detention center.

For the benefit of the onlookers more so than myself, I staged a show. While thrill seekers cheered me on, I foolishly circled the block repeatedly as the police officer tailed me. An intuitive nudge warned me to put an end to this spectacle. Ignoring this flash of insight, I turned on an alternate street, rounding the block again and again until another police officer stealthily appeared using his patrol car to obstruct my path, leaving me two choices: plow into the car or drive onto the sidewalk into someone's well-kept yard. I chose the latter, resulting in a blown tire.

Now on foot with the heated police officer in pursuit warning me, "Stop or I'll shoot," foolishness combined with adrenaline propelled me to keep running. My decision to further elude the police officer was partly due to the crowd. I wondered how they would view me after getting apprehended. Would I lose my faint renegade status?

I called his bluff. I ran. That successful evasion would be my first recount of God *carrying* me. The gun was drawn, but the blast to my back never came.

If I wasn't immersed in that rare blend of Funk, I was disco skating. We kids had an appointment every Saturday at the roller rink, Skate King, in Burien, Washington. Skate King was the place to be. Everybody who thought they were somebody was there.

It would be a downright lie if I were to say disco skating enhanced my dancing; in fact, it got worse. None of which prevented me from hitting the floor with the other party-goers. Especially when the DJ dropped a Cameo song. I had the inclination to bust an ankle to that ol' muffled gorilla sound of Cameo. I could not be left holding up the wall to a Cameo song!

Skate King was also where I met Kenny and Dwight Thomas––the twins, two Filipinos—who held an appeal equal to that of Dana.

Kenny had more of a propensity for corruption than Dwight. He sometimes ended up in juvie. Mostly as a "weekend warrior." That is, the judge had shown him a bit of leniency, sentencing him to do time only on weekends: Friday through Sunday. I couldn't resist asking him why bother with the Life? Laughing, he said, "You know man, I love the rush."

A part of me still didn't understand because whenever I visited his family's lush pad everything was intact. The cars we were stealing were at his command; his dad would even lend him a car oftentimes. I supposed he just wanted to integrate with the in-crowd.

Dwight, on the other hand, was the good twin. He was incorruptible; he wasn't about to risk his freedom. However, to my astonishment some decades later, I would see him in prison. He had started entertaining the incorrigible and had yielded to the Life we—Mark, Dana, and I—had succumbed to during the disco era.

From Skate King, we evolved to a joint called the Money Tree, an elaborate discotheque which boasted dance floors both upstairs and downstairs.

Other than the love I had for slow dancing, this would be the only time that I genuinely relished dancing. It had everything to do with a popular dance called the Gigolo. The Gigolo best suited my close dancing. The Gigolo, unlucky for me, was short-lived. It became dated, as did my fast dancing.

Right before doing a stint in juvie, I was getting my groove on at the Money Tree and that's where I met Ashley. We hit it off instantly. Her looks that night rivaled that of today's video hotties.

Two days before doing my time, Mark and I made an unannounced stop by Ashley's home in Bellevue, Washington. She, a young party animal, was still in bed. Nevertheless, when she joined me, we spoke at length about making the most of our coincidental meeting. She professed to understand what I was up against: incarceration. It sounded good. Imprisonment is unfathomable unless one has been sandwiched between those lonely walls. I also knew that for my own good, I had to be proactive; I had to get my mind right to be housed in juvie.

In juvie time crawled. I spent most waking hours obsessed with thoughts of not being in the mix with Mark and Dana, weekend jaunts to the Money Tree and Skate King, joyriding in other folks' vehicles, and of course, getting to know Ashley—more intimately. In today's terms, I would be called a hot mess, a young philander addled by the excess of girls, corruption, and largely a reprobate mind. The mental energy expended on Ashley proved worth it. We connected, perhaps, through some extrasensory means.

Through fabric interwoven amongst kin, Mark felt me, too.

Two weeks into my tired stay, Mark appeared in a fashion not unlike himself: in a stolen car. I reveled at the moment as the familiar sound "beep beep" (our evacuation code) pleasantly interrupted a courtyard basketball game.

Beep beep. If by chance I was in the yard, Mark was intent on letting me know it was him. To my dismay, the dark colored slats woven in the fence didn't allow for any viewing.

Out of pure desperation to see lil' bro, I inspected every slat until a quarter-inch hole magically appeared. Squinting enabled me to catch a glimpse of the ol' illicitly borrowed gray 1978 Thunderbird, of which we'd previously, for months, taken ownership. Seeing him for that brief moment, knowing that he had thought to stop by to break the monotony of big bro's time, took the sting out of my predicament.

I was surprised even more to see some pretty young thing at the passenger door waving as though she were in a parade. Upon further scrutiny, I learned shortly that it was Ashley.

A scrupulous individual would've been elated that a hot chick (or any chick) had journeyed from an adjacent county exhibiting such exuberance for the mere sound of her encaged friend's voice.

I, on the other hand, was distressed. I knew the young master manipulator would expect compensation of some form for doing what Ashley might have mistaken as a brotherly deed.

As crazy thoughts sped through my mind, a staff member yelled, "Hill, I'm of a good mind to think you're planning an escape. If I were you, I'd get away from that fence and don't let me hear you talking to those civilians again. Do I make myself clear?"

In full view of the fellows, I sucked it up and said, "Yeah, man!" in a loud, defiant voice.

That night, my imagination provided alternate scenes of what the tiny view had offered. Of course, I added yeast—blowing it up like Mount St. Helens. In juvie, even more so than the free world, inquiring minds lived for this sort of trivia. I poured it on till the pre-dawn hours until the guards came through ordering us to keep it down. If we didn't, we'd suffer the loss of any favorable privileges.

In juvie, summertime was the most difficult time for me; I knew others were having fun without me. So, I wished for clouds to cover those blue skies. Rainy days meant there would be no cavorting, no frequenting the beach, no hanging at Lake Washington. *Straight hating.*

Lake Washington, especially Seward Park, was where we gathered during summer months to barbecue and cruise our candy painted rides. If there was a heightened vibe that day, house speakers, or even perhaps car speakers, were set out for those of us who wanted to shake our pants to some Cameo, or just plain ol' girl watch.

My reminiscing soon passed, rather than focusing on happenings on the outside, happenings on the inside started to garner my attention. Besides, those considered to be of note, who I aspired to emulate, were now on the inside also.

If we weren't swapping tales, we were lounging on bean bags in the library, infecting our minds with tales from other hoods by way of urban fiction. In no way was I a good reader, but I did possess the uncanny ability to trade places with the character vicariously. Back then, my heroes and role models were the unprincipled and unscrupulous.

*****

There were different times when tension had us *wound* tight. To unwind, we played basketball. Sometimes on a Saturday morning a staff member, Mr. Murray, with NBA-like potential, took us to school on the hardwood.

Funny, another staffer professed to be a spade-ologist–supposedly the best in the business. He was great, but even the great are delusional. Many times we took turns playing as his partner, and there were many times he wanted to slap our heads. He was also great at playing the blame game, for we had—in his mind—"trucked off" the game by playing the wrong card. Although the blunder had been his, we faced the situation and went back to our cells until tedium got the better of him. Besides, he was one of the primary distributors of our late-night snacks.

144

In truth, my liking for him outweighed the brown bags; though unknown to him, there was a character reference—he reminded me of a man back at the Juke Joint.

Perhaps my scant experience with boldness attributed to my believing magic lies within it.

With a snack in my hand, a staffer approached me: "Hill, I have an extra sack for you tonight." Like most gluttons, I trailed him into the hallway to retrieve an extra sack from the cart. With my mitts not yet wrapped around the bag, he remarked, "Hill, I need you to take care of something for me."

"Sure, what?"

"You see that punk ass white boy over there?"

"Yes, but I don't know nothing 'bout him being a punk."

"Well ... he has been using the N-word. That racist bastard needs to be taken care of. I need you to kick his ass for me. If I kicked his ass, I'd lose my job."

"You're the punk, for letting the dude get under your skin," I thought. My mind raced. I'd never been one to fight another's battles unless it was a family affair. I once learned this the hard way while rending service to a friend, whom in a panic-stricken moment *took flight*, leaving me to contend with the herculean foe.

My mind continued to search for solutions. What is this guard going to tell the homies? Would he lie and tell them I punked out? And what if I ended up back in the Hole? A rat hole of a place!

Last time I was in the Hole, what I found to be of utter interest was the haunting door right next to my cell. Months earlier, to the surprise of many, the door was kicked down and served as a passageway to freedom for several juvenile offenders.

Most everyone who has ever been incarcerated has fantasized about being Houdini. *Escaping.*

Escapism has much to do with location. Most detention centers and prisons aren't sitting right in the hood like the local Youth Center, so if you made it to the opposite side of the infamous door, you were home-sweet-home.

Most correction centers I've had the displeasure of serving time in are out in the boonies. And if the gunners in the towers didn't lay you to rest, it's for certain the gun-toting good Samaritans will.

As the head-trips slowed, I motioned for the staff to bring on this alleged racist, and he did. As we neared the squabble-room, I confronted him: "Dan, what's your prejudice?"

"Terry, you know I ain't like that."

"I kind of figured that—"

"Don't your white ass get scared now," the staffer chimed in with the key inserted in the door, "Get your ass in there."

"Terry, ain't got no problem with you," he said, walking away.

I walked back to my unit with the extra sack for which I'd long since lost my appetite. I flung the sack on a vacant bunk for my cellie. Dan was the smart one, for he had no way of knowing what was going to happen once he entered the squabble-room. He determined to walk away, tucked his pride to fight on equal terms.

*****

Healthcare at the Youth Center was unmatched. Remissness didn't play a part here as it did with other health administrations; I wasn't looked upon with disdain because of my welfare coupons.

During that stay, I had to have worn out my welcome. I visited the infirmary for both real and imagined ailments, especially my tinea versicolor which resulted in the experimental usage of every antifungal cream on the market. At last, that awful itch was remedied with Selsun Blue, a dandruff shampoo, smelly stuff.

Since the getting was good, the next order of business was my grill. My way of thinking was 'a quick cavity check and I'd be on my way'. *Right.* On my way with eight cavities. I'm still confounded as to how one without a sweet-tooth could be stricken by such a decadent enemy.

Same as my dutiful health provider, the dentist scheduled two appointments, giving me fillings that have lasted even 'til this day.

*****

The fun in juvie didn't start until Mark arrived.

Third period as I sat studying for my GED, a note shaped in the form of a football streaked across the floor landing underneath my desk:

"Hey bro, it's me. They won't let us talk, but I'm on the Southside. So, we'll talk to and from class. Yeah man, this girl named Stacey likes me but she says I'm too young, so she asked if I had an older brother. Her class is next to yours. I'll have her slide you a note. Anyway, it might be a minute before we're together again because I think I'm getting sent to Echo Glenn (a juvenile institution)."

Love you, Mark.

Sure enough, a note breezed right by my desk. In her brief missive, she ran down her pedigree. Like the story often goes with rich Daddy's girls, she was the typical good girl gone bad:

"Terry, you might not know me, but your brother Mark said it was cool for me to write you. My name is Stacey. I'm 5 feet 6 and a 125 lbs., with blonde hair that reaches the middle of my back. And yes, it's true, blondes do have more fun. Anyway, I should be getting out soon. I'm serving time for being a repeat runaway. I guess my parents are trying to teach me a lesson by allowing me to remain in custody."

The remainder of the note was pure blather. Stacey lived in Magnolia, a well-to-do section not far from downtown Seattle. She explained that her Dad was a doctor and his rigidity had forced her into seeking a life outside the home.

Stacey and I never got the chance to interact beyond our hallway gatherings; however, before she was released, she slid me a final note:

"Terry, when you get out of juvie please pay me a visit. My parents are gone most of the time. They work late into the night.

"Love your smile, Stacey."

My mind was more warped than ever—in reverie about Ashley. Now... Stacey.

When I left juvie, home was not my first stop. A priority that morphed into a trend (upon future releases), was that there were always more intimate things that needed my attention.

Since Stacey lived in the same county, she was on the top of my to-do list. Furthermore, I was learning early on how to welch off the System. If one couldn't contact a parent after being released, then his caseworker was obligated to provide bus tokens.

With tokens to spare, I hopped on the nearest transit bus headed downtown, then transferred to whichever bus would take me to the ritzy Magnolia district.

If the matter for which I'd come calling hadn't been of utter importance, there would have been a change in plans. Stacey was nowhere in sight, which didn't help my paranoid state of mind.

Ms. Prissy finally showed up and escorted me to the family's mansion.

Inside, the black maid stared as Stacey led me up a steep staircase. Her eyes followed me as if to say, "Negro, you know you're not supposed to be in this house!"

My instincts cautioned me; I didn't belong in these folks' home.

There's something about the libido that influences one to ignore intuitive nudges. Stacey and I walked hand in hand into what looked like a dollhouse as the maid glared ominously.

Stacey's bedroom was a laid-out arrangement: a fluffy, ankle-high carpet, hot-pink wall paper, matching dresser and bureau, and a pink, queen-sized canopy bed.

Flopping onto the mattress, Stacey began disrobing and motioning for me to follow. In the beginning stages of post-release adjustment, I couldn't lose my nervous tic. It was hard for me to fit back into society. At that point, I knew I couldn't lay this girl. A little light smooching and the promise of next time was all I could offer at best.

On the bus ride back, my load was not yet lightened. Hard stares came from passengers which had little to do with my thought of being perceived as an intruder, but more to do with Stacey's face cover smeared all over my face (a mime-like resemblance). The stuff wasn't easy to remove.

Later, I ran into Stacey waiting at the monorail for a trip to the Space Needle. Accompanied by a brother who just *happened* to have the last name Hill. Though torn apart by time, I still gave her that knowing look of approval. She looked damned good. For those times (the late seventies), she was a blonde gone gothic.

Which held a freakish appeal.

Chapter Twenty

THE SUDDEN APPEARANCE OF ASHLEY, a block from mom's, stunned me. She was hanging out a second story apartment window (the Flintstones, another one of Seattle's scant projects). Her family had downgraded from Bellevue to the hood. Again, my trip home was put on the "back burner."

Having been on the shelf, so to speak, and testosterone-led, when she invited me to join her I answered tersely, "Be right up!"

Inside, the complexion of things instantly changed. Ashley's Isaac Hayes-looking step-father greeted me. His name slips my memory but not the austere way he made my acquaintance. Reflecting now, I understand that he was doing as all fathers should—protecting his daughter and home.

I had observed the man's fly ride at gambling shacks and after hour joints. He was one of those cats who I was destined to pattern myself after. And the man sensed the dog in me. He perceived that I wasn't just a schoolmate in his pad taking in a movie and conducting myself like a good-natured young man. He saw through my transparency; he rushed out. The Life had summoned him.

Hearing the engine roar was my cue: "What's up with Isaac Hayes?" I asked. She laughed. "Terry, don't pay him no mind. He's cool. He ain't tripping off you being here."

"I can't tell," I said.

She sashayed over to the turntable and put on Rick James and Teena Marie. With passion, Rick and Teena belted their hearts out like two lovebirds as they sang "Fire and Desire." She then pulled out a fat marijuana joint, wrapped her lips around it, and licked seductively. "Since you're being all nervous, try this," she teased.

The bald step-father immediately faded. "Let's blaze!" I said.

Weed has never been my friend; it serves to heighten my paranoia along with giving me a ravenous case of the munchies which then results in fatigue.

Come to think of it Ashley was faster than I thought her to be. After a couple of long pulls, Mary Jane (marijuana) did her *thing*—intensifying *everything*. During my launching a litany of friendly explorations, she blurted, "I got a waterbed. Are you just going to sit there? Or, are you joining me?"

Under normal circumstances, I wouldn't have sat there like a dunce but that awkward feeling of being fresh out of detention overshadowed me again. It would be awhile before I learned to shed the dross of imprisoned. When I did learn, I learned in a sinful manner: Seagram Gin. Gin forever did the trick in steeling my nerves.

I would've loved for there to have been *motion* in the ocean, as the term went regarding waterbeds. That wave of paranoia, along with images the Isaac Hayes-clone abruptly keying the door, all factored into turning me into the "American Pie Guy." It was over before it got started.

However, Ashley never afforded me the opportunity to recoup the loss of my exalted manhood that day. Why? Because the Life had both of us stretched thin. Our paths never crossed again. She went off in the direction in which promiscuity often leads one and I went off chasing the elusive nature of the Life.

Though I'm not a total believer in fatalism, I can easily give testament to the raw deals of which the Life offers up. I also know that with better choices one, for the most part, can keep out of harm's way.

As time went on and the events of my life continued to unfold, one time after returning to the neighborhood (you guessed it, post-release) I found out Ashley had been killed by the Green River Killer (Gary Ridgeway).

Unbelievable. Ashley, a teenager, fallen prey to the Life.

Several of Gary Ridgeway's victims and I moved in the same circles. Just kids hanging out on the streets of Seattle. Some of us were runaways; others, like myself, had a strong liking for Seattle's underbelly. It served as my training ground. One of my favorite haunts was First Avenue. Having the nature of a reconnoiter, I made it my business to survey the area: The Public Market, the Piers, and sometimes quickly ducking into an Adult Show. Dropping coins into a slot for a little visual pleasure became a pastime.

Despite the fun I was having, Seattle's rain always had the final say in the matter. When it poured, I would enter the haven for runaways: the Donut Shop. Though we co-existed, we were antitheses—they were victims, and I, on the other hand, was probing the area because of my strange addiction to the Life.

Thirty-four years later, reality smacked me in the face: I, too, was a victim of the Life...

Chapter Twenty-One

DANA AND I STARTED STEALING CARS AND JEWELRY FULL-TIME. We'd go out to the airport, or any of the other rental lots, where masses of cars were stored. With the keys usually kept behind the visor, or often in the ignition, we'd just get in and go. Periodically, there'd be a bit of difficulty requiring us to request a test drive; no problem, we'd drive off just as the salesman would reach for the passenger door handle. We'd use these rides to go to school, house parties, or for getting to and from the jewelry stores we'd hit.

(My sister, Patricia, was heart-broken when word got back to her. Of the hundred dollars sent to the Western Union in Louisiana for me to go to Seattle, half of it had come from her. Now she was having second thoughts about whether she had done the right thing; and with our relationship, we saw each other less and less. When I did visit, even if just to see my new-born nephew, Ronald Jr., and his sister, K.K., she'd be so appalled by who and what I'd become, she could hardly look at me.)

Mom had stopped allowing Dana to visit at the house. His mother felt like I was a bad influence on him, too, though she never stopped me from visiting him. Instead, she'd give me a dissatisfying look whenever I'd show up. Making matters worse, Dana and I started associating with other thieves, robbers, and hustlers. A whole different plateau had been reached. Though my actions were quite sick, I saw my abuse and criminal activities as normal, fun even, and after a while, able to stomach no more, Mom finally kicked me to the street.

Every once in a while, Sharon and Robert's friends would let me stay over at their place, but sometimes with a price—that of my youthful stamina. To their disappointment, however, my vigor was starting to fail. Too many other partners were sapping my strength. Eventually I had to find my slumber sleeping in cars or out on park benches when I was unable to call on these friends, who invariably were busy entertaining "other company."

One morning after having overslept, a crying baby awoke me. Wiping my eyes to clear my vision, I noticed it was Donna, 20 feet away and on her way to daycare, pushing her baby in a stroller. Fortunately, Donna happened to be looking straight ahead and didn't see me.

Later, I went to Mom's to get some fresh clothing. Not able to take seeing me so tired and weary, she begged Samuel to let me come back. He relented, and I moved back home.

It was less than a month before Mom received a call from a screener at the juvenile detention center giving her the choice of getting me—since my record was clear and the charge was only shoplifting—or leaving me there. Opting to leave me there, I suffered the same fate as Mark. But rather than placing me in a group home facility, they put me in a transitional home in case Mom had a change of heart.

The transitional home was on the classier side of town, a place run by church people. My bedroom was in the basement, as was their son, Kenneth's room. A few days had passed, and he and I had not yet spoken. I noticed Bruce Lee posters all over his door and bedroom walls. Catching me looking at them, he started to talk. Anything concerning martial arts made me think about Karate Joe. The difference between him and Joe was Joe had been taught by an instructor. He and I started hanging out together, which wasn't the greatest of ideas, especially with me as the rotten apple.

There was a beautiful girl who lived upstairs, their daughter. Forbidden to go to the basement, she'd steal peeps from the many windows as I came and went, swapping flirtatious smiles with me while still managing to exercise good judgment and refusing to come out and hang whenever I'd try to beckon her down. Shockingly, I would see her years later. She had become a prostitute. I didn't remember her, but making up for lost time; she quickly refreshed my memory.

Kenneth decided to come with me one weekend. Not the best of plans.

Thanks to me, he scored his first criminal charge: robbery in the second degree. *Senseless.* I knew he could fight like a well-oiled machine, but I wanted to test his bravery for crime. Worse, we did our deed downtown, two blocks from the police station. When the call was dispatched, the patrol cars didn't have far to go. We ran in circles for twenty minutes before they caught us and took us to the detention center.

It was awful seeing Kenneth's sad face in the chow hall every day. He was smart enough, after the fact, to avoid me. Detained for months until all the court procedures were over, they finally cut us loose with Kenneth going home, and me released to a juvenile facility called Maple Lane.

Maple Lane wasn't what I thought it would be. Instead, it was a coed facility. And even though the girls lived in cottages separate from the boys, it didn't stop the guys from sneaking in whenever the staff was preoccupied with other duties. Over time, of course, several of the girls got pregnant.

Maple Lane was in the backwoods of Centralia, Washington, a logging town. It felt like an extended summer camp with a host of indoor and outdoor activities, even schooling if one was inclined. There were two math teachers, a gentleman and a lady, that I truly favored. The entire staff treated us fairly.

My stay at Maple Lane didn't last but a few months. Being that I was a first-time felon the system was quite lenient. Arrangements had been made to place me in foster care, which was how I met John and Jackie Horn, a couple with three daughters of their own, a niece, and another foster son named Steve. Before my arrival, Steve had things going on with Laura, the niece, but no sooner had I made my way into things did I get the girl pregnant, and with Steve, had made yet another enemy.

Dana had a car waiting for me when I got out—a stolen car, a loud, ugly, orange-colored stolen car. Unlucky for me, someone saw me exiting the car at a local mall, and within ten days, I was back at Maple Lane pending investigation for auto theft. It was an all-in-all uncomfortable situation, especially since Maple's staff had just wished me farewell, and had even personally driven me to the bus station. Now they were welcoming me back.

How crazy.

Chapter Twenty-Two

TO MY SURPRISE, ONCE AGAIN, THE HORNS WELCOMED me into their loving home. But no matter how nice they were, or how structured the environment, something had come inside me and taken over, and it wasn't letting go.

I'd even enrolled in a predominantly white school by the name of Ingram High. As usual, things worked out fine from the start, but that didn't last long. Self-destructive behavior was fast becoming an ordinary part of my life. For years to come, I'd be enthralled with unruliness and entangled within the judicial system.

One cherishable thing that came from attending Ingram was making the acquaintance of a young gentleman by the name of Manny Franklin. He was the only friend who hung out with me that hadn't been corrupted, either by me or by anyone previously. He also talked me into joining the high school football team. Though fun while it lasted, my other activities took precedence.

Graduating, Manny went to the University of Washington. I often wondered why Manny's mother allowed him to hang out with me. She knew of my status, the transitional home, the juvenile detention center, all of it. Perhaps she knew of God's plan for her son. He no longer goes by Manny. Now he's addressed as Reverend Franklin.

Mark decided to pay me a visit at school during lunch break. We loitered in the halls, taking in the view of all the females passing by. Ingram had strict policies concerning visitors, a fact that everyone knew. Several senior classmen patrolling the halls began casting racial slurs at Mark. To their surprise, Mark reached into a duffel bag and pulled out a gun. Students were running and yelling. It was only mere chance that Mark didn't fire off a round. Mark was the family's gun collector. He got a charge from a smoking gun.

With school security alerted—along with the nearest precinct—personnel began closing in on us from both ends of the hallway. To this day, I don't know why I burst through those side doors with Mark. Maybe it was brotherly instinct.

We heard sirens and K-9 dogs in pursuit. We ran through wooded areas, trailer parks, and hid under mobile homes. Seattle's expansive transit system allowed us to make our escape unscathed.

The bus ran every thirty minutes, and after several hours of not hearing footsteps, dogs barking, or patrol cars, we got the nerve to go to the bus stop. Following this fiasco, and fearing an inquisition, I never returned to Ingram.

The Horns weren't too pleased with my school conduct—or lack of it. They were tolerable because they had dealt with troubled children before. But Jackie was more patient than John. He was ready to give me the boot. John had the vision to recognize a losing fight. I had already been to Maple Lane twice, and there were no signs of reform.

Mark had started visiting me, imposing his charm on the Horn's household. Further, Laura had started taking joyrides with Mark on one of his stolen motorcycles. At first, I thought nothing of it, but after seeing her dismount his bike while wearing the hot pants she'd won me over with, I realized that the young manipulator had been pulling a fast one. And shame on me for thinking he'd spare his brother when it came to her. The one plus was Laura aborting our baby. I wasn't ready to be a father, nor she a mother.

(Some twenty years later, Laura made things even clearer. Talking to me on the phone while I was in jail with a boyfriend of hers, she called me brother. I thought to myself how back in the day when I was busy knocking her up she hadn't called me brother. Then, asking how Mark was doing, she said, "Mark's always going to be my baby. He taught me how to steal diamonds out of jewelry stores and money out of department store safes." Deep thoughts for a moment. Even though it had been more than twenty years, Mark, the adventurous little fellow, had struck close to home.)

A recipe for disaster, Mark and I enrolled in the same preppy high school, Nathan Hale High, an institute not remotely close to being ready for this notorious duo. One memorable bright spot was that Marline went there. We even shared adjoining desks in typing class, an arrangement that worked fine until the teacher saw that I was more attentive to Marline than my lessons.

Mark and I began parking our stolen cars in the school's lot, an act, at least in our minds, that made us appear more aristocratic than we were. Our outrageous practices would continue for at least a few more months before ending.

On our way to school one morning, with one of our roguish friends riding along, a white guy threw a rock at our car. Our friend, a karate enthusiast, leaped out of the car while it was still in motion, an attempt to impress Mark and me. He began kicking the guy in the head and chest. Before we could back the car up to stop the assault, our friend had beaten the man to a pulp. The following morning, the principal called us into his office and expelled us from the Seattle public school system.

There were alternative schools for delinquents, vain attempts to complete our high school education. But we had to pass through downtown to get to and from these schools. Most of the time that meant deviating to the public market, car lots, jewelry and department stores, or whenever possible, to the ferry to get to Bremerton—all for happy pilfering. At one point, our G.E.D.

was nearly in sight, but corruption had a far stronger draw. Kleptomania being an irresistible force and the disciplined structure of a prison environment still on the horizon, schooling became irrelevant, and our last chance at public education was blown. We'd been self-reduced to criminal life—full time.

Having paid my dues under Mark and Dana's apprenticeship, I had finally come into my own. It was about evolution; just like so many other areas in life, if you're not moving forward, you're going backward. If you're not growing, you're dying. With me, evolving was necessary and I did, surpassing my peers, especially in communication.

Then Mark had a little twist of fate: after one of his solo escapades had caved in, he was placed in juvie.

While living with the Horns, my car boosts had markedly dropped. The whole neighborhood had turned into a big watchdog and a patrol car was regularly parked in front of this one house down the block. For all I knew, the officer could have been dating the woman living there or she could've been a family member. Whatever the reason, there was a policeman nearby at all times. For the time being, it wasn't going to be best dropping it in my own neighborhood.

A burning desire to see my little brother led me to steal a car and drive more than a hundred miles to where he was being held. He was one elated fellow knowing that his big brother had come to see him. While guaranteeing that soon we'd be back together, that big smile of his flashed at me over and over.

Those few months went by fast. Before I knew it, Mark was once again visiting me at the Horns. He was living with a man of substance named Carlos, a brother of the gentleman who'd ran Mark's previous group home.

With Carlos being a former pimp and gambler, I quickly grew fond of him. My poisoned mind had me thinking he was my kind of guy. What I like most was the free reign he'd given Mark with his house, and with Carlos gone most of the time, that meant the place was all ours.

The Horns treated me as if I were their own son. On the other hand, I was envious of Mark's conditions at Carlos's. So after he convinced the man to take me in, the Horns and I parted ways.

Jackie Horn, her three daughters, and I remained close for years, and until I fell prey to cocaine, we always found time to sit and talk.

Many years elapsed before I'd see Jackie again. I had been faithfully serving my master (cocaine) when I met her. She embraced me as if a day hadn't passed between us. The love was still there.

*****

Dana introduced me to a free-heeled woman whom I'd visit from time to time. We'd shoot billiards or get into whatever opportunity presented itself. Hanging out one day, Nadean, her girlfriend, came by. We'd all set our minds to partying: shooting pool, laughing, playing music. When it got late, I was asked to escort Nadean home.

With a touch of Indian descent accentuating her beauty, Nadean stood an attractive five-foot-two. "What's a nice guy like you doing with her?" I told her I only came by from time-to-time to hang out. She laughed and said, "Oh. I know how my friend is." I couldn't say anything except offer her a smile. We had exchanged phone numbers before the walk ended and I swore I'd soon give her a call.

For the brief period it lasted, our teenage love affair was hot and steamy. Nadean was one of the few that escaped my destruction. Putting what we'd shared behind, she moved forward with her life.

Nadean's mother and sisters showed me the utmost hospitality. Her brothers and father had a different take on the matter. I was transparent to them. Being males, they knew what I was up to. Along with that, they heard about my activities on the streets, and that wasn't good. Baby sister wasn't going to get far in life with a guy like me.

Nadean and I began having unprotected sex, so the tension between us increased shortly after she became pregnant. Her Dad's tight jaw reminded me of how Samuel had once acted towards me. Regardless of how they looked and felt, I had to give Nadean the only support I knew, and that was through visitations and the promise of future financial contributions. All she required from me was that I show that I cared, and not to put my roguishness before her and the baby. A hard sell, seeing that I put my roguishness even before myself. When an individual truly loves himself, he doesn't continually put himself in harm's way.

*****

Umbrellas are must-haves. Being caught in Seattle without one is like being at a sale with no cash. For some reason, Mark and I kept losing ours. During one of our downtown trips where we were looking to lift a couple, along with whatever else we happened upon, I unexpectedly ran into Marline. It had been awhile since we'd last seen each other. This time she was a bit more receptive. Perhaps by this time I had acquired a swagger more to her liking. So, when we traded phone numbers this time, it was for real.

Marline had no idea I was soon to be a father, but she'd soon be finding out. Word of mouth travels fast. After all I'd been through, and everything to come, she was the one true love of my life, standing by me despite the many tribulations I subjected her to. It would be many years before coming to the realization that she needed to abandon my sinking ship.

*****

One rainy Saturday afternoon, Mark and I went to a local Safeway where we noticed a guy that had just parked his green Cadillac. By chance, once inside the store we ended up next in line with the man where we saw that he was paying his bill with a wallet full of hundred dollar bills. Moving fast, we ditched our items and moved outside. Remembering the man's car was left unlocked, we snuck in the back.

After placing his groceries in the truck and slamming the lid, he got in, put his key in the ignition, started the engine, and drove off. After making it out of the parking lot, we sprang up and told him to pull over. We then told him to give up his wallet, park the car, and leave the keys. The man got startled, so he veered onto the sidewalk, barely missing a pedestrian. Then as Mark grabbed the steering wheel so we wouldn't crash, the man grabbed a can of mace and sprayed me. The pain was intense... and new. I'd never been hit by mace before, let alone blinded in both eyes. While I floundered in the backseat, Mark proceeded to pummel the man. Some moments later, recovered enough to squint out the tiniest bit of vision, I pulled Mark off long enough for the man to throw down his wallet and haul ass.

We kept his vehicle for three weeks, parking it around the corner from our house. One morning when we awoke, it was gone. Later, seeing the man patronizing the businesses in the neighborhood, we supposed that he must've just found his car. Regardless, from then on, every time he spotted us, he'd bolt like a rabbit.

So many preposterous things took place between Mark and me that it was no surprise when I found myself back in Maple Lane. Things were different this time. I was now a father. Nadean had sent pictures of my firstborn, a lovely little girl named Renata. I had seen baby pictures of my mother, and to me that's who Renata resembled. Nadean expressed her many disappointments, especially about bringing our girl into the world alone, and I expressed my many regrets. Nonetheless, I don't believe she ever forgave me, and the sad truth is that it is completely understandable.

Maple Lane was no answer; there, all I did was fuel myself on corruption, from books to stories and lessons-learned from the other "guests." Incarceration was different back then; one could receive incoming calls.

Today, that's a fantasy. Back then, however, it was not only available but it was a lifeline. Marline, called daily and wrote, one of the many reasons why I was always partial to her; consistently, she did her best to be there for me, even during my darkest hours. Her influence and time spent in contemplation almost bore fruit.

By the time my stay at Maple Lane had ended, I was ready to take things in a different direction. The intent was to discontinue the stealing and robbery. Instead, I had other plans: gambling, pool-sharking, and any other type of hustle that wouldn't land me back in juvenile hall or jail. I was now seventeen and had already butted against the law several times; one more offense and I wouldn't be looking at getting tried as a youth, but as an adult facing real prison time.

The revolving door needed to stop. Dana was getting ready to move into a juvenile facility and I had just gotten out of one. With my eighteenth birthday fast approaching, I was ready to leave behind my youthful shenanigans with a heart towards having money in my wallet—earned rather than stolen—and a car purchased rather than jacked. Alas, change isn't always possible when a person doesn't change their environment.

I found myself hanging around the house more, playing dominos and listening to Carlos talk about the glory days of hustling and pimping. When not at home you could find me at a club or other various house parties. At one house, I found the pleasure of meeting a voluptuous sister named Gwen. Being like-minded, it wasn't long before we started spending time together. Although she was only sixteen, she had the mind of a woman in her twenties.

Donna was often a sight at these parties, too, and every time I saw her, a queasiness would hit. She'd greet me, sure, but there was no longer that radiant smile from her anymore. Seeing who, and what, I'd become didn't match the man she'd once met. Watching her gaze from afar, the disapproving shakes of her head mixed with her beauty made her feel like an angel—a disapproving guardian angel..

*****

Every now and again, Carlos would leave his cocaine in the freezer. When Mark and I would stumble across it, we'd snort a few lines, enjoying the euphoric rush. I particularly enjoyed the hit; the cocaine instantly catapulted me from my usually laid-back demeanor. Mark, on the other hand, was always high-energy, and though he enjoyed the jolt of the coke, when he came down, he crashed hard.

The first time I ever saw Carlos come unglued was when we accidentally threw away some of his cocaine. We practically took the house down searching for it. Finally, out of desperation, he suggested ransacking the dumpster in the back alley. The weekly pickup hadn't yet arrived. Fortunately, we found the coke in a trash bag that we'd thrown away. At the time, I remember thinking how ridiculous the whole event was. Years later though, I'd find myself searching through trash time-and-again, hoping to find some crack. Later we learned that Carlos was not only snorting his coke, but he was also taking it intravenously. The man's fits of depression and rage were no longer a mystery.

Serious about not returning to theft, Mark and I went half-and-half on an old Cadillac. Thinking it a bad idea, Carlos tried talking us out of it.

Shortly afterward, we wished we had listened. Arriving at the owner's apartment alongside Mark and Carlos, we saw the writing on the wall. The car was a lemon. Just to turn the car over required a jump. However, it was a caddie; a car that can hypnotize a young man and only Carlos stood impervious to its allure. Ignoring our friend's pleas to our common sense, we handed over our cash, a whopping $800, and drove the beast home, the entire ride all sputter and smoke. Not a problem. Whatever challenges the car might have had, we could fix them--after all, it was a caddie. Days later, the engine died. And of course, fixing the beast would cost more than we'd already paid-- a lot more. Our only recourse? Taking it to the wrecking yard and getting what we could.

Amid all this, I still found time to make half-hearted attempts at being a teenage father. My beautiful daughter was now four months old and sometimes I would take her to visit my sister and mother. It didn't take long for Renata to melt their hearts. Wouldn't be long, either, before I'd lose the love of my precious gem, especially with my life-decisions forcing her to grow up without me. To date, our relationship has remained unrepaired.

Seattle's underworld and night-live continued its siren call. I wanted to be like the infamous characters I had read about, the suave players of the boulevard. Thus, I started sneaking into adult clubs and cozying up to the well bred, making friends, contacts, and selling marijuana. Some of these people, especially those on the way down, didn't give me the time of day. Still others, the partying kind, saw me as an up-and-comer. Then there were the girls, the sexy kind, the kind like me, corrupt and full of pipe dreams.

Either due to my stars lining up, or a blessing from Satan, those pipe dreams came into view; I started making my mark and in short order amongst my corrupt circle, became a person of note, someone to be around and know. Despite this, and despite the women attracted to my dark ilk, I never became vain.

Despite the fact that I was now living the life that Carlos had always bragged about, the man wasn't happy with my transformation. He started lashing me with his tongue, especially when I'd be busy entertaining, yelling at me to answer the phone, take out the garbage, run an errand, or do the dishes. First chance I had, I'd be getting out.

*****

Beforehand, the morning of my eighteenth birthday, Marline paid me a visit. She came bearing gifts of designer jeans and my first two golden cans of Old English 800, otherwise known as liquid crack.

Years later, my Mom and sister would ask why I ever started drinking that nasty concoction. Apparently, my addictive tendencies were too far beneath the surface for them to identify.

Brian, a man who lived in Yakima, Washington, was a play-cousin of mine.

My mother had met his mother while in prison, and occasionally we'd visit. That is, if Samuel was up to the three-and-a-half-hour drive to get there. Coincidently, one evening I ran into Brian at the gym. After a short verbal exchange, he told me he had an apartment in Seattle and a car that needed a brake job. I offered to fix it and he extended me an invitation to move in with him.

It was a perfect opportunity to put some space between Carlos and me. Living with Brian would give me the chance to become the street magnate I wanted to be, but without the hindrance. I appreciated Carlos, his stories, his dope, giving me a place to crash, and a place to lay a lot of pipe, but I could no longer take his abuse. He didn't want to see me leave either, but his ego wouldn't allow him to ask me to stay.

Living with Brian was all I expected and more. The one throwback was that he loved smoking grass, an activity that didn't sit well with me. I never liked the ensuing fatigue.

One night while I was high as a kite, Gwen called to tell me she was pregnant. She went on to say that if I didn't honor my responsibility as a parent she would seek child support. I hadn't been spending enough quality time with her because my lifestyle didn't allow me to.

Marline and I were still communicating by phone. Knowing my address, one day she and a girlfriend paid Brian and me an unexpected visit. Upon arrival, Marline saw another girl ironing the jeans she'd bought for my birthday. Within the twinkling of an eye, things turned wild. Words were slung back and forth and a catfight started to brew. Having known Marline for the better part of three years, consoling her was as simple as taking her on a moonlit stroll down by the lake. Her mood was quickly lifted.

*****

When Dana got out of juvie, he started pleading with me to assist in a robbery that he, supposedly, had all mapped out. His reasoning? He was down on his luck and felt I should help. Naturally, after he laid out his plan, I felt compelled. Brian wanted in, too. Dana was to be the getaway driver. Brian and I were to be the muscle.

As Dana had said, there was a dwarf of a fellow working alone in the store. Casually entering, Brian and I let the man know that it would be wise for him to hand over all the available cash, including the bread in the safe.

To his credit, he made an honest attempt to hand over the money, but before he could finish Brian senselessly started wailing on him. Before he lost consciousness, a customer came in. On the way out, I tried snatching the phone cord out of the wall but must've failed because in no time at all, the authorities were on their way.

Brian and I ran as fast as we could to where Dana was supposed to be but he wasn't there. Instead, he had parked on the other side of the road ... five blocks ahead. *Shit.* He had the driver's window down as he talked to a girl. With the robbery within the city limits, the police didn't have to travel far.

With sirens blowing, the police cars came in from the east to west. With Dana sitting west of us, we had no choice but to run northward. We made it eight blocks before the neighborhood watch assisted in our apprehension and a couple of K-9s forced our surrender.

Now I was on my way to the Big House, and decided then that I'd never forgive Dana. He had failed me in the worst way. My memory of meeting him the first time in school was of him messing around with girls. When I needed my little Casanova friend the most, he'd be messing around with a girl.

The cell I'd been trying to avoid was now beckoning.

Chapter Twenty-Three

THE COUNTY JAIL WASN'T WHERE I'D planned to spend the summer of 1981, but when one submits to peer pressure, this can often be the result. Mentally, I was stuck in neutral. Compared to jail, my previous juvenile experiences were like Boy Scout Camp.

Jail's about survival of the fittest, and disappointedly, I wasn't one of the fittest. Nor was I the only one. Heavy sedation was required for some to deal with the strife. The most common form of escapism used was a drug called Thorazine.

Though jail was now my new home, and would be for several more months, if I were to make it, I'd have to accept that the judicial system left much to be desired.

For one, the violence that took place was gut wrenching, with the walls and bars nothing more than a concrete jungle with a nauseating life all its own. And whenever weakness shined its timid head, the stronger inmates would pounce like blood-hungry lions. After an initial assault, other inmates, like hyenas, would also want a piece. Whatever the prey possessed, rest assured, it was taken. Often, sodomy would follow. Most of the time, these things were swept under the rug.

With thoughts of how I landed myself in this mess constantly plaguing me, I had to find a distraction. Jailhouse poker came to the rescue. At least I thought so for a time. At first, things were smooth. Then I noticed something. The biggest guy in the joint, who just happened to be playing in the game and wiping us all out, was cheating. After several more hands it was plain to see that the other three players were letting this big brute clean us out. Either they were blind, or perhaps with me being the new guy in the tank, they were selling me out. Having them take me for a sucker knowingly was not acceptable. I started accusing the behemoth. The words had hardly left my mouth before everyone cleared the dayroom. All but paralyzed with fear, I made a feeble attempt to square off. He stood there staring, large eyes dilated, nostrils flaring, and clearly not impressed or threatened by me. He told me to apologize. Ain't no lie when they say, "Don't let your mouth write a check your ass can't cash." I stood there with my fists clenched, my mouth frozen, my tongue having just kited the biggest check of my life. He finally said, "Youngin', you don't want none a me," before storming off to his cell. With the beast's departure, the room came back to life and blood started flowing through my veins again. I might not've completely manned-up, but neither had I backed down. Now was that due to having some stones, or was I simply too scared or too stupid to back off? I'm not a hundred-percent on the answer, but either way, deserved or not, I gained some respect.

(Years later, again in prison, I ran into this same big brute. I was sitting in the audience taking in a heavyweight-boxing match where he just happened to be the main card event. After pounding his opponent into the canvas, he exited the ring on the side I was seated. He had those same wide eyes and flaring nostrils. Once again, he stared at me ... intensely. The impression received was of him channeling the message, "That could have been you." Right then, the realization hit that those many years ago the only thing that had saved me was the fact that there would've been no braggin' rights for beating down some stupid, skinny-ass kid.)

During this time, Marline lent as much support as she could, but the delight of summer was too much of a distraction. That and the fact that she had yet to turn eighteen meant that she wasn't allowed visitation rights.

And then there was Nadean. She'd written me off as a deadbeat Dad. We occasionally talked on the phone, but the fire was gone — my despicable behavior had long since extinguished it.

Around this time, there came another demoralizing slam. Brian's mother bailed him out. Now I was alone and left to rot, or so it seemed. We'd already spent some months together, and they'd been a boon; having someone around you know, that you can trust, is practically a necessity.

My lessons weren't over.

I would soon learn that an individual stands a better chance battling the system from the outside as opposed to within. Most court-appointed attorneys don't give a rump's care about "proper representation." The many that have represented me behaved more like prosecutors than defense attorneys. May sound funny coming from a person in my shoes, but even when a client is an inmate, their attorney should put forth the best defense available. It's about ethics. Inmates may or may not have those, but attorneys are officers of the court. Their principles and ethics shouldn't be left behind once a person passes the bars.

Brian had never been in trouble so they offered him a deal he could live with. Pleading guilty, he was sentenced to a year in work-release. Meanwhile, I remained in limbo, deadlocked with the system and a lawyer trying to sell me up the river.

Finally, a guardian angel came by way of a phone call. With my sentencing date approaching fast, I was feeling doomed. With no support from family, and with past acquaintances dropping like flies, an overwhelming feeling of despair started to set like concrete. A person could easily lose their sanity under such conditions. And some have. Surprisingly, while under lock and key, pharmaceuticals held no appeal. Who could have guessed? Instead, peace of mind, or what of it that I could find, came from withdrawing back into the person I was before succumbing to the wiles of the world. Enduring throughout, if even barely, I still hit a point where I needed contact. And like so many, I sought my mother; hoping for a chance to unburden myself, if only a little, of the weight being carried. Placing the call, however, a funny thing happened. Mid-ring an operator came on. "Can I help you?" Saying yes, and that I'd like to place a collect call, the operator came back with: "Oh, my GOD. Terry … is this Terry?"

"Yes."

"This is Donna. Terry, you did it, didn't you? Got into trouble." Out of embarrassment, I gave her the party line that I'd been framed. Next thing I knew, we were catching up on the past and I let her know that it must've been fate that had brought us back together. She sympathetically promised to visit before my painfully awaited sentencing date. Afterward, she put the call through to my mother.

Mom and I became absorbed in the conversation. Like any mother, she loved me but was also ashamed. She reminded me of Inez and how my foster mother would've felt. She went on to say that Inez was probably turning over in her grave due to my behavior. Still in denial about my hand in things, it would be much later in life, and several prison-trips later, before the truth of her words would hit home.

A woman of her word, Donna visited as often as she could. She was paying me my last visit before sentencing when suddenly Marline and her big sister appeared. Not yet eighteen, Marline had to be accompanied by an adult. I appreciated the kind gesture but their timing was truly bad. Donna had just disclosed that if I were sent to prison, she'd be there for me every step of the way. It hurt to do it, but I turned Marline away. I needed to visit with Donna. My life was filled with pain and more was looming on the horizon. Donna had volunteered to take some of the pain away by promising to come inside prison walls; it was a promise I couldn't risk losing.

There is an old saying, "In the hospital or locked behind bars, a person finds out who's who." And then there was Brian and Dana, my partners in crime. Rumors abound, even behind bars, I'd been hearing about my compatriots celebrating while I was stuck in this hell-hole. Neither of them had written, and neither had come to visit. And with that, dark thoughts stewed and brewed.

Finally, the sentencing day arrived. I was sweating so hard; the perspiration alone proved my guilt. As for my attorney, the man was there in body only; he just impassively stood as the judge proceeded to dress me down, reproving me for my improper attitude, and how I carried no remorse, not for the crime or for the victim. I asked my lawyer, "What the hell's he talking about?"

"You didn't tell the court and the victim you were sorry."

"If you'd have prepared me, I would've known. Top of that, you told me to plead guilty, told me to endorse that piece of paper. Now I'm looking at ten years?"

This was just one of my many tours through the correctional system, and the first in a long line of relationships with court-appointed cutthroats. Public defenders are nobody's friend... least of all their clients.

Chapter Twenty-Four

AFTER ARRIVING AT THE WASHINGTON CORRECTIONS CENTER BACK IN THE EARLY '80'S, guards disinfected, showered, shaved, and buzz-cut my hair before anything else took place. In-processing complete, I descended through a tunnel to the lower receiving units. That's where they housed and evaluated me, and had my medical needs met. Until a parent institution was assigned, I remained at the Washington Corrections Center.

With just about every felon in the State of Washington taking a run through this place, I had the displeasure of meeting some of the most disgruntled individuals one could ever have the displeasure of meeting. God help the man who catches one of these people on a bad day. Creeds applied on the streets carried even more weight in prison. Snitching, for example, was an intolerable act. One that caused many a head to roll. The inmates despised, sifted out, and severely dealt with snitches. Choices for a snitch were slim: get administrative protection or die!

Stealing is another taboo. They frowned upon jailhouse thieves. At best, the act would bring revulsion from the other prisoners, and at worst, the offense required blood.

And whatever happens, don't mess with another man's bitch. Same as in the free world, in prison people kill for the sake of love.

In the old days, homosexuality was a different animal. It was something either forced on an inmate through various forms of coercion, or the result of incurring debt.

Veteran prisoners were the most adept at "turning" situations their way. A person, especially a newbie, could pick up debt by something as innocuous as accepting a candy bar — an unbelievably costly "gift." Bolder moves like whistling or blowing

176

a kiss were also commonplace. Real or imagined, just about anything construedas an invitation if a person came off as prey or otherwise vulnerable. How a person responded would be the guide behind a predator's next move. In some cases, bold advances brought on bold responses, with a new inmate savagely retaliating against a sexual aggressor.

Individuals falling victim usually slipped into oblivion. On one occasion, I remember walking down the tier to take a shower when I noticed a guy clinging to the bars of another cell, his midsection crammed against the bars while some kid pleasured him. Rumor had it the kid had amassed a sizable debt from the "accepting" of gifts. All over again, same as in the county jail, the hyenas pounced.

After weeks of medical needs being met and a psychological evaluation completed, it was now time to receive a parent institution, the location where I'd spend my time, possibly even all of it. Fortunately, I was assigned to another segment at the Washington Corrections Center, a place not as gruesome as other prisons. Here, I'd have more of a chance easing my way back into the incarcerated scene.

One thing for sure, one worked and went to school. Like other things in life, when it comes to self-improvement, some people needed a push; I was one of them.

Even in prison, negativity attracted me like a magnet and I found myself hanging around guys with dark aspirations like my own.

Early on there was a squabble between another inmate and me. With televisions not allowed in the cells back then, only one T.V. in the dayroom worked to service a legion of inmates. On this day, I wanted to take in a Sonic's game, and this corn-fed, white fellow wanted to watch a John Wayne Western. No compromise in sight, we moved to settle things the old-fashioned way... fighting from one end of the tier to the other. My punches were no more effective than bee stings and when the man saw his opening, he took it. Diving on me, he stripped away what meager boxing advantage I had.

Rolling on the floor hadn't been part of the plan. What had been hoped for was the quick-giving of an ass-whuppin' and then a resumption of the game. With that not happening, the guards infracted, and locked us in our cells. Today, we'd have both been cuffed and taken to the Hole. The one lesson learned, painfully so, was that it was time to bulk up.

*****

One evening playing basketball, I saw a slew of new arrivals heading into one of the buildings. One pigeon-toed fellow with a full beard instantly reminded me of my brother Robert. Ballgame forgot the closer they approached, the more curious I got. Could that really be my brother? The reason for the doubt was that this man was easily 60-pounds heavier than the man I knew. Just to be satisfied, I yelled out, "Hey, Robert." Recognizing my voice, he turned in my direction and his face instantly spouted the traditional Hill-family smile. The guard escorting him into the building gruffly told him to keep moving and stay in formation. I yelled once more to reassure him that we'd be getting together soon. Out of nowhere, I found myself hit with a devastating sense of sadness and embarrassment, for him and me; we were here, after all, both of us here. Still, it was good to see him. The solidarity between us was already making me feel more secure inside of this zoo.

With Robert being the most athletic out of us siblings, I knew that at some point, I'd catch him in the gym or out running the track, and when I did I asked him what had happened since I

178

knew that he hadn't been in trouble since Louisiana. He went on to say that while between jobs, and facing a hopeless situation, he'd tried his hand at robbery.

Not long after that, around noon one day while taking a breath of fresh air outside the chow hall, I kept hearing a whistle. I looked over in the direction of the lower receiving units, and there I saw an arm waving at me from the catwalk, "It's me, Mark." The only thought that passed through my mind was, "Whoa! Mark, my other brother, had joined Robert and me at the Corrections Center". Having escaped from a juvenile detention center, Mark was now in the Big House.

Now there were two more backs for me to watch.

Listening to Mark gripe about his situation, I encouraged him with the advice of just keeping his nose clean, that if he could just do that, he'd be all right. But that was the problem. Something about Mark always begged for conflict.

Even within our relatively small prison community, Mark, with his boundless reservoirs of energy, stood out—rising early and retiring late. Then there were the fights. During his first few months, Mark swapped paws more than Robert and I combined. Throwing down's a prison reality. Sometimes it simply can't be avoided. On the other hand, like with many things in life, an inmate has to be choosy about which hills to die on. Fighting, for example, on top of potentially risking an inmate's life also jeopardized their "good time." Due to my dayroom-dance, I had already seen my release date pushed out. Then and there, I swore to myself to mind my manners; I had to get out, and to that end I quickly determined to not let anything get into the way, including my ego.

What continued to get Mark in trouble with the other inmates was his arrogance ... that and the fact my brother knew he had me and Robert watching his back, a truth that my brother

179

was quick to take advantage of. During one quarrel, Mark had a con so stirred up that the man was ready to take on the three of us at once and damn the cost. Fortunately, the guards broke us up, and once reprimanded, we went our separate ways.

*****

Mom received mail from the three of us several times a week. Mom wrote back that her man, Samuel the grouch, was getting fed up with all the prison clutter in his mailbox. That and he was pissed about footing the phone bill. From then on, my brothers and I did our best to minimize the collect calls. For me the cutback wasn't that challenging, could hardly enjoy the calls I did make, not with Mom having to live under that man's thumb. It was enough to be thankful for the guy finding just enough compassion to let Mom come maybe once a year to see her sons. When she did come to visit, she'd bring a friend, someone to come along to help her calm her nerves. Anyone would do, so long as they weren't Samuel.

An ex-con herself, the visits were torturous. Not only did they bring back reminders of her own served time, but it rubbed in her face that her own three boys were now in the joint. With an all-too-intimate understanding of the perpetual frustration, loneliness, and despair inherent in such an environment, she would often just come and sit, mouth bolted shut. Despite the silence, I could still feel our connection and am sure she did, too.

Sometimes it's more than enough to simply relish sitting in the presence of a loved one.

The couple of times Samuel did come along, he made sure to do his best to ruin our time spent together. Never believing that any of the kids were going to amount to anything anyway, he'd sit in his chair, arms folded, and make faces: looks of disdain, of disgust, frustration, and disapproval.

On one such occurrence, Mom had hardly arrived and hugged her three sons tight to the chest before she was ready to leave, her spirit nearly broke under Samuel's constant barrage of complaints.

Nonetheless, having to take the good with the bad, these visits still imparted endless joy, even if I did always find myself back in my cell mentally exhausted. Knowing my mother was paying the price just in her coming, and not sure how steep the bill was or how close it might be to pushing Mom over the edge, was a constant stressor.

*****

With Donna's visits, those blessed moments of reprieve, I could momentarily forget the walls around me and just listen to her voice. She'd tell me how much she cared, how different I was, how there was more going on within me than what my exterior might have suggested, and how she was determined to persevere through any of my shortcomings. And then there was also the physical beauty of Donna's to enjoy: her eyes and lips ... that blessed backside poured into a pair of jeans. Having something you want and can't have, and then having to watch it walk away was nearly unbearable. I wish I could have shown more affection during our visit, but first, there were rules and limitations on displays of affection, and then there was also intimacy problems of the heart ... mine. Must've been something from my childhood. Affection lived within me, but I didn't know how to let it out.

With school, I went through the motions but there was no heartfelt application; rather, school-time simply served as a meet for Mark and me to discuss our prospective futures and how to further take care of our partying present. Despite the extra hoops and ladders, even behind bars there's good times to be had: prune (prison booze), pills, grass, and even the hard stuff, though my brothers and I refused to take anything intravenously. We didn't believe in piercing our veins.

After school, I'd come back to the unit where a couple of the fellows and I ran a poker game, took bets on football and basketball, and regularly played boastful games of dominoes. Another common form of fun and distraction and profit came from extortion, the charging of "rent" to the newbies fresh to the grinder. A friend and I, with seniority established on the tier, numbered amongst the prison's numerous landlords.

Coming into the unit one Friday after school, the Unit Sergeant asked me to stop by his office. Once there, I was handcuffed and barraged with a host of allegations, then hauled off to the Hole where, pending transfer, I'd spend the next several months.

My friend and I weren't worried about any evidence being found, at least not with us. Yes, we kept a ledger, after all, like any business, one had to manage the books. On the other hand, no inmate ever stores his own wares. Rather, things get parceled out, with some stuff here, some there, and with things kept separate any individual piece found just appears as an innocuous item. The one thing we had no control over, however, was testimony, and that poured out by the bucket-full. Result? Transfer to Monroe Reformatory.

The Hole sucks. No surprise there, after all, that's its job. But effects reach further out than just its wall. Visitation, for example, is highly affected. With Donna, the whole point of her coming was all but taken away.

Now with her arrival, there could be no face to face, no kissing or hugging or hand-holding, no walking to the vending machine together—no contact, save sitting on the opposite sides of glass. Meals were taken in-room, with trays slid under the door. Rumor mill circulated that food would often be contaminated with thoughtful additions of spit and other things. Anytime my own suspicions—real or imagined—raised its ugly head, I'd find myself sliding my tray back under the door, hunger being far preferable than contaminated by anyone's sick sense of humor. Showers, too, were hole effected; now they came only once every couple of days, and with five-minute time limits. All of this and more made for a miserable time, but I still endured and the days, some flyin' and some draggin', went by.

Unexpectedly, Mark dropped in as my cellie. Make no mistake, the man's my brother and his company was welcome beyond compare. At the same time, being cooped up with somebody of his deep levels of boundless energy was taxing. One either had to have the skills of a psychologist or by the end of the day they sure as hell would find themselves needing one.

After months of waiting for my transfer to Monroe, it was finally approved.

Arriving at Monroe was akin to what was expected. After all, stories get told, lessons passed along, and then I had my own set of experiences reminding me of what it's like being a new arrival at any corrections facility. But the going *through* it part is always stark and in one's face: the catcalls, the whistling, and kiss-blowin' and even more insensitive body gestures; it's all part of the game, the ritual, the rite of passage of gaining entry into the den.

The lion's den. "He's mine!"

"No, he's mine and that one, too."

"Look at that guy, man, is she fine!"

Pointless to yell back. The best one can do is project that, indeed, they are not prey, that they have teeth, and if necessary, will bite back. In some cases, the taunts are just that, fun barbs thrown out not by homosexual predators, but by guys looking to distract themselves from the boredom of their day ... at the other guy's expense. In other cases, these threats were of a truth, promises that would be kept. For me, I was happy with just making it inside and getting put behind lock and key. At least for the night, everyone was safe.

Morning came and the orientation process began, which for me was a fast and typical process. For others, those with enemies or who otherwise feared for their lives, there were additional hurdles to clear.

Protective custody for one. There may not be honor amongst thieves, but there are boundaries, codes of the street if you will, and I'd always done my best to adhere to them. One of the biggest, if not the most important, was not being a snitch. On the street or behind bars, there's hardly a mammal more hated and despised than the rat. And for those with time under their belts, there's the stigmata attached if one's ever needed protective custody— for any reason. A couple of the other incomings were placed under protection. I didn't know why, nor did I particularly care, but I feel a certain degree of pity. For them, prison life would now be forever different. Never having snitched or needed protection, I carried with me a certain base-level form of respect, something I'd milk for my own safety as much as I could. Otherwise, whatever might come up, just would, and with it, I'd have to man-up.

During the orientation process, I was let out to mingle with the general population to seek out a roommate instead of being thrown in a cell with a total stranger. Blessed with luck, I happened to run into a guy I'd been acquainted with from my trips to the detention center in Seattle, a man called Junior. Shortly thereafter, I moved in with him.

While searching for a workout partner, I ran into an inmate from Yakima who knew Brian. He was a dedicated exercise partner. He and I worked out together until Mark unexpectedly showed up. With three being a crowd, Mark became my mainstay in the gym. But even then, Mark had to rock the boat and get transferred to a different cell block, furthering more discord into what should've been unity amongst two brothers. A painful epiphany when I realized it wasn't all roses having a brother with me, especially with all the contradictions that came with the package. The biggest, with him being family both by blood and by heart, I had the responsibility to stand with him. On the other hand, his idiosyncrasies were such that with the load he seemed to be adding daily, he was going to have to start carrying his own weight ... especially when it came to fighting. Men are funny animals. Get enough of them together, especially under controlled, cramped, and stressful circumstances, and they have a tendency to revert to childhood— and fight. I won't try to defend the tendency, it just is. Now, if that's true—and it is—add to that that the group is predominately made up of a bunch of dysfunctional inmates and there's bound to be some scrapping. The problem with my brother was two-fold: with the numerous bouts he'd been in he had discovered that: one, he was good at it and two, that he liked it.

The reformatory being what it was, fostered a climate that tried to channel the population's inherent drive for violence— even encouraged it. Hence, the gym and the boxing ring being home to a slew of fighters of every weight division. Eerily, the big brute I'd faced-off with back in the county jail was there, ceaselessly annihilating any opposition. Along with that, I found his daily smirks unnerving.

Prison, anywhere, is never the place to show weakness but Monroe was especially troublesome for the weak-willed. During my time there were several guys that didn't survive intact. One young blonde guy, with a lot more wants than money, found himself in debt. Worse, he discovered that to his horror, in the eyes of his creditor and new cellie, he resembled Farrah Fawcett. Soon, he found himself living inside his cellie's insane fantasy world, even to the point of being renamed, Farrah.

Visitations at the reformatory were prone to far fewer restrictions. It was great. Donna would often visit and spend the evenings with me. These testosterone-heavy courting sessions were intense, physically and emotionally. Having waited for me the better part of three years, she'd often ask about my release date, to which I could only reply, "Whenever the Parole Board sees fit."

Then the disappearing acts started.

Why's she standing me up? Why now? What's going on? The questions would roil in my gut as I paced the floor in my cell. I knew she cared about me ... maybe even loved me, but in my insecure gut I suspected another man had entered our equation. Wasn't long before I found my suspicions were correct. Finding out wouldn't have been so bad if it could've been delivered to me straight; instead, however, I got slapped in the face with the news. During a Sunday morning call, I could tell she was acting peculiar. She'd be talking for a minute then put her hand over the mouthpiece. Tired of the game-playing, I finally asked, "What's going on?" That's when this fellow named Corey snatched the phone away and proceeded to tell me the good news.

I was out and he was in. That whatever I and Donna had, had finally run its course. The final words? "I'm payin' the phone bill now ... don't call here again."

As I've said, there are times to man-up. Some of the occasions are a lot harder to deal with than others. In this case,

I would've preferred getting it handed to me by that beast in the boxing ring. Still, it happened and I had to move on.

One day, Mark and I were walking the track when the usual occurred. New arrivals. Everyone in the yard ran to the fence. Deciding to break the monotony, we joined in.

Robert happened to be one of the inmates departing the bus. Mark and I were happy to see him, but still, it saddened me. Prison was no place to continue having these family reunions. The one good thing was that Robert wasn't into making waves, not for himself and not for anybody else. Like me, all he wanted to do was make-date, and do so without adding a single unnecessary day. We'd both been to the Parole Board already, and had been denied. I'd be having another shot within the year. Hopefully, so would he.

Having kept my nose clean for a space of time, good conduct had finally awarded me a piece of luck. I was given a chance to do the rest of my time at the honor farm. There, I worked at the dairy, dispensing milk into two-gallon containers. The honor farm didn't have an infirmary, so once a month I'd fake an illness to go back to the reformatory to see my brothers. For the most part, Robert was all right; Mark, however, was a concern, and always would be.

Someone else I came upon at the honor farm was Jackie, Nadean 's older sister. She was there visiting another inmate. For some inexplicable reason, Nadean never wrote to me. I asked Jackie how Nadean and Renata were doing. Each time I'd see her, she'd say the same thing: "They're fine."

Nobody owed me a damn thing, I knew that. Still, I was devastated and knew in my core that I'd never have anything close to a conventional relationship. There'd been too many people who, in my skewed view, had let me down while I'd been incarcerated. The truth? I'd let everybody else down.

It was summertime, I was twenty-one years old and I was scheduled to see the Parole Board. Again, the butterflies in my stomach were working at full capacity. With the Parole Board, you never knew what to expect. I learned that when dealing with them that it was best not to say a word sometimes. If asked a specific question, I'd respond. Other than that, I remained an active listener. The Board consisted of three people with the power to either parole or detain you until the next meeting the following year. After the hearing, they asked me to step out of the room while they made their decision. I did, sweating and pacing the hallway for what seemed an eternity. In the end, they summoned me back. Two of the three members voted for releasing me as soon as possible.

I was to be released in ten days... and for the next ten days I hardly slept.

Chapter Twenty-Five

FINALLY, THE DAY ARRIVED ... PAROLE. I had greeted the morning more anxious, more excited than any day ever before in my life and still, the fates were not done with me. Problems with my paperwork needed to be fixed. Some T's yet to be crossed... well, of course. Not to be daunted, I got my stuff together. Months prior, in preparation for this glorious occasion, I purchased an old, overpriced, O.D. green penitentiary storage chest.

When I'd first arrived at Monroe, the chain bus had driven through two retractable gates within the walls. Now that I was leaving through the front of the building, carrying my chest as I walked between giant white pillars and down a long series of steps, it didn't feel like I was leaving a warehouse of men, but rather the Capitol Building.

Citizens of the tiny community of Monroe didn't want ex-cons loitering around their town—too much history of crime committed by the newly released—so a prison van waiting in the parking lot drove me to the local bus depot. The officer waited until I boarded before driving back to his place of duty. My old chest wasn't much for looks, but I lugged it onto the bus headed for Everett. I knew my first day out would have its ups-and-downs, but the hard looks, stares, and scowls as I came aboard the bus hadn't been anticipated. I wasn't wearing prison garb, but still must've had the look. That or people didn't like O.D. green. Whatever the reason, I immediately felt isolated ... alien.

Then it hit: PARANOIA.

One little misstep and BAM! I'd be back inside, rotting away. Wrestling with these dark thoughts, I made my way to the few empty seats in the back. At least I'd be close to the bathroom.

Some minutes later, a courageous young lady came and sat next to me. "Hey, you just got out of the joint, didn'tcha?"

Could she have spoken any louder? Damn, the whole bus had heard; I even saw the driver through his mirror cast a glance my way. Biting my lip and holding back the desire to dress this young girl down for embarrassing me, for interrupting my privacy … I did my best to ward off any conversation.

Not fazed by my quiet, the girl continued to talk, with me only responding every occasionally with an obligatory short answer. I remember thinking: If only she'd just leave me alone. But then I realized that she wasn't the only person interested in poking their nose into my business.

There was another, a slightly older young woman up around the middle of the bus who was sitting busily making out with her boyfriend. And this girl, between her back-patting and smooching, was giving me the eye as she winked, grinned, and waved her fingers. *Gawd, please just get me back to Seattle!*

It had yet to hit that I was now a hot commodity. Wasn't about my charming looks, either. No, I'm not going to self-deprecate about my charms, but the reality is that there are a few women out there with a fetish towards the recently incarcerated, the sexually deprived … the sexually hungry. I know this of a truth from first-hand experience.

The same was going on with the harmless young thing on the bus yapping in my ear.

After having finally arrived at a station in Everett, I took my chest and departed the bus only to find that the young, nagging woman had no plans of letting me leave. Seeing that my next ride wasn't for 45-minutes, she invited me to stroll with her in a nearby park. Nervously, I obliged. It was a beautiful sunny day. The landscape at the park was pristine. And I was walking with a woman instead of leaving a cell, or the gym, with somebody smelling like *pit*. I decided to take a seat on the lawn. No sooner had my butt hit the ground did this woman all but sit on my lap. My previous mode of being sexually out-of-control, coupled with my newfound sense of paranoia, was leaving me in quite a straight, and this girl could sense it. Her answer?

Pulling out some reefer and lighting up, right there in the park. The result?

Increased paranoia. Deciding to be frank, I let her know that there was no need wasting her smoke or her time, but not wanting to let her go empty-handed, I gave her my mother's number, and she promised to call. Not long after, I was back on the bus and back in Seattle.

As for meeting my parole officer, I had a gracious 72-hour window in which to report. However, with the bus depot being in the heart of Seattle's downtown, I decided to knock it out right away. My P.O. was surprised and impressed— a good thing. I'd wanted to show my willingness to comply. Making sure that I understood just how fast I could end up back at the reformatory, the officer still made sure to go over every piece of stipulation paper he had before making me sign each one.

Not believing in my ability to make good time, Samuel hadn't expected me to be released so early. So after a long day's work at a construction site, it was a brow-raising experience for him to come home and find me waiting. I understood his stress, and I shared it. First opportunity that arose, I knew I'd be taking off.

Mom, though, was glad to have her 21-year-old son back home. And thank God for it. I remembered those days at the Juke Joint when, after a few beers, she'd finally seem to be able to unwind and loosen up. I stopped by the local convenience store and picked up a 12-pack of Bud, her favorite. She took the beer and put it in the freezer while I put my chest away. Then we started to talk, the easy stuff at first, the way to just open things up after having been separated for so long. Then we moved on to the elephant in the room. When that started, Mom moved in, reminding me of how my reckless living was destroying my life— throwing it away. "If Inez were around right now, how'd you think she'd feel about the way you've been going?"

The question needed no answer.

If the conversation turned a bit unsettling to my mind, it was just fine with my stomach. For years, I'd been longing for some good ol' fashioned soul food ... and dear ol' Mom had known it. While we talked, we feasted over collard and mustard greens mixed with ham hocks, country fried chicken, dirty rice and red beans, candied yams, and more. A homecoming to service a king.

Once filled with some southern down home, my mind went even more south to thoughts of Donna and how I needed to re-introduce myself to her. Throughout my incarceration, we'd often laughed about her sexual timidity. I'd wanted to help her release the wildcat that I knew was waiting to break out. The problem? Corey. That Fort Lewis veteran who'd given me the what-for on the phone, whose intrusion into my life and mine and Donna's relationship had left me in a nigh-permanent state of angst. Those barbs, lying on my bunk filled with loneliness, had stung––and they still did—wedged in the convolutions of my mind.

I didn't know Donna's work schedule and since Corey had heisted her heart, there had been no need for me to know. With so many previous parole opportunities crushed, Donna had no doubt presumed that I'd again be denied, and with that, had no idea that I was now a free man. I figured it about time to let her know.

With timing akin to winning the lottery, when I was going for the door to enter Donna's complex, she was grabbing the knob to leave. Whether from shock—or real fear—I don't know, but once she saw my face she started to scream. If the shock was due to fear, I could hold no blame. After all, an embittered con with a score to settle has nothing but time on his hand to plot, plot, plot. A moment later, our tug-of-war abandoned, Donna asked if she could make a call. Being fine with me, I followed her back to her apartment where she phoned into work and, wonderfully, took the day off.

Glancing around the apartment, I saw she had a bunch of pictures I had sent— pictures of me. They were artfully placed on the walls and lamp stands like a little gallery, proof that I'd not been forgotten and that I might still have a chance.

I asked how Corey felt about having all these pictures everywhere of her former boyfriend. Apparently, he'd tried to get her to take them down, but she couldn't. Pressing on, I had to ask exactly what had happened between us. She answered that Corey had caught her during a moment of weakness, and later had introduced her to cunnilingus. And then there was the simple truth that I'd been away, and he'd been around. What to say? What to feel? I didn't know.

Despite the conflicting feelings, we talked, and later that day and into the evening, enjoyed one another's company in a far more intimate way. Holding each other, a knock at the door interrupted our time together. "Who could that be?" Donna just stared, frozen on the couch. The knocking continued. I remembered, suddenly, that earlier Donna had turned off the ringer on the phone. The person at the door couldn't be anyone other than the man with the *unbridled* tongue. Damn!

Jarred from her paralysis, Donna went to the door and looked out the peephole. In a flash, she was off to the bedroom then back, body wrapped in a robe at the door. "Corey, why don't you come back tomorrow? I've had a busy day and I'm tired."

Having a sense of the man, I knew he wasn't going to just take off. This needed to be dealt with. Penitentiary-mode kicked in, "Donna, open the door and tell the man the news!"

She opened the door.

Corey stood there, wide-eyed and drenched with nervous sweat. "I know you!" Donna stood in place, frozen and breathless.

"Go on," I prompted, "Tell him it's over." I wanted to get back to business, get this man outta here. Hadn't been a day of me getting out and I was now dealing with this drama — didn't seem a bit fair.

"So that's it, huh?" Corey bellowed. "I've been played?"

The man was fuming; I couldn't blame him. I'd been there. He went on citing off a laundry list of everything he'd done for Donna. There was no way I was going to sit through any more of this. I got up. "Why don't you try coming back tomorrow as you can see, we've got some business we're tending to." No, the words weren't brilliant. And they weren't meant to be. They were meant to stab.

"Oh, you're gonna tell me to leave?" The man, eyes bursting with tears, yanked out a gun out from under his jacket. My mind started to race: Oh God...

I was standing there, nothing but a pair of shorts on, and I thought to myself that I was going to die. Crazy thoughts flashed through my mind of different ways to get out of this situation unscathed. Wanting to go out like a warrior, the thought occurred to me that I could knock his gun hand away like an old-school Jim Kelly, or I could get Donna, the person I suddenly loathed, to do something to fix all of it ... after all, it was all her fault. Shit, it was my fault. I had gone there unannounced, unprepared, unarmed, and with no plan ... *Yeah,* I scolded myself, *that's the thing to do ... go and surprise the broad.* I had wanted to show her who the man was, and now I was left hoping Corey'd miss, leaving an opening for me to make a move. But with him being a vet, I knew there'd be no missing. He was probably a damn sharpshooter, even the army's worst shooters were still rated marksmen!

Corey stood trembling with bloodshot eyes that leaked tears, his nose running. Donna was still frozen and from the look of her, there was no coming unstuck. It was time for *me* to make a move. "Corey," I called out, calm, hands up, palms forward. "C'mon in here. We don't need the neighbors butting their noses in, and for God' sake, ain't nobody needing the cops right now so keep your gun. Get in here and we'll talk."

Corey appeared to listen, the words apparently giving him some way out— and that was a good thing. Having been behind the wall, I know there's a lot of guys that end up on the inside simply because they got into a spat where they felt they'd had no options left. Closing the door, Corey started in on Donna, yelling and pleading his case. Donna, now un-stuck and arguing back, I got dressed, and seemingly invisible to the feuding lovers, made my exit, quick and proper.

Only later did my mind start to wonder what would have happened if Corey would've flipped out and settled things with Donna a bit more permanently.

A few days later, the girl from the bus called and what good timing did she have. By then, with my sexuality and my bravery back in full bloom, we agreed to hook up over the weekend. She commented that even if a bit strange, I was still a handsome guy and she was looking forward to our time together. Then, perhaps shooting myself in the foot, I left off with, "Strange, hell! You try spending the last several years with the state's most notorious beasts and then we'll talk." After some nervous laughter, we hung up. Our weekend get-together didn't happen and I never saw, or heard, from her again.

The next few weeks saw me through some dark moods. Unwillingly, I ended up telling Mom what had happened, and that I wasn't taking any calls from Donna. Mom felt my pain, but she also felt Donna deserved another chance. Giving me a female's perspective, she was able to lighten up my temper. Reserving the situation, she put it to me like this, "With all them years ... would you have waited for Donna?" What could I say? Gotta hand it to them Moms.

Back to Nadean and Renata, my daughter.

Nadean now had a boyfriend, a man by the name of Paul, whom she was head-over-heels for. Things weren't the best between them but they were working on it, and with me, well, at least Paul was polite whenever our paths happened to cross. I don't want to think I caused him to bolt because I only came around at times to connect with my little girl, but the man did know about my past and where I'd just come from, but I can't help but think that perhaps he was concerned about being around a possible ground-zero. Regardless, he wasn't around for long.

I spent as much of my free time as possible with Renata doing my best to reconnect. I hadn't seen my girl since she was four months old and now she was just under four years. Trying to be a dad now, after all this time, was a challenge unlike anything I could've imagined. The problem? My daughter didn't know me, didn't trust me, wasn't comfortable with me, and, of course, none of that was her fault. I hadn't been around. If all that wasn't enough, there were also my parenting skills which were practically nonexistent.

Believing that necessity can truly be the mother of invention, I did my best to take Renata without Nadean coming along,

196

figuring the time to be ideal for us to bond. Unfortunately, we'd hardly be down the walk before my girl would start crying out, "No, no, Daddy ... I want my mommy."

Adding to the fun, I had to rely on the public transportation system. As soon as we'd board a bus, Renata would start kicking and screaming and people would begin to stare, their thoughts readily apparent on their faces, "My God, is this an abduction?"

Thankfully, not every excursion on the bus was bad. One nice woman, obviously filled with empathy towards the problems I was having, offered to help, even commenting on how beautiful Renata was and what a pair we made with us looking so much alike. Despite the embarrassment of needing a stranger's assistance, I welcomed the woman's help in calming my girl.

As we hit up McDonald's, Renata's mood stood appeased temporarily, but later, on our way to a children's store, she started in with one of her temper tantrums again. Once again, peace on the bus was not to be had. Some of the older passengers viewed me with apparent sympathy, obviously aware of some challenges I was facing being a single parent.

Reaching the store, a woman working the floor in the children's apparel section helped me. Her product knowledge and ability to connect with kids helped me save the day. Both Renata and I left as happy campers.

When Renata and I returned — after an exhausting day — Nadean asked what any mother would: "So, how'd your day go?"

Such a simple question. An obligatory question. And nothing that I could find any fault with. At the same time, those simple inquiring words were rhetorical. Furthermore, they were rife with waves of smarmy "knowing." I know how your day went! It sucked. And it's all your fault. Daughter doesn't know you ... wanted me, not you ... and now you've gotten just a smidgeon, just the tiniest tastes of what you've missed, and how there's no way our little girl sees you as any kind of father. Neener-neener-neener.

When it came to being a Dad, my self-esteem was shot. I had fathered this girl, but I was no father and I knew it. Worse, my daughter knew it, and she showed it. I was the boogeyman. I was an inconvenience, an interruption to my girl's day. She could be playing with her dolls, having fun with the neighbor's kids, doing anything, going anywhere, being with anybody, and any of these things would be better than being with me, a stranger.

Before the man ended up making his final exit, my heart would ache even more when Paul came around, when I'd have to watch as my girl would run and jump into his arms. Paul might not have been the best potential stepfather around, but he was likable enough, one could even describe him as a slightly tamer version of me, with just enough of the bad-boy type to attract someone like Nadean. Nonetheless, watching him garner favor from my daughter, filling to a better degree the shoes that should've been mine, caused more than pain. It made my heart burn.

Let's not forget Gwen, either, my son Terrell's Mom, the woman who hadn't taken the time to tell me about my son's birth. When I did get to see her, she seemed happy that I was out, seemingly pleased to see me, yet her actions — or inactions — during my incarceration told me otherwise. I was an interruption with her, too. She was now involved with a man named Al, a guy I'd met when I'd first arrived in Seattle.

With Terrell, his grandparents were the real gems; Gwen wasn't around much whenever I'd come to visit him. The boy's grandfather owned a corner store equipped with a pool table. I'd come by, shoot some pool, and play with the boy — but always under grandpa's wise and watchful eye. In the man's youth, he'd run the streets and could plainly see the direction I was headed.

198

There were times that grandpa's attitude was inconvenient, but his attitude didn't bother me, after all, on my best day I was still the capricious fellow.

Terrell's grandmother was a bit more compassionate, or at the least, a bit more flexible, allowing me to take my boy places without subjecting me to the third degree. For the most part, Terrell and I enjoyed our time together, but it didn't take long for him to get homesick. He hardly ever cried, though; he'd just ask to go home or inquire about his grandparents. Most of the time his eyes were set upon me, trying to discern who this stranger was that came around from time to time. I'd take him by Mom's and Patricia's, and then by Renata's to get acquainted with his sister. To this day, they share a special bond.

*****

Donna finally called to let me know that Corey had settled down, put the gun away, and understood that they were done; that while I was away, he'd simply caught her at a vulnerable time. I found myself only partially sold on the news. Apparently, the two of them were finished as an item, were separating themselves from each other, but at the same time, the two of them were still employed at the same workplace.

Donna repeatedly apologized for the whole sordid mess, and I did my best to be as understanding as possible. One way or another, if we were going to see each other we had to work our way past these challenges. It amazes me how soon people forget just how dangerous it can be to mess around with affairs of the heart.

Back in high school, Donna had been a cheerleader and though her pompom days were over, there was no writing off how graceful she could be on the dance floor. Hitting the clubs on the weekend became our mainstay activity.

On top of Donna's addiction to dance, she also had Pac-Man fever and she would drop rolls of coins, oblivious to time, all for the sake of gobbling those yellow dots. Finally, between the two of us, things were starting to level out.

The one-speed bump? My past. Donna was aware of my sexual proclivity and my penchant of entertaining hosts of women. At any moment, she was expecting to find me back in my old ways.

So often drama seems to walk hand-in-hand with love. Even parental love.

At home, Samuel was readying to go back on the warpath, his grouchy ways already pressuring Mom about the two of them housing a grown man. It made no difference, either, that I was doing my best to stay clear of the home. And then there was Samuel's curfew, something I thought insane to stick on a guy old enough to drink, and let's not even discuss how such a rule impacted my nightlife. I needed to get out, but to where? There was Donna's place, and presuming she was amenable to the idea, then perhaps that would work. But there was that drama: Corey! Would he show up agai ... armed? Would the place end up riddled with bullets after the guy had a bad day at work, got lonely, or otherwise went postal?

Encouraging me to endure for just a bit longer, Donna started looking for a different place to live. After weeks of searching, things finally started to look up. The difficulty was in finding a landlord willing to rent to an ex-con. After more than a month of house hunting, we found a place. Next stop: notifying my parole officer. Tentative approval was set with the condition of my P.O. getting to meet Donna. Afterward, the man said Donna was good people, a template for me to follow, and bid us the best of luck.

Samuel, my mother's live-in, had finally retired. *Oh, goodie. More jibes to put up with.* Fortunately, I didn't have much longer after his last day of work before I, too, was ready for a change.

The day of the move, all I had to put up with was walking by him carrying my ugly, heavy, loud, green prison chest, and looking at his disparaging gaze; lip stuffed with Copenhagen, a fifth of Jack in hand, and his body chillin' in a recliner. He couldn't have been happier.

Neither could I.

The house Donna and I were going to share was perfectly situated—at least for me. The cottage rested alongside several parks and didn't sit too far away from gorgeous Lake Washington. A convenient tavern, with an even more convenient billiards table, stood only three blocks away, a perfect opportunity to test out my pool-hustling aspirations.

First opportunity I had had me racking-and-smacking balls. Quick discovery, however. Most of the gentleman hanging out there were alcoholics, functioning alcoholics. I didn't know how they functioned at work, but I quickly found out how they functioned shootin' pool with them playing better while blitzed than I did dead sober. I had already been playing around with alcoholism, but a good habit takes time and I wasn't quite there yet. But I would, and when I'd arrive, there wouldn't be anything functional about it.

Moving in together did wonders for Donna and me, the biggest of which was that for some reason it allayed her fears about me messing around. Instead, the expectation was that with her, her son Ryan, and me all living together we'd all just move on happily ever after. Didn't happen, however. Our problem, of course, was that I wasn't too skilled at getting along with kids, and with Ryan, I never seemed to gain his trust. At the time I didn't understand why. Now I do. Ryan was Donna's little man, and with her being all he had, he was too busy standing the watch to let his guard down with a relative stranger.

The bus system was quickly getting old. Word had it, though, that a successful brother owned a nearby car lot, and better yet, that he'd be willing to give a first-time buyer a break. With the cash I'd scraped together and Donna's good credit, there was no way the dealer was letting us off his lot without a deal. And I got one, the only one available … a green Cadillac. At first I thought a jinx, what with the car being the same make and model of the one that Mark and I'd had such hell with. Whatever fears I had, however, paled compared to the headache of taking the bus, and with a deal comprised of making bi-monthly payments, I embarked on a new adventure, that of being independently mobile, a necessary launching pad for me to start in the many illegal activities that I'd been lusting after. With four wheels now underneath me, things would never be the same.

Donna's only expectation was for me to drop her off and pick her up from work. But even with this Godsend of a stipulation, my past had to find fault. Mark and I had once burglarized the home of one of her co-workers. And though the charges against us had been dropped, the co-worker knew that I was one of the guilty parties.

With Donna's job downtown, the lure was irresistible. Back in the day I used to ravage the place with Mark and Dana. And not a lot had changed. Opportunities abounded, but there were still things to be wary of. My parole officer for one. His office was only eight blocks away from Donna's place of work, and then there were the cars to be watchful of, both plain views and unmarked, reminding me that parole's not a good time to get busted. My P.O. had told me I needed to find employment; I was looking at it right here.

*****

One fine evening while strolling through downtown Seattle, I ran across Marline and a boyfriend of hers while they were sitting at a bus stop. She stared at me with incredulity. She'd thought I was still locked up — a lot of people did. We didn't talk. I just walked by. I did hear her whisper my name, though, no doubt informing her man who I was — her first love. She might've denied it, especially given her company, but when she'd first seen me there'd been that sparkle. Without a doubt, our paths would cross again.

Extending my leisurely walk deeper into the urban jungle, I ran into an eye-catching brunette named Tamika — a girl who I quickly found out needed a tour guide on her first trip to Seattle. We planned to hit the Space Needle as the first of many stops at the city's various tourist traps and scenic pit stops, but first, we opted to stop at my car to share a joint. With the weed magnifying the intensity of the shared moment, it was all I could do not to explore the sexual temptations that threatened to overpower me. Fortunately, I maintained a modicum of self-control.

The Space Needle was a hit, with Tamika enjoying the diverse cultures busily mingling there. Afterward, with the day still young, we visited Pike Place Market before closing out our evening with the ferry ride across the Puget Sound.

Things with Tamika soon developed into an "open" relationship with both her and Donna aware of the each other. Of course, Donna didn't agree with the idea of me having another woman in my life but at the same time, with Tamika being Caucasian, Donna didn't feel that threatened. It's been my experience that sisters tend to view white women as passive distractions rather than serious competition.

At twenty-one, Tamika still lived with her parents, the overprotective kind, who were already sensing that their daughter was getting knocked off track.

And they were right.

Tamika was a prime example of a good-girl-gone-bad — and that, in record time. Hanging with me wasn't helping, either. One example of her growing bad-girl persona was the way she treated her grandmother, a wealthy woman; when Tamika would visit, there'd always be a hand-dip into the jewelry box, just a karat here and there that never seemed to go noticed.

As my relationship with Tamika grew, so did the tumult within her home.

They didn't approve of me, and who could blame them. I went for the whole meet-the-parents routine, but all I got from the father was a gruff voice, and from the mom, an overly inquisitive eye which led to her copying down my license plate number after leaving the residence with her daughter. Asking Tamika if this was typical behavior for her Mom, she replied that it had only grown typical since of the start of her coming home night after night past two in the morning, smelling of booze and grass.

In fact, Tamika's newfound habits bothered her mother so much that, wanting me back in prison, she placed a call to my parole officer. My parole officer warned me to back off, but legally he could do nothing as Tamika and I were two consenting adults. The man, however, did try to draw out the sense in me: "Just what're you doing? Trying to find a one-way ticket back to prison?" But there would be no listening to common sense — not now. I'd already begun drifting past the point of no return.

Amazing how so many clichés can be so filled with truth, such as, "association brings on imitation." With relationships, there's "open," and there's "open," and one doesn't make a self-centered man comfortable with the other. With Tamika, the girl had seen me socialize with any number of different girls and apparently felt it was time for her to expand some horizons. Entering one of my favorite watering holes, I found Tamika standing between a man's legs, talking away while nursing a drink in her hand. Things between us the way they were, I had no call to get possessive, but still...

"What are you doing?"

"Nothing," she gave me a look, "This is Devon, an old high school frien ... bought me a drink 's' all, while I was waiting for you!"

Giving her a look in return, I responded with, "Looks like he's bought you several," before turning around and walking out the door.

Astonished that I'd dare give her the cold shoulder, she followed me out and before I could unlock my car door, exclaimed, "What's with you, anyway ... hell, you're the one living with another woman!"

Driving her home, I let her have the brutal truth: a man does what he does, he gains respect, becomes a player, a stud ... when a woman does the same, she's a slut, a skank, a whore. Getting to her house, she bolted, slamming my door, obviously unable to cope with the dated, caveman philosophy that I'd thrown at her. Far as I was concerned, it was good riddance— I didn't need the bother anyway ... not with her, and not with her mother who seemed intent on calling my P.O. more than me.

Weeks later, Tamika called to say we had to meet. We did— at one of her favorite Chinese eateries. Once there, she told me the news: She was pregnant. *Damn!* I'd noticed her face looking puffier, the few extra pounds, but had attributed it to her wild lifestyle. Wrong again, and this time in a big way. Last thing I needed was to father another child. Flashes of my father and his many failings instantly came to haunt.

There was a clinic not far from Seattle. She made the appointment, and I coughed up the necessary funds for the procedure. With the doctor taking his time, Tamika told me not to bother hanging around, that her mother was taking her home. I left thinking that the abortion would be carried out as planned.

With Tamika, there was no more drinking and smoking, which was fine, but what did quickly beg the question was her swelling belly. She said there had been an equipment problem and that she'd have to reschedule. This line worked to keep my fears at bay for a little while longer, but soon things became very apparent. There'd been no procedure, and there wasn't going to be one in the future. Tamika's family were Jehovah's Witnesses, so for them, there was to be no consideration of such an "evil act."

When the call came, the call that most fathers welcome with excited anticipation, I found myself filled with dread. Tamika's parents had left the hospital, and if I wanted, Tamika said I could come and see our baby. *Man, oh man.* I went, I had to, but it was one long strenuous trip. The final months of Tamika's pregnancy up to this moment had found her family on the hunt for me. Not only was I no longer welcome in their home, but even their neighborhood was now off-limits. A fact I found to be true the few times I'd tried to come around only to be warned off by the city's police. And Tamika's mother had not stopped making her phone calls!

Entering the room, I found Tamika holding our baby — a girl. I froze in place, felt numb and distant. "Look," Tamika said, "she's got your eyes. Looks just like you."

I'd walked into a nightmare! The baby had a pale complexion with slanted eyes and jet-black hair— straight hair. The baby was not mine, and with Tamika, she had somehow deceived herself into thinking I'd fathered the child.

So many situations in life where there can be no winner, when someone, sometimes everyone, is going to come out hurt. This was one of them. I was uneasy, even if understandably relieved, and Tamika, she would be devastated when the realization hit that there could be no way for me to take responsibility for the child — and for the baby, herself; there'd be the pain of not knowing her father.

Looking at the sad picture in front of me, I stopped myself from bursting Tamika's fantasy. Now was not the time. I'd let her savor the moment. Later, with her and the baby safe at home, we'd have the inevitable heart-to-heart.

A sad blow to the soul when that day finally came, and through blinding eyes Tamika revealed that she'd been date-raped by an Asian.

I had to ask, "Why didn't you tell me?"

"You'd have just gotten pissed."

Our relationship ended not long after. The baby cried constantly, remained sickly, was angry all the time with a mood ever worsening the more that I hung around. And with Tamika, with quite a burden to carry, began accusing me of not giving a damn, of being mean to her and her daughter. Faced with a deteriorating situation, Tamika threw herself into her religion. After spurning an obligatory invite to join her with the local Kingdom Hall, we finally parted ways....

Chapter Twenty-Six

THOUGH AT THE TIME I DIDN'T SEE IT, and if I had I probably wouldn't have cared, I'd begun setting a bad example for the teenagers in the neighborhood. With them, boys and girls, looking at 'the attitude', the cars, clothes, and women-under-my-arm as an elevated status they wanted to emulate. With the young men, it was all about P.R.B.: pussy, respect, and the Benjamins. With the girls, the glitz-and-glam was delusional, offering up a facade of the kind of guy they wanted to be with; they had no concept of the kind of abuse that went with it.

Some of these same young men I would see many years later on the streets, and even worse, jail or prison. Being older, and having a changed nature, the sight of them squandering their lives pierced my heart. Especially true, when they'd tell me how they had once wanted to be like me.

*****

Robert and Mark, my two endearing brothers, called every so often to see how my debut back into society was working out. Mark was no longer at the reformatory. He had transitioned to the honor farm at McNeil Island. Whenever we had the chance to speak over the phone, he disclosed how much he enjoyed the atmosphere there, which had a spectacular view of nature, trees and greenery, and the Puget Sound. But that restful feeling soon vanished; inevitably, Mark ran into some snag that landed him back in the Hole.

His yearly parole meeting was approaching and by the parole board's standards, this behavior was unacceptable. Whenever possible, he'd call and tearfully tell me how he was dreaming of his freedom. I didn't help matters much telling him about how exquisite it was being a free man. After my many prison stints, I have painfully learned that freedom isn't only something to be cherished, but respected and stewarded. I went on to share the various opportunities I'd had both taken and missed. During our conversation, I could feel Mark's intense emotional desire to breathe free air once again and get on with his life.

During this time, things were more lenient and I was granted the privilege to pay Mark a visit at the Island. One of the requirements was that a person with a clean record accompany me. Donna was that person.

I had never been inside this prison before, yet I felt they were all the same — detestable. Donna watched as my complexion changed and beads of sweat formed on my forehead. She asked if I was all right and I told her that I was fine. I didn't think she believed me because of the sideward glances she kept giving me. Whatever the feeling that was oppressing me, it left without a trace once I saw my brother's sunny smile.

Mark and I shared a strong, heartfelt brotherly hug. Donna stood amazed at the sight of two brothers smiling like Cheshire cats. Naturally, the sight of my face overjoyed Mark. We sat there for hours talking about what the future would hold once we joined forces again.

Then, having smiled and laughed the day away, a guard alerted us that our time had ended. I could tell that Mark was dispirited. Giving one another our best final wishes, I left and lost no time getting off the Island.

*****

Donna loved cooking, and even more, loved experimenting her gourmet dishes on me. One evening, Donna and I were dining on one of her many cookbook specialties but before we could finish our meal, the phone rang. It was Robert calling to apprise me of his impending release.

On the day of Robert's parole, I brought a friend of Mom's so that I wouldn't have to set foot in the administration office. I felt hexed being back on the grounds of the reformatory. Sitting there in the parking lot feeling uncomfortable, Mom's friend went inside to let them know Robert had a ride. He wouldn't be boarding any prison van like I had.

Another reason behind my angst, I had brought a drug on the premises. Even though it was only one rolled joint of marijuana, I was still in violation. Sitting there nervous as hell in the parking lot, it didn't take long for the paranoia to set in. I was superstitious to the point to where I had the rear of my car facing the administration building. That way, all I had to do was glance in my rearview mirror to see if Robert and Mom's friend, or whoever, were headed in my direction. Finally, my brother came out. I don't think I've ever seen Robert's smile so radiant. His pace wasn't far from a jog. I teasingly asked, "You being chased?" He didn't find this too funny. Remembering how I felt getting out, I didn't pour the humor on too thick. I understood that it was only natural for a man's temperament to be a little different after imprisonment, especially the first time. Just so Robert would feel better, I screeched off towards the freeway, quickly leaving the small town of Monroe.

I told Robert to reach into the compartment. He didn't know I had a thick stick of marijuana as a surprise. Mom's friend didn't see this as a good idea. He didn't think a person should be filling their clean lungs with the taint of marijuana smoke. After Robert's first inhalation, he went into a coughing fit. Mom's friend was concerned about picking up a contact-high. He was also concerned for Robert. With Robert's lungs sounding like they might collapse at any moment, he asked me to pull over. Not wanting to pull over, not wanting to stop until we reached Seattle, I rolled the windows down and told Mom's partner to pat Robert on the back. There wouldn't be any more tokes for Robert. That and I couldn't wait to drop off Mom's nagging friend. At least the rest of the day turned out to be fine, and later Robert even enjoyed a triple shot of his favorite juice — Vodka.

Something on the to-do list for any newly released inmate is to hook up right away with a female. Knowing this, and realizing that Robert's day wouldn't be complete without giving that mission a good ol' college try, I gave my brother a ride to his girlfriend's house. Dropping Robert off, I couldn't help but hope that he wouldn't be met with the same level of drama I had found on my first day out.

*****

Renata had the right to be merry; her birthday was right around Christmas. The occasion called for a dual celebration. It truly set my heart aglow watching her attack the wrappings on her presents. Right away, thoughts drifted back to my childhood and Christmas, which were some of the best times of my life, spent in the loving arms of Inez. No one noticed, but it was with moist eyes that I sat there basking in my precious daughter's moment, musing about what her life would possibly be like beyond the gifts and childhood, and how instrumental I'd be in it.

Some of the gaiety was disappointing to little Renata. She was extremely pigeon-toed and bow-legged so she often tripped over her own feet. In the process of walking, she sustained injuries to her knees and legs. She was the cutest little tomboy anybody could ever lay their eyes on. She wasn't going to allow anything to hinder her when it came to her big wheels, tricycles, bicycles, and romping with her friends.

She also had an exceptional fascination for Michael Jackson. I enjoyed watching her being captivated by the creatures in Jackson's "Thriller" video. She'd watch it a thousand times, and be in awe with each viewing. While Nadean did her chores in her household, Michael's videos were Renata's sitter.

*****

At one point, Marline staged a coup of her own. We had been running into one another at various clubs and even at the gas pump. She knew that after enduring my prison stint, I was still mad at the world. I had no right to think this way, but I hadn't grown through it yet. Most the time she'd send one of her girlfriends over to tell me she'd like to speak with me. Our verbal exchanges involved her saying how we needed to rekindle our teenage flame. She couldn't see that life and prison had turned me callous; there'd be no recapturing of any glory days, but being who she was, Marline would not let up.

One fall evening, I stopped over to watch a few videos with Renata. Respectfully, I knocked on the door and became startled when Marline opened it. Questioning about her being there, she said with a smile she was Nadean's new roomie. I knew Nadean was gracious and all, but never in my wildest dreams would I have expected to see my two previous girlfriends under the same roof.

For the most part, whenever I'd stop to see Renata, Marline would be there, too. One time, stopping off at Nadean's to pay Renata a before-bedtime visit, Marline, in a see-through negligee, answered the door. I inquired about my daughter. She said that Renata had gone to spend the weekend with her grandparents. Saying that I'd be taking my leave due to the fact that it was looking like she was set to greet some fortunate guy, she stopped me, saying that I was that guy, that the whole point of moving in with Nadean was to get closer to me. Then, grabbing my hand, she led me into her bedroom like a helpless lamb. Though the sex was sweltering, it wasn't enough to reunite us.

*****

Sometimes I would encounter my brothers, Ronald and Jimmy. With Ronald being the consummate Momma's boy, I'd catch him stuffing his face at Mom's. He'd never drifted too far from that southern style cooking. Whenever I'd come over, he'd lay into me, criticizing my way of life, warning that it was just a matter of time before I landed back in prison. Being law-abiding citizens, Ronald and Jimmy knew how to live life on its own terms, something that I hadn't even started dreaming of yet.

Those hard-working qualities that were instilled in Jimmy when he was a young farm hand in Louisiana were still shining through. He worked as a sanitation engineer driving trucks. Sometimes I'd see him in the back alley, driving his route, picking up garbage. Infrequently, my garbage was set out late and I'd see him. We'd talk for a while then he and his two coworkers would move on. I remember how he'd always frown at my clothes, my stuff, my bling. He'd sweated for his two cars, boat, motorcycle, and house. Off and on, we'd meet somewhere and have a drink or two. Then we'd lie to each other with promises of getting the family together. I had plenty of respect for the way my big brother lived, but my doom had been sealed from the first time I'd caught the street merchants and players out on Yesler Boulevard.

*****

Turning 22 called for something special — Louisiana Cajun theme. Not sure if she could pull it off, Donna made me settle for a large pot of gumbo. Having little experience preparing gumbo yet wanting my first birthday back in society to be over the top, she consulted her grandmother who provided her with the necessary assistance. I invited every family member that I thought might be able to make it while asking Mom to lose Samuel for the day; I could do without the man's negative mojo messin' up the festivities. Mom didn't respond, but I figured she thought of it as a great idea.

Robert gave Mom and Ronald a ride to my party. For some reason or other, Patricia and Jimmy were a no-show. With the handful that did arrive, our little gathering was still a hit. Beforehand, I made sure to have Mom's favorite beer on ice. Truly enjoying the affair, Mom was also impressed with how nice the gumbo turned out. For the time being, she let go of her worries, loosened up, and even found herself warming up to Donna. Donna smothered me with so much love and attention, that Mom commented, "You really love my boy, huh?" Donna could only smile and blush. No answer was required; her actions showed it all.

That day with Mom, my siblings, and all of us there sharing, loving, and laughing ... it was the last occasion of its type, all of us bonding under the same roof, an experience never repeated.

Patricia gave me some half-baked story as to why she couldn't make it. She was my second mother; I was so disappointed she didn't come. Another reason was that Donna and I often looked in on her and her husband if for nothing more than to enjoy a card or dominoes game. Plus, I'd take Renata by every chance I'd got. Patricia still carried with her that country air, with Renata able to enjoy rides in the back of their pickup truck, running around barefoot at their place, and eating greens and cornbread with her fingers.

And then there was K.K., my niece, whom I could always amuse myself with, watching her dress up like Michael Jackson and moonwalk across the living room floor. Whenever she became burnt out on Michael, she'd don some lacy garb and transform herself into Madonna. Either I would grow tired of the exhibition, or she'd collapse from exhaustion. Then I'd go down into the basement where the pool table was located and hone my shooting skills. Often, Ron, my little nephew, would join me. A boy growing so tall that even at ten- years-of-age, I figured that one day he'd be the tallest male in the family, a lad so mannered that he was always a joy to be around. Even today, he gives me that special kind of attention that makes me feel the way my favorite uncle Otis must have felt.

Chapter Twenty-Seven

IN 1984, AT THE AGE OF TWENTY-ONE, I took a turn that would miserably change my world for the next two decades.

I drew in my first breath of crack.

My girlfriend Donna and I habitually went to her mother's house. Like me, she hadn't outgrown her mother's cooking. Even if her mother wasn't there, the pots on the stove would still be raided. Donna even turned me into an accomplice.

One humorous instance, Donna's mother came home early from work and caught me with pork chop grease smeared across my mouth. "Donna, you and your penitentiary boyfriend better quit eatin' up all my food."

For some odd reason, whenever she addressed me, it had to be penitentiary-*this* or penitentiary-*that*—her humor quickly grew on me.

One time stopping by Donna's mother's to fill our stomachs, we found Donna's brothers there, Donald and Jeffrey. Having served time with both, I felt like I knew them well and enjoyed their company. Donald was around when I had courted Donna back in high school, and Jeffrey's life ran pretty much parallel to mine— meaning a lot of brushes with the law.

They asked for a ride home.

At the time, I was a loner. Besides, with three parolees in the same vehicle, if by some fluke the police stopped us, I'd automatically be in violation.

Another phobia? If stopped by the police and any of the passengers stashed anything illegal, like drugs or a gun, the charge would be against me because I was the owner of the vehicle. I wasn't planning to go back to prison, but if I did go, it would be on my terms.

As I started in with my excuses, Donna asked, "Please, give them a ride home?"

"Sure."

We were halfway to their destination in the middle of a suburb when, unexpectedly, they needed to make a stop. I didn't think much of it as long as they didn't take too long. I parked the car on the side of the road while they headed towards a convenience store. Once there I watched in shock as they kicked the front door off the hinges. Instantly, I started my engine and was just about to drive off, when I remembered what had happened to my cousin, Brian, and me when my best-friend, Dana, had ditched us. Against better judgment, I watched Donald and Jeffrey burglarize the store, hoping they would hurry up. Greed, however, kept them going back in for more. Finally, feeling they must have had enough, they waved me forward. I quickly pulled forward and told them to hurry. The stolen goods were placed in the trunk, and I accelerated the process of getting us out of there without any confrontation with the law.

On the way to their home, though, there was one more detour.

We stopped at what must have been their fence to get rid of the stolen goods. The idea of having all that unlawful property out of my car made me feel better. After they returned, they split their earnings. I didn't require much because I knew we'd never travel again in this manner.

In the end, we arrived at Jeffrey's place. They invited me in for a drink or two. I accepted and took my position at the dining room table. My drink was hastily prepared and placed on the table. They then moved at a frantic pace in search of their drug paraphernalia: baking soda, a pot for boiling water, and their glass pipes.

Of course, I had heard and read about freebasing, yet I never thought I'd be subjected to it. In a sense, it was a tad bit amusing watching them in their mad-chemist state trying to turn the cocaine from powder to liquid, and then into rock. They finally solidified the cocaine and I watched as they fired up the rock. It popped and sizzled as it melted and evaporated into smoke. The vapor swirled in the glass bowls of their pipes as they inhaled. Once they had descended from the stratosphere, they realized I'd been sitting there for close to an hour, my drink consumed, the whole time with them ignoring me.

I was offered a pull. I turned it down.

They shoved a smoking pipe in my face. I said, "Oh, well, it's only cocaine ... a toke or two and I'll be on my way."

To this day, I wished I would have stuck to my guns and stood firm on my initial decision: No. From the very moment that I wrapped my lips around that glass instrument, the whole course of my life rerouted. The cocaine penetrated the pleasure zone of my brain. At that moment, I had my first mental orgasm.

It felt too good. Sensational.

Today, reflecting on many, many, many years of cocaine abuse, I wish that first pull would have made me puke, or given me a headache from hell. But no, it enslaved me. With that very first inhalation, the crack monster was conceived.

The sad part was, for years the monster would thrive in an embryonic state biding its time, till finally, needing to feed. Once again, my laid-back demeanor was disrupted. The altitude of the cocaine's high went beyond the clouds, with the crash of the low far beneath sea level. That very first hit had ripped me to shreds. I didn't know to what degree or the kind of beast now fermenting inside.

These days, when I hear the word "abstain," I fully understand and wish I had held fast years before. The course of an individual's life can forever be changed by a single hit.

Some are fortunate, with divine providence moving in their lives. Others never make it back from the dark side. But still, I am in the shadows.

Driving home that night, dealing with the overwhelming depression from the plummet of the cocaine wasn't easy. My body had become feverish. The foreign substance I had subjected it to was having an adverse effect, not to mention guilt. Would Jeffrey and Donald tell their sister I had gotten high with them? Would she then view me as a despicable crack-head? Would she stay with me?

These were just a few questions tormenting my foggy mind.

Before going home, and with the windows down, I cruised the viaduct and Seattle's waterfront, letting the chill breeze off the Puget Sound slash against my face until I was close to being sane again. Despite giving me several more invites, Jeffrey and Donald never did inform Donna of my drug use. And though still obedient to my will, the crack monster remained within, a baby that was growing hungry — famished.

Donna and I went on living together for almost two years, a time that I will always hold dear. I hadn't yet been caught in my sea storm. There was still a fraction of desire to remain at shore. The monster within had yet to reach its epic proportions.

In our relationship, I was continually making bad decisions. Donna had become pregnant. For over a year, she had desired to give birth to my child. Seeing it differently, I convinced her that at this point in our lives an abortion would be best. Sitting there holding her hand through the abortion process was a despondent time for Donna and me. And I don't think she ever forgave me.

Years later, when I fathered two more children with someone else, she told me with a heavy heart, "You wouldn't let me keep my baby." Hearing these heart-wrenching words let me know that I had made one of my biggest mistakes of my young life. This was the result of having misconstrued priorities and living my life like a runaway freight train.

Donna was hurt beyond repair. She left behind a scarred part of herself that day in the clinic. She still loved me, but her love had faded over time. Her behavior made me think, "What if my parents would have aborted me?"

Once again, my thoughts had me second-guessing my decision.

Donna had begun giving me ultimatums. The choices weren't many. Either her lifestyle or mine. Painfully, I chose mine. The quarreling between us began to disturb her son, Ryan. He'd wake up scared, thinking I was harming his mother. This eight-year-old kid loved his mother and he'd damn well protect her.

One occasion, Donna and I were both exhibiting a strong amount of "assertiveness." Taking it for more than what it was, little Ryan snatched a lamp off the table and slammed it into me. He said, "Punk, leave my mother alone." I couldn't help but admire his courageousness, but then he ran to call his grandmother and great-grandmother. Twenty minutes later, I heard a car screeching in the driveway. From the view I had from the living-room window, it appeared to be a carload of irate black folks. Then came that loud police sounding knock, and a voice yelling, "Open up!"

Donna opened the door and the crew rushed in with shouts of, "You better not have harmed my granddaughter and grandson!"

Little did they know, I'd never harm a child. While I sat there composed on the sofa, her grandmother said, "Put him out! What he needs is a job. Girl, you can do better than this."

Donna's grandmother was in her seventies. Not daring to disrespect her by making a derogatory comment, I sucked up all that they said until the storm blew over.

With Donna, our relationship had become so unhinged she threatened to move in with her mother. She was hoping I'd heed her warning and at least try to change, but the call of the wild would not leave me alone.

Coming in early one morning from one of my nocturnal outings, I noticed Donna waiting up for me with puffy eyes and a tearstained face. Hurtfully, she told me that the lease was up on the house and she wasn't going to renew. Her immediate plans were to move out of the house by the first of the month. She'd given it one last try, hoping I'd do something ... or say something that would prevent the demolition of our relationship.

She even spoke of a suitor.

We hadn't been spending much time together like we once had. My corrupted endeavors were taking up most of my life. We had cast aside our previous dance nights and she had started frequenting the N.C.O. Club at Fort Lewis.

While there, she had met an army fellow and just like her ex-boyfriend, Corey, he was from the east coast. Because our future was so bleak, she was letting me know she was considering giving him a chance. My waywardness wouldn't even allow me the dignity to register some good, old-fashioned jealousy. Corruption was leading me, and I wouldn't dare turn from it until I was either derailed or deceased. The baby cocaine monster inside was coming to fruition.

Once Donna and I parted ways, I knew a new chapter in my life was about to begin.

From the very first day when Donna and I had met at school and made eye contact, I knew there was something special about her. She had dedicated a nice portion of her life to me and would have wholeheartedly loved me until the end of time. Sadly, I couldn't return the favor. The things we wanted out of life weren't in alignment. I wanted overnight success, and she wanted to toil for hers legitimately.

I shared my dilemma with Mom and my sister, Patricia. They feared what lay ahead. Foolishly, I didn't consider the potholes and ditches reserved for me. They were fond of Donna and couldn't believe I was allowing her to walk out of my life. Instead of a righteous life with her, I chose pipedreams.

Corruption had its giant claws in me, and it was leading me to a land far, far away.

That dreadful day inevitably occurred and my brother Robert and I backed a rented U-Haul up to the front porch and loaded the furniture and other belongings while Donna milled around the house.

After taking the last load to a storage facility, she rode off in the U- Haul with Robert to her mother's house, presumably to continue her productive lifestyle while I climbed into my car and drove off into Never Never Land.

Chapter Twenty-Eight

NOW THAT MY GUARDIAN ANGEL AND I had parted ways, I was out to sea and hopelessly adrift. Life now consisted of everything except becoming a productive citizen.

Then there was the club scene, irresistible and necessary—like in many areas of life—for networking. One individual I befriended was a notable cocaine dealer. If I'd known then what I know now, I would have avoided him like the plague. Instead, I became just another casualty to the ever-spreading crack epidemic. He'd often share his private stash with me, stuff more potent than what he usually passed around. We'd head off to the bathroom between stints on the dance floor to snort coke through hundred dollar bills. Cool stuff ... inhaling poison. Just toy with it, I had thought, play a little. What's a little messin' around going to do, anyway? And besides, you only live once, right?

Never did I imagine that what I thought was harmless recreational drug use would wrap me in chains.

Another backlash to this euphoric rush was in losing my virility. Snorting this perilous drug was not only freezing my nostrils, but it was also freezing other vital organs. Also, being addicted to sex, for the time being, drugs would have to be more of a sporadic pleasure.

Around this time, Bessie, my grandmother, along with her granddaughter, Debbie, paid the family a visit. They lived at mom's during their Seattle stay. Listening to grandma, it was apparent that things had been hard on her, swapping California sunshine for Seattle's rain. Not having a memory of ever seeing my grandmother, she had turned out to be much more than I'd expected. We bonded as if we'd always known each other—a bond that never broke until the day she was called to heaven. When she grinned, I suddenly realized that my own smile had come from a long lineage.

At that time, I had too many distractions in my life for me to realize that they needed help putting an end to the abandonment, neglect, and dysfunction that had been violently uprooting our family. Family members that cared were a dying breed. My grandmother, however, saw the caring spirit within me and was hurt by the fact that I was not willing, or didn't believe, that it could ever surface. If only she could see me now! Although I submerged myself in a sea of drugs, from its murky depths my caring spirit finally emerged.

Grandma and I shared many lengthy chuckles about my attempting to get her to the stove while she was vacationing. With her having cooked since she was a little girl, it would have been nothing for Grandma Bessie to dole out a southern style meal. But Mom wasn't having it, said it was inconsiderate of me to be pestering grandma about cooking while the woman was on vacation. Emphasizing her point, Mom said that if I wanted grandma's cooking that bad, I should make my way down to California. Little did anyone know that I'd be doing just that.

Good manners and being a good hostess for her mother aside, there was perhaps a bit of jealousy, too, seeing that Mom's cooking in the house had always been first and foremost. To keep out of trouble, I said that I had only wanted to see if she got her good cooking from her mother; seeing the broad smile come across my mother's face, I knew I was back in her good graces. Being a man with a serious dependence on soul food it would have been an awful thing for the best cook in town to cut me off from her food.

Grandma said that if there were ever a need, her home would always be open to me. She went on to enjoy her stay in Seattle, even to the point of becoming temporarily immune to all the rain. We laughed about how it had to rain to keep the Evergreen state beautiful. She even dealt with those crowded, smoky bingo parlors that Mom and her patronized.

Bidding farewell to her and my cousin Debbie was rough, but my heart rejoiced when my mother and grandmother embraced each other farewell; they were the cornerstones of the family.

*****

Being single leaves one with a lot of idle time. I filled mine, especially around the pay periods of the 15th and 31st, by hanging around soldiers and airmen from Fort Lewis and McChord Air Force Base at the various clubs throughout Lakewood, and Tacoma, Washington. I'd show up alone and look like an easy mark, but was always ready—especially after some beers or shots had been passed around—to lay down a friendly wager over a game of pool.

One night there was a lusty, six-foot brunette who was eyeing me and my earnings. I wondered if the other players had strategically placed her there to distract my game. Probably. I didn't care, at least not at first seeing as she had legs going on for days, skirt hiked high, and heels made to stab. And as my wallet was emptied, my question was answered; whatever my mind was on, sure wasn't the cue ball.

Having previously seen me win several games, she sashayed over to the table and in a whiskey-moon voice, offered to play. Not wanting to sound biased, I politely told her that gambling with a lady wasn't my policy.

"You afraid to get it handed to you by a woman?"

I plead the fifth.

I was stuck, too, as I was sure that there were female hustlers out there, though I'd never run into one ... until then, at least, as I had one stand before me. Now I could get away with saying how I felt: Ain't no way I'm getting beat by a freak. Quick thinking saved me, however, as I instead said, "Tell you what, winner buys a round of drinks. I'm Terry, by the way."

"Jasmine pleased to beat ya."

I smiled. "We'll see."

After dropping some bills and having some drinks (that I had the privilege of paying for), the conversation took a sharp turn. She asked if I'd like a date. "Sure ... Friday's good, that work for you?"

"No, I mean do you want a date?"

Her right thumb and index finger rubbed together, the universal sign for money. Though I had never been approached by a hooker in so brazen a manner (let alone while shooting pool), I decided to have some fun. "No, baby, I ain't that tough to land... you don't have to pay me."

"Never mind, this was a mistake."

Her face turned downcast. For a moment, I was puzzled, and then I understood. She was new at the game, and I don't mean pool. "Now wait a minute, hang on ... we got our drinks, let's sit down a bit, talk some ... least you can do after making me play so hard."

Grabbing a table, it all came out. Some friends of hers suggested going to work; she had the looks after all. And besides making same green, she might get lucky and land herself a Sugar Daddy, or even better, maybe a husband, some lonely soldier or airman, perhaps, looking to rescue a damsel in distress. Whatever Jasmine's motivation, it was clear that there was something dark going on inside the girl, some hurt or wound. I can't say I understood it, but the recognition was there. After all, I had my *own* demons.

Our talk lasted quite a while, which was very unprofessional of her, but then again, it became quickly clear that with me she was no longer working. Instead, something had clicked and we'd struck a fancy.

Friday was fish night, an indulgence of mine since my Louisiana catfish days. For better or worse though, I was no longer in Louisiana and getting some good catfish was a bit of a stretch. Still, there was Ivar's, a restaurant located on one of Seattle's piers. I invited Jasmine to come along for a meal of fish and chips. That was when I told her of my upcoming trip to California.

My plans were to make a brief pause through San Francisco before going on to Fresno and visiting my grandmother. After that, it would all be about getting back to Seattle before my parole officer got wind that I'd left. Besides seeing my grams, of course, I'd been sold on checking out San Francisco by a gentleman I had befriended at the reformatory I'd lived in. Plus, seeing Eddie Murphy in *48 Hours* foot-loose and running rampant through the city and the Tenderloin district ignited my interest.

Jasmine with her own bad case of California dreaming asked if she could come along. I let her know straight-up that a life with me, let alone a trip, wasn't any kind of way to live for a struggling single parent, that my operating mode consisted purely of illegal activities; the only legal thing I'd done was to get a driver's license, an emissions inspection, and tags for my car. Having her own agenda, she could have cared less about my warnings.

"I'm a big girl, Terry, don't worry about it."

"Okay."

"Besides, with Frisco I won't have to be walking red when I'm red-lighting it."

"What do you mean?"

"You know, red-faced ... embarrassed ... when I'm working the red-light district."

"Embarrassed? About what ... the johns—"

"No, don't be silly. With everyone else. I know too many people here, friends and family. And they ain't too thrilled about what I do, if you know what I mean."

"I do."

"What's your story, anyway?"

I told her the bitter truth. "Look, Jasmine, been fun for you up to now, and that's fine ... but the Life ain't no joke, got the police, the joint, the competition, rough clients, feuds, you name it, and if you're not careful, and sometimes even when you are, there's the morgue."

She wrapped her arms around me. "I don't have to be afraid, Terry, not with you to protect me."

I broke away. "Look, you ain't listening, hooking up? Yeah, we can have some fun, and I don't mean you any wrong, but we ain't no thing. We get down there, and you butt heads against it, you're on your own."

"Really? And what, you don't think I can handle it?"

"Ain't about that ... you gotta have the spirit for it, and I don't know that you do."

"And where'd you get yours, huh? Some kind of Louisiana voo-doo or something?"

"It's 'hoo-doo' not 'voo-doo,' and no, I ain't saying that. Just that at least with Seattle, which isn't all that bad, you know the tracks; San Francisco's new and ain't your turf." I went on to advise her about setting up her own call-service. That way, she could better pick her clientele, even charge more, and not be walking the strip. She wouldn't have any of it.

Instead, she told me she needed the street. Needed the instant gratification.

"What's that supposed to mean?"

She then gave me her laundry list: the abuse, bad boyfriends, two dead-beat Dads that had left her, and her kids without fathers. She said she had it nailed: men were pigs. Having johns pay for it, up front, then working 'em quick to get the job done, she got to see men shamed, got to be in control, no pillow talk, no false promises ... just pure business. "I'm a big girl; you don't have to worry about me. All I need from you is a simple yes or no. Can I go, or not?"

I don't know if it was her boldness, her foolishness, or want, but suddenly, having her tag along didn't seem like such a bad idea. "Be ready in a couple of days."

With a couple of days on our hands and with the backhanded hope of perhaps having Jasmine change her mind, I took her to the northern section of Seattle so she could give her pumps a trial run. To my surprise, Jasmine was a natural. A lot of girls starting the walk are soon arrested if for no other reason than for the police to give themselves an introduction and to let them know that they know what's up. To add another strike, Jasmine was flying solo, having no pimp; that could only bring a girl heat from both sides of the fence. The thing was, Jasmine was a chameleon, blending into the environment like just another patron window-shopping or taking a stroll. She was invisible. Not even the local business owners called her in for loitering in front of their establishments.

The night before making my California trip, while sucking down a neck bone at one of my favorite soul food cafes, a man walked in that I'd spent time with at the reformatory. I invited him over for a drink. After exchanging a few pleasantries, he asked what was going on with me. There's something to be said about loose lips. Not realizing we had the same parole officer, and that this guy might use the Intel as a bargaining chip, I innocently and ignorantly told him about my morning trip to Cali.

The next morning, parked out front of Jasmine's house, I waited as my new "girlfriend" happily placed her luggage in the car as her kids mournfully peered out the living room window. Before Jasmine could get into the car, her friend rushed out to give her a tearful hug. For a second I thought I might have to tear the two apart. Later I found out this woman was more than just a friend; Jasmine didn't have any trouble working it, seeing that the men were just johns, but when it came to intimacy, she'd found safety in being with the same sex.

Fantasies started running through my mind, imagining the two of these ladies together. Sometimes women wonder why this is such a common head-game with men. No mystery to it. Women are beautiful. Two women together, well, it's double of everything us men like.

Maybe Jasmine was right about men being pigs.

Crossing the California border, Jasmine lowered the boom, saying she'd told her girlfriend that I was an insurance salesman on my way to a convention in San Francisco, and she was vacationing with me and would be back in a few days.

I knew what was up. She was cutting out of town. *Damn.*

Knowing about abandonment all too well, I told her she was wrong. Explained how it not only happened to me as a child but was a crime I was also guilty of, having two children of my own; I was no different than the men with whom she found so much disgust. Her tear ducts burst. Seeing her grief stream down her face from those pretty green eyes, I knew what I needed to do: turn around and drive back, or at the very least, drop her off at the nearest Greyhound station. Unfortunately, she urged me on, and for another stain on my soul, I gave in...

Arriving in San Francisco was such a special moment that I had to insert some Herbie Hancock into my cassette player even as my mind was swept up by the magnificence of Treasure Island, the crossing of the Bay Bridge, and the spectacular view of the Pacific Ocean. And then there was the city itself, the Paris of the West Coast.

The city was like Seattle, except the hills were steeper and there was less rain. Another thing that instantly stood out was the manic traffic, with the flow of cars moving so fast that I felt I needed to turn into a racecar driver just to keep from getting horn-blasted by everyone for slowing down business.

With our excitement starting to wane, we finally found a hotel close to the action that we were looking for, a place near Powell Street and Union Square. With its underground parking, Union Square was key. I needed to be able to conceal my car bearing Washington plates as I had a record and was an ex-con out on parole. My P.O. had made it clear that I wasn't to cross the county line without written permission. The last thing I needed was my party crashing because of some bored cop running a random plate check and finding out I was two states away from where I was supposed to be.

We made ourselves at home and Jasmine quickly discovered that she did have the spirit needed for the street. We tried checking out the main tourist attractions, but Jasmine could have cared less.

Working the streets had become not only her line of work but her favorite pastime as well. Finally, out of morbid curiosity, I had to ask, "If you're so turned off by men, how'd I wind up getting so lucky? Or were you just looking for a taxi to take you out of town?"

"Easy... we're both like minded, honest with each other about who we are and what we want. And, don't forget the great sex!"

But Jasmine had it wrong. We were not like-minded — not in the least.

The hatred she bore faced out, towards the world, her clients, and such. Mine, if anything, faced inward.

In no time at all, Jasmine went from not only working the street, but operating out of several ritzy hotels as well, and she soon started her own lesbian love affair with a fellow prostitute, a beautiful sister with cocoa-colored skin.

How did I know about all her shenanigans? I was her sounding board.

Jasmine loved to share her various exploits almost nightly, seemingly drawing intense pleasure every time she sensed that she'd caused a shock, or otherwise surprised me. Many of her tales were simply variations of one theme; that of entertaining some nervous john out for the first time, angry with his wife, looking for something other than ten-toes-up and ten-down. But then when she'd start to share her rising role in engaging in various BDSM practices, her eyes would protrude and her face would turn aglow as she'd start to share how "··· you wouldn't believe the tip I beat out of the guy."

Life became surreal and I began to question my own sanity.

Jasmine's intense passion and tolerance for extreme sex fed my own out-of- control desires. Doing our thing while looking out our high-rise's windows at such a strikingly beautiful city had me convinced that we were living.

Breaking into the Tenderloin district was a different matter with the area nothing more than a thousand rats fighting over a piece of cheese, and absolutely no tolerance for new blood trying to piss out their own little section of turf. The fact that I was new to town reversed the role of hunter versus prey for me, a fact not to my liking. Needing better hunting grounds, I found it in Chinatown. There, it was like being a single rat inside a cheese factory.

After making the necessary rounds reconnoitering the area, I ran into a woman I'd seen visiting many of the same clubs. Needing to network some contacts, I approached and we started flirting with one another. My coke stash was running low and I needed to make a score. The woman, after making sure I wasn't a cop, promised to hook me up and took me over the Bay Bridge into Oakland.

Some say cats have nine lives. For some reason, though, I've seemed to be graced with having ninety-nine. And that night one of them got called.

Only a moron would've pulled into a no-exit alley. And I was that man.

I gave my "friend" a hundred bucks for product and another twenty for her brokering the deal. Then I waited ... for 40-minutes before, with a startle, she suddenly appeared and got into the car. I stared at her for several minutes as she sat, scratching and nodding. Finally, "Hey! Where's my stuff?"

"Uh ... oh, yeah, here it is, jus' a second."

I waited another ten minutes, watching in stunned silence as she fumbled around inside her bra. Then, thinking I'd have to go in myself, fumbling around her enormous can to find my stash, she flung a small packet that looked to be worth about $30.

Mystery solved.

I'd been had — taken like a cherry. How embarrassing.

This woman was a junkie, the scratching and odd behaviors were all tics from her heroin grind. And I'd been the dunce to fund her fix – and all for a lousy, half-teaspoon of coke.

Live and learn. Huh?

Getting back to my hotel, I found Jasmine in a tuff. She'd been having some close calls with the police and had been chased off by security out of some of her favorite hunting grounds. And she was jealous, having seen some of the other working girls wearing furs, jewels, driving fancy cars, and being helped out of limousines. She didn't understand why she wasn't getting some like play.

"Jasmine, you can't be working dusk-to-dawn and not expect to have some run-ins with the boys in blue, and with your clients, think about it, they're registered and you're not — it's going to attract attention. Be happy hotel security didn't just call it in and have you picked up."

Following my advice, she started making inquiries amongst some peers. One professional she found had been working nine years, another who sported a mink had been hitting it for fifteen. I even told her about one gal in her sixties who, niche market or not, was still out there hawking.

She started to get it, the understanding that the life wasn't a picnic and that these girls she'd been turning green over had busted their... backs to get to where they were.

With time starting to tick away, I reminded her that the main reason for my going to California was to see my grandmother. It was time to move on.

During our trip to Fresno, I shared what I knew about the town. What with its industrial and agricultural bases, and the people too, who, by and large, worked long, hard hours, and who, to Jasmine's chagrin, might not have as much disposable income as their counterparts in San Fran.

Jasmine's various issues were going to have to take a back seat.

There were uncles and aunts I had never met, kitchens I'd never visited, and when we finally arrived, to Jasmine's joy, she found I hadn't been joking. She stuffed her face right along with me, even started her own hankering towards soul food. I got a kick out of seeing her get past the smell and relish and taste of my grandmother's chitterlings. I introduced her to a couple of my uncles, J.J. and Junior, and my aunts, Betty and Loretta. With Loretta, her and my mother could've been twins; the only noticeable difference between the two was my aunt being five to six inches taller.

Jasmine and I spent most of our time at Grandma Bessie's. She had two shade trees in her front yard just like some of the houses I remembered in Louisiana. We ate big red and yellow meat watermelons, swatted flies, and made up for years of lost time by enjoying numerous chats. Grandma loved seeing me eat. Jasmine, on the other hand, was a little uncomfortable being the only white person around all these black folks. I told her that these weren't the 50's and 60's. My folks had seen plenty of interracial relationships.

Time spent in Fresno was woefully short, but the few weeks it did last, I would forever cherish.

Jasmine's phobia with the law was the real reason I had to leave. The streets she worked were only so long, and with her running and leaping over fences to make her various get-aways, she had worn out her welcome and for the first time ... was headed for jail. With Jasmine's arrest, I now had my own paranoia, that of the law going through her and getting to me.

My car could be seen, plain as day, parked in front of my grandmother's house — not good. I hadn't seen my parole officer in 60 days, which meant I had missed four appointments — again, not good. My name had surely gone out to the system that, along with my out-of-state plates, left me in one hell of a vulnerable position. I had to get back to Washington.

With Jasmine's release, we immediately took off for Seattle, but she wanted to make a pit stop back in San Francisco first. I shouldn't have, but I did; it's hard saying no to a woman who's consistently rocking your world.

Frisco was the same. We even stayed at the same hotel. Or ... it started out the same until I came in from a weekend romp only to find my room empty of not only Jasmine but also all of her stuff. There was, however, a note, a tearstained Dear John letter sitting atop a lamp stand:

Dear Terry,

I'm sorry to have done this to you, but I had to face reality and seize an opportunity. You don't love me. That's not a dig, just a fact, but that did mean our days were numbered anyway. And now, I've met someone. A rich gentleman. We're going to elope. I'm getting off the streets, and he's going to take care of my kids and me.

I wish you the best.
Jasmine.

Having been around the block a few times, I should have seen this coming. And why not? It's every hooker's dream. And normally, it wouldn't have been a thing. But this time was different. Jasmine had grown on me. Just in case things didn't work out for her, I stayed an extra couple of days, but she didn't come back, and there was no call. With a hardened heart, I left for Seattle.

Or started to.

Before I made it out of the city limits, my mind drifted off and I rear-ended the back of a car. The car belonged to a guy who happened to be a law student. I tried calming him down, but he started signaling for anyone listening, or who may have seen the accident, to call the police. The only thought that registered in my mind was that I had a parole violation and that I was going to lose my car, and go to jail.

With the panic of going back inside jolting the rational side of my brain, I reached into my pocket, pulled out a wad of bills, and asked the man how extensive he thought the damage was to his car. He couldn't seem to think of a number, so I gave him $300, and he let me go on my way.

Jarred from recent events, I decided to stop by the nearest liquor store before continuing. After picking up a six-pack, I took off for home. After driving hundreds of miles under the influence, I picked up a hitchhiker, something I wouldn't have done otherwise. He told me he was headed for Salem, Oregon. We shared some shallow conversation that didn't amount to much. From the alcohol and constant driving, I started swerving a little and asked if he'd mind taking the wheel. More wiped than I thought, I was out in minutes. Four hours later, late in the night, I woke to find myself parked at a rest stop in Medford, Oregon. That had not been part of the plan, being way too easy to be spotted by a curious trooper. With a mind more set to business, I made it back home.

The moment of truth had arrived. This time, when I walked into my parole officer's office, I wasn't greeted with the normal. "Mr. Hill, have you done anything productive with your time lately? And while we're at it, how was the weather in San Francisco?"

With the blank look on my face, he knew he'd caught me off-guard. "Don't ask me; I haven't seen the weather report."

"Mr. Hill, I have a good mind to send you back to prison. Furthermore, I would be mindful of who I mention that I'm leaving town to. From the last speeding ticket you have, it appears you're driving a better car than I am. Care to explain that?"

I wanted to say that maybe I had a better girl than he did, but I bit my tongue, opting instead to say that I simply made several trade-ins off Donna's credit.

"Got way too much time on your hands, Mr. Hill, way too much time." He went on to say that from now on he'd be expecting me once a week, and with proof that I'd been looking for work.

I left the man's office glad I hadn't made the crack about having a better girl, as it was I had just barely missed being sent to prison.

Chapter Twenty-Nine

MARLINE AND I HAD STARTED HAVING MULTIPLE chance encounters. What a fine time for reconciliation. I'd been getting antsy and needed a different wind in my sail. Actively employed, she worked full-time at one job, part-time at another, and lived in a posh apartment near the Renton airport, out on the outer limits of Seattle.

It was in quick, enjoyable, and foolish fashion that we embraced our reunion and in a blink, I moved in with her; me, my debauchery, and my growing drug problem. Marline didn't have a clue.

There was another situation, too. Marline had just ended a relationship and her ex-boyfriend was having a hard time letting go. How right she was. One night, just as we were sitting down to watch a movie, her former beau came in having gained entry using a key that Marline had forgotten to get back. Situations like this make a man start to wonder just how many times he can roll the dice. Fortunately, this situation didn't get as volatile as with what had happened with Corey. Marline simply talked to him, telling him the obvious, that things were over, and they needed to part and go their separate ways. The man professed he understood, but later, he continued to pester and prod and "hope" that things between them could get back on track. I was troubled, myself, with thoughts inevitably realizing the truth ... that I had no idea what this man was capable of, or just how many times God was going to grace me with getting over.

At the end of one day, while Marline and I were kicking back and enjoying some light banter, things took on a more somber tone. She voiced concerns about the possibility of being infertile and her sorrow at the thought of never having children. Apparently, she and her former boyfriend, consciously or not, had been trying. Wanting to be supportive, I brought up the obvious, that perhaps it hadn't been her, but that he had the issue. She smiled, comforted, if only for the moment.

However, sometime during the next four months, things changed, dramatically. Marline had gotten pregnant. And I was the father.

Marline's mother didn't quite know what to think of this. She trusted her daughter was making the right decision and even if, at times, she didn't, she at least wanted to. Since I was a teen, her mother had always shown me the utmost hospitality. She'd at one time thought of me as a noble young man, and had treated me as such by opening up her home, blessing me with numerous meals of fine down-home cooking, late night movie watching, and fellowship. Inevitably, though, things changed— she changed. And I was the cause. Corruption can so easily nullify the good in a person. It's with a strange mixture of laughter and shame that I look back on all the occasions of jumping out of Marline's window, shooting out the back door, crouching in the closet, and the regretful day of Marline's mother snatching her daughter out of one of my stolen cars. I'd abused the woman's good graces, and now, with the pregnancy, had still done nothing to earn them back. Nonetheless, the woman, class act that she'd always been, was doing her best to treat me with a light hand while fully supporting her girl.

*****

I received a call from Mark, him giddy and all but hyperventilating. He was earning parole in a couple of days...at midnight.

Back then, McNeil Island Corrections Center would parole an inmate at midnight so long as they had a licensed driver there to pick them up. I wasn't too familiar with the Steilacoom area, having forgotten the route Donna and I had previously taken; so, to be on the safe side, I decided to do a practice run. The woodsy back roads weren't my favorite place to be at midnight, but I knew from personal experience how critical it was for any person who's been behind those prison walls to get back into the free world. Another thing I knew, this time out, there'd be no Mary Jane —marijuana — surprise as part of the welcome package. Despite my personal hang-ups, I still wasn't going to throw all caution to the wind.

While driving to McNeil Island, I was thinking to myself that this would be my last trip ever to a prison. Arriving with a few minutes to spare, I backed up to a loading dock and waited, keeping my eyes glued to the rear-view mirror.

A short time later, Mark arrived and I popped the trunk, getting him loaded up.

Mark had no cause to be reminded of the previous scuffle we'd had in the green caddie. Since then, I'd traded in the beast for a newer model.

Fresh-faced and newly turned twenty-one, Mark was still a kid at heart, and with no surprise, immediately wanted to take over the wheel. Brothers ... what can ya do? Saying we'd wait till we got out of Steilacoom, I pulled over just before we hit the freeway to make the switch. There are a lot of things, some good and some bad, that a newly-released man might want to scratch off his list; I figured this was an easy one to cross off. With Mark now happily navigating the road, I directed him to a particular lounge wanting to introduce him to what Donna had introduced to me when I'd first gotten out, a very special drink: an electric iced tea, a stomach-burner built over ice with squeezed lemons and sour mix, holding a healthy dose of vodka, rum, tequila, gin, and Blue Curacao, and when one of these are missing, don't be afraid to sub in some bourbon whiskey.

Doesn't take too many of these to drop a normal man, let alone one who'd been behind bars for four years, but I was treating Mark, a brother with a well-trained rot-gut.

With Mark released at midnight, everything that needed to get done had to be accomplished quickly; time was ticking, and we still had a 30-mile-plus trip to make it back to Seattle.

I also threw out a hint that Samuel had been getting worse over time, grouchy and crotchety as ever. If Mark was going to be pitching his tent at Samuel's place, then the sooner he got there, the better. Mark, though, was like a young, stout Rottweiler that had broken its chain, with everything there for the taking. He said to me, "On second thought, I don't want to be dealing with that old grouch. Not on my first night out. Take me over to Jean's."

Jean was Mark's on-again-off-again girlfriend. Wanting to cater to my little brother's needs, I headed over, but soon, tinkering with thoughts of my first day out and the chaos that ensued, I began to have second thoughts, especially about showing up at some woman's property at two in the morning. Mark, however, couldn't be dissuaded.

Arriving at Jean's, we found the place dark—surprise, surprise. Again, I just wanted to bug out, but I knew where Mark was coming from. A man fresh out of the joint … if he even thinks he might have a shot, he's gonna go for broke.

Standing next to Mark, I started to cringe, the man's knock sounding loud enough to wake the neighborhood. A light came on in what might have been a bedroom. I listened as a pair of light feet made their way to the door. Then the fumbling began, she must've looked out the peephole to see who was barging in at such an indecent hour. Jean opened the door. She wasn't smiling. With hands on her hips and a frown on her face, I looked at my brother. "Call me if you're alive tomorrow." He just smiled back and went inside. I knew they'd be have some issues to work out, the least of which was showing up in the dead of night, and yeah, Mark would have to do some apologizing but in the end, I had no doubt that my brother, the master charmer, would have his way.

Mark, indeed, ended up having some good early morning hours with Jean, but their enjoyable reunion soon turned sour. Making matters worse, Mark, still irresponsible and with nothing to do but get in trouble, started badgering me to borrow my car. This soon became a burden, started interfering with my plans, but wanting to do my best for the man, I asked Marline to loan him her car for a while, vouching for my brother. Mark bitched it up. Soon, and on top of dealing with all the pressures of a first-time pregnancy, Marline started receiving tickets from all over the city and beyond. Then there was me adding to the pressures. I'd started getting nosebleeds— a lot of them. Coke'll do that. Especially once you hit a certain level of tolerance, and I was way beyond tolerant. No amount was enough. I just couldn't reach the heights I once had.

When the occasion allowed, my brother and I would hit Seattle's hottest nightspots; fun times filled with all sorts of thrilling shenanigans. One of the things I enjoyed was how the women would make such a fuss about how good Mark and I looked, and how much alike we stood. All but twins, the only thing differentiating my brother and I was a few years and a bit of height. But where I enjoyed the fuss, Mark was competitive, a narcissist, and dead-set on upstaging his older brother.

When I'd first arrived from Louisiana, he couldn't believe how much we resembled each other. Before my arrival, his sweet-

243

faced look had the limelight often turned toward him. Guess that's something a person can get used to. But since I'd hit town, there were times he felt threatened. I remember him asking childhood girlfriends who they found more attractive, and the famous Hill smile that would spread ear to ear whenever they would answer, "You, Mark."

We were enjoying a typical night out, parleying with two appealing grown women, discussing what restaurant we were going to have breakfast at when Mark asked a kid a question, "Who do you find more attractive between my brother and me?"

I hadn't even asked the question, but I felt more ill-at-ease than any of the four of us. In the blink of an eye, it became clear that Mark had blown it ... for the both of us. Thanks, brother. The ladies suddenly remembered they had something else to do.

"Damn, Mark, when's this shit gonna end?"

Laughter. "Don't sweat it, bro ... they just wanted some free drinks." Part of me wanted to pursue the matter, but knowing how argumentative he could get when confronted, I defaulted to mommy-wisdom: Don't cry over spilled milk.

While we were getting ready to leave, I ran into a straight out, busty piece of chocolate delight, a woman by the name of Karolyn. I'd seen her out before, on the town, occasionally looking at me, smiling, then turning her head away. Shame she'd only just introduced herself because Mark and I had to leave. Still, her heavenly beauty had damn near hypnotized me, and later, she'd tell me that she'd left that night with a heart warmed from my own smiling eyes. Something had happened in that moment of our meet....

*****

As the blistering cold of winter set in, California sunshine was the only thing on my mind, and soon I decided it was time for Marline and me to make a venturesome trip down south on I-5. Along the way, Marline was concerned. She hadn't grasped the concept that there were times I retreated to a quiet place in my mind, a needed self-defense mechanism brought on by having to deal with the constant stress of my abnormal lifestyle; the threat of jail and prison, death, the feast and famine of my wallet, and my never-sated desire to get high.

Marline's concerns suddenly took a backseat. A deer had crossed our path, stood frozen in our headlights. Terror filled my eyes. We were going 80-miles per hour. Brakes squealed. We started to fishtail.

We struck.

The deer flew. Our car began to smoke. Thankfully, though, we had come to a stop. I got out, assessing the damage to the car.

"Terry, you've killed that poor deer."

"Cry over Bambi later."

I felt bad about the deer, but my mind started to reel with the financial hit. Just a month earlier, on this same freeway, I had totaled my front-end after hitting a patch of black ice and had to cough up two-grand.

Marline was sullen for the rest of the trip to my grandma's. When we finally pulled up front, the first thing my grandmother said was, "Boy, what on earth have you done to that pretty car?"

"It was terrible, Grandma. A deer came out on the road. Suicide by car."

"And you left all that good venison on the side of the road? You should have thrown that deer in the trunk, and grandma would have shown you what to do with it."

Years following that incident, I would have the satisfaction of sinking my teeth into some choice venison. I'd go on to enjoy this beef-like meat every time the opportunity presented itself.

While we were in Fresno, we stayed at my uncle J.J.'s house. It wouldn't have been right for me to subject grandma to my nightlife. But with J.J., we had things in common, and the man didn't mind making a few dollars on the sly. Where we markedly differed was: my uncle knew how to balance work and family, knew to come home at night, and didn't share in my many addictions.

Marline was happy to have the opportunity to get acquainted with the other side of my family, a closer-knit bunch than my Seattle kin. These were down-home folks who lived their lives as if they were still in the south.

Having her own down-home spirit, Marline fit right in. I was in turmoil— and still am to this day. God had surrounded me with such beautiful, loving, and caring people, friends and family deserving of my sincere love and support. But stain-to-my-soul, I couldn't return it.

Finally, it came time to make our return to Seattle but our car, by now, was pretty Humpty-dump. An acquaintance made while working the street turned me on to a car dealer in San Diego, a guy who didn't require a big down payment, and who'd also take jewelry on trade-ins.

San Diego turned out to be my kind of city, with a Louisiana-style soul food cafe at every turn. Unfortunately, I'd barely arrived when I witnessed a crack-tragedy. A young man pacing back and forth on a freeway overpass, obviously distraught and disoriented. I had to pull over to make room for advancing first responders: firefighters, police, and paramedics. Out of macabre curiosity, or a subconscious recognition of my ever-deepening plight, I circled to see the outcome. I did. The young man, crack addict according to bystanders, had swan-dived off the overpass. For him, the fight was over –perhaps had been for quite some time.

Tragedy aside, Marline and I found the car dealer we'd been looking for and successfully haggled our way into not just one, but two cars. About our combined pieces of bling, I overheard the dealer say: "My wife's going to love this stuff!"

The pieces I had offered up weren't meant to stand as payment, but as collateral. I remember thinking, *don't be gettin' too attached, 'cause I'm coming back to get mine.*

Making our way back to Seattle, the tomboy in Marline got the better of her. We had to visit Disneyland. Frolicking with me on the rides, she must've forgotten she was pregnant, and after a rousing fun time on a killer bobsled roller coaster called *The Matterhorn*, she got sick. Bittersweet fun. Unfortunately, it would be Terry's, my unborn son, first and only trip there, and from the jostled position of his mother's womb.

While still in California, I called home to check in with Mom. There was bad news. Mark was in jail and headed back to prison. He hadn't been out ninety days. Insult to injury, he'd gotten arrested while driving Marline's car. He had abandoned the car, with the windows down, in rainy-ass Seattle. Then as proof that the Devil is real, the ride had become home and hearth for a vagrant. The I-told-you-so's from Marline never let up, and I had to just take it. After all, she was right—had been right.

Guest of Seattle, my brother, was being housed in a newly-built jail, a tall facility just some yards from the freeway. Mark made the mistake of gazing out the window at the traffic, wishing he were out there free again. Deep depression made its way into my younger sibling, and he told me that he would no longer be making any calls, that he needed time to set his mind for the trials and the time that lay ahead. This was now the second of

247

what would be Mark's many tours through the correctional system.

Chapter Thirty

RICK JAMES HAD IT RIGHT. Cocaine's a hell of a drug. Of course, he just as easily could have said, "Cocaine's a drug of hell." I started to recognize that, though I was helpless against the budding realization. At this point, my entire life revolved around the substance.

A handful of exclusive friends had been pooling their money to binge off some free-basing. Receiving an invite to join in, I quickly agreed, my mind curious about this relatively new and potent form of my favorite drug. The logic was simple. Why get high when I could get HIGH? And drinking hard liquor to hide the effects of the drug ... well, that was just a bonus to my demise. With a drug as powerful as crack cocaine, it doesn't take long for the mind to start playing tricks. I could have thousands of dollars on me and be convinced the whole while that I'd only be picking up twenty dollars worth of blow. Back in the day, a $20 rock could blast four people into orbit. And oh, that initial high ... nothing like it. And that's the problem. Shit's worse than popcorn, ya can't have just one, and that's the thing, once you've had the first hit, from then on you're on a marathon tryin' your damndest to chase that first high. And an addict like me will spend the roll tryin'. But not the next time. The next time, I'll just do the $20 ... I mean the next time, next time, next time, next time.

And Marline was with child. I'd be coming home at dawn, day after day, only to find her zombied-out, wiped from another sleepless night, or being hit again, first from the stress I was causing and then by morning sickness. Depressed, I collapsed into a beanbag by the door. But was it Marline and her condition

249

that had me down? Of course not. Neither was I concerned about what her problems were, let alone interested in her chewing me out with her ceaseless, fruitless nagging: What are you doing to me? What's happening to you? Who am I, anyway ... the woman carryin' your baby or just same piece of meat you happen to screw? And let's not forget the drug lectures. Blah, blah, blah. I didn't want to hear it. And I didn't. Couldn't. It was all I could do to wrestle with crashing—not falling asleep, that didn't happen anymore– before passing out.

Words, written or spoken, can never wipe away the shame, but then, at the time, there was an amber within that vainly wished for things to be different; I was wrestling with my own monster. The crack monster. And I was pinned.

One day, by chance, I awoke only to overhear Marline on the phone with my brother, Mark, busily telling him about my degeneration, all-nighters, exhaustion, and the fact that I hardly ate; I'd go days and days without eating. Marline didn't specifically know that bellyfuls of crack had robbed me of my appetite, but she wasn't stupid, she knew I was tearing myself apart, and that it was drug-related.

Marline's friends weren't stupid, either, and were quick to let her know of my car being spotted frequenting the high-traffic areas—drug traffic that is. Time after time, demon-led and demon-followed, I visited these crack houses answering their irresistible siren's call.

Marline's family and friends warned her to sever all ties with me. I didn't care. Didn't need help, and would be damned before I asked for something I didn't need in the first place. Yeah, there was a problem. I knew that. I wasn't a dummy. And I had a plan to deal with it. To fix everything. And I would...

... next time.

Unfortunately, I stayed pinned — ass-out on the mat for the next eighteen years.

Out of embarrassment, I started taking my crack away from Seattle. With the impeccable logic only available to those who have perfected denial. I presumed that by putting some distance between my current haunts and myself that nobody would recognize me as a crackhead. My answer was close-at-hand with Tacoma, the third largest city in the state.

Self-deprecation aside, even self-delusional addicts can learn a lesson, and one night I surely did. What was the pearl of wisdom? Be careful who you get high with.

While holding up in a motel, I ran into a woman I had gone to high school with. Even back then, the attraction was her supersized lips. If I had known better, I would have left this woman and her lips alone. I'd been using to the point where the cocaine had somehow become an aphrodisiac for me, with it and my sexual addiction becoming inseparable, and with me not indulging one without the other.

Lil' Miss Lips was no ordinary drug user; supposedly, she knew how to make rock. Always nice to have some skills. Not having enough money to get some coke on her own, we decided to combine our loot, get what we needed; she'd cook it up, and then we'd split it down the middle. Easy peasy. And seemingly fortuitous. I didn't have the know-how on turning powder into rock form; after hearing about Richard Pryor, my favorite comedian, doing the flaming streak, I was nervous enough as it was. Why all the trouble in the first place? The high, of course. Buying in powder assured getting the highest percentage of cocaine possible. Buying rock straight-out was risky; you never knew what you were buying, or what other ingredients it included. I once watched a guy drop 30k on some rock before I, in turn, bought a grand of it off him. Once I set fire to my stash, it smelled and tasted like burnt rags— we'd both been duped.

Watching Miss Lips's frenzied actions as she cooked the cocaine put me in the same frame of mind I had when I was first introduced to crack by Donald and Jeffery, that I couldn't wait. What I should have been doing was paying attention to her erratic behavior, the way she was moving, the way she'd talk to the substance as she'd stir and cook away. She was a loon. But love is blind — love of the drug. Plus, I had crossed the Rubicon, having already laid down my bread. Finally, with the stew lifted from the cauldron, she placed it on the table and took off for the bedroom to get her kit.

When she returned, I sat there twirling my thumbs as she sliced through the large rock: half hers and half mine. Wanting to check the drug's potency, she lifted her glass pipe and fired up. I soon followed suit and started sucking on my own piece of glass. While I continued to inhale, I noticed her pupils dilating larger and larger. Seeing her take in this much smoke made her appear inhuman, as if she had the lungs of a large mammal. By now, I had exhaled and was seriously wondering if my partner was going to go into heart failure, have a seizure, or if her lungs would collapse. I wanted to say something, tell her to stop, to exhale — but I couldn't. I was mute. Crack can, and does, do a great many things to a person's body and brain. For a lot of addicts, and me in particular, losing the ability to speak was quite common. Whenever I did crack, it could take fifteen to twenty minutes for me to be able to speak again.

Finally, before she collapsed, she filled the kitchen with the smoke she exhaled, then dropped her pipe on the floor where it shattered into a thousand pieces.

I sat there, wasted, unwilling or unable to move, waiting for the inevitable decent from my high. *Miss Lips... had she gone?*

252

Yes, out of the kitchen, but only for a moment. She came back in, but this time not alone. With her, and pointed at me, was a double-barreled shotgun. She started to rant that I'd stolen her drugs when she went to test the rock. Not able to speak, my hands tried to "sign" defense, pointing to the rock still on the table.

"Get the fuck out."

Feeling helpless and sobering up by the second with my life in the balance, I swallowed my pride, eased out of my chair, found a wall with my back, and made my way to the living room and out the door, twin barrels staring me down the whole time.

By now, my voice was back, but I didn't say a thing. Just getting in my car and driving away alive were good enough for me. Driving back to Seattle, I could not get that shotgun out of my mind.

The evening was shot, and all because of a pair of lips. I was angrier with myself than her. It was the drug. Crack caused people to steal from their parents, abandon their families, and to pawn their children. A night like this, a normal person would've gotten a clue. But there you go. When a person is in the clutches, they're clutched.

My relationship with Marline started to deteriorate, with her constantly giving me shit, reminding me of the man I once was, how she'd been attracted to me, but now ... who the hell was I? Marline, ah Marline, who can be angry at Marline?

My drug use was out of the closet.

The accusations thrown hurt, but that's the thing about self-denial, it's a skill too easily perfected. I considered telling her about the terrible creature living within me, but the revelation might've been too much for her to handle, at least in terms of her staying with me; and let's not forget shame. There's always shame.

Somewhere inside, I still had the idea I could beat it, that I would beat it. The idea was clear. Reality, however, was a different story. I was in too deep.

*****

The day had arrived. The baby was coming. By chance, after a drug-fueled marathon of a night, I just happened to get home a minute before Marline's water brake. Panicked, I rushed her to the hospital. Shortly after our arrival, it was found that the contractions were still far apart; things were going to take a while. Marline was afraid of going through everything alone and wouldn't let me leave her bedside. I understood. I'd been no good for her and I knew that, but there was no way my third child was coming into the world without me being there to stand witness and lend whatever support I could. Renata and Terrell had both been born while I was on the inside, and I'd never hear the last of it, not from others or myself.

After a fair amount of reassurance, Marline reluctantly calmed down enough to let me leave to get myself cleaned and freshly dressed; after being out all night, I was nasty. Unbelievably, drug urges still hit when I took off, but these I could beat down. Getting home, I donned my navy-blue suit and returned as quickly as possible.

There, standing bedside as nerve-wracked a father as ever there was, I watched with wide eyes as a giant needle was inserted into her spine. The contractions had become unbearable, and she'd needed a pain killer. For a moment, I felt woozy and had to steady myself even as Marline's bravery outweighing my own humbled me. A moment later, the epidural started working its magic.

Marline was fine.

Birth, the process of it all, including being the Dad, is a profound experience of the kind I'd never imagined possible. And, of a truth as sappy as it may sound, standing there and watching my seed brought into the world was, indeed, a gift beyond compare.

Little Terry came into the world with a head full of curly black hair. Next thing I knew the doctor slapped him on the butt. Who'd've thought a child's cry could sound so wonderful. Or so loud. Terry's little lungs bellowed out like trumpets. The moment was wonderfully surreal, even the part where the doctor shaped my son's funny-looking boxed head. There was no one there passing out cigars, but that was all right. I stood there proud and studly. Marline and I had done this. Never again have I witnessed anything as grand as the birth of my son.

Once the doctors cleaned the little fellow, the features he favored from his Mom and Dad became even more apparent.

The family moment between Marline, little Terry, and I will always stand as one of my too-few special memories, a clear still shot of something beautiful, something with which during dark moments of the soul, I could always recall in my mind's eye.

With Marline exhausted and needing her rest, it was time for me to leave. However, during the drive home, instead of precious memories of the day's grand events filling my mind, I found myself heavy-hearted. There was a war taking place within me, two screaming voices; one of reason and the other from the lungs of the crack-monster. What I wanted, though, at least for the moment, was to simply be a man who loved his family. Not wanting to be alone, perhaps too afraid that the monster would win, I soon found myself back at Marline's bedside. Now, family and friends had stopped by. They were mindful of me, but wonderfully supportive of Marline, and understanding of the need for two new parents to have some time. I stood amazed at how Marline had blossomed into such a beautiful woman and thought of how much had changed since we first met downtown on Fourth and Pine Street when she was merely fourteen. I remembered, too, how she'd initially been swept by the looks of pretty boy, Dana. My perseverance, however, had paid off. Now, here she lay, face swollen from the pregnancy but looking as bright as the North Star.

Then things turned somber within me. There were things to sort out and questions that needed to be answered. And the scariest of them all: Where was fate going to take my family and me? And would the monster win?

Sadly, I was going to find out.

It was around this time when I truly became afraid. If you don't want to dance with the Devil, don't go to the hall. I should've never taken that first hit in the way-back-when. All I had done was light an ember that would become a flame.

And fire burns, consumes, and destroys.

*****

Mark was back at the reformatory and whenever we talked, the conversations were piercing. One can imagine what a younger brother would say: I always wanted to measure up to you, man, but how the hell can I do that now with you being a crackhead? And how does an older brother answer? Sorry, but you see, for whatever reason, I have an obsessive/compulsive addictive personality with a predilection towards self-destructive behavior once I've been put on the hook by multiple substances and bad habit patterns, and it'll probably take me the better part of my lifetime to learn how to channel that disposition into something positive?

Yeah, right.

256

Connecting with my brother on the phone started happening less and less; after all, I was never home. I heard of his love, his castigations, his concerns, laments, and reproofs, through Marline. It wasn't my intention to neglect my brother, or hell, anybody, but there it was. My real mistress wasn't Marline or any woman. My real passion wasn't a job, my children, or anything positive or remotely lofty. It was the monster. A love affair that would last the better part of two decades. Only by the grace of God, was the monster's hand stayed from killing me.

The power of this drug—if not any drug—is unthinkable. Guys I went to school with turned into drag queens, others buried into sexual depravity the likes of which would make the Marquis de Sade blush, and with women ... oh, women have it worse, with more always expected, slavery, and the loss of children— a person lost their sanity, their soul.

The horrors of drugs are endless.

Chapter Thirty-One

THERE WAS NO EMBER, not anymore, not even the pretense; my addiction was now in full-bloom, an omnipresent driving flame that made it nearly impossible to enjoy any aspect of life that might be deemed as normal. No matter who I was with, or what I was doing, I found myself constantly jostled by the need to light.

I did make an earnest effort to keep the holidays festive for my three children. Little Terry was now two-years-old and no longer so little. Seemed like only yesterday he'd been just a tiny bundle. I'd been there to hear his first words, "Da-da." I'd watched him take his thousand-plus Mom-assisted steps before he was finally ready to step out on his own, and I was there to see how he'd wonderfully taken ownership of the home, with the beds, the furniture, our stuff ... everything becoming his as springboards to jump, to play with, or to adventure with. And with the month of December, every day held Christmas cheer for my piece of flesh and blood, my son.

*****

Even after our breakup, Donna and I were somehow able to keep, if not an unconditional friendship then certainly an amendable and friendly one. And with Renata, my daughter, the woman loved her as if she were her own; Renata stood sweet on her, too. There were times, however, when I looked upon their relationship with disapproval. Now, why'n the hell would that be? Easy. Envy. Donna had her stuff together; I didn't. She had a lot of love for kids. Affection that children could not only perceive

258

existed, but that they could feel, which translated into a knack with children—her children and my own—especially during Christmas time when she'd literally dole the stuff out.

Unfortunately, this would be the last Christmas Renata and Donna would spend together. They would never see one another again. After everything that I had put Donna through, she still always made efforts to maintain, if not mend, our dysfunctional relationship. I understood her to be earnest, but I was off to the races for the sake of a monster. After finally accepting the inevitable, that I would always be unattainable, perhaps to anyone, she eventually told me she'd be getting married in June. She asked if I'd be there to share in her happiness on her special day. In candor, I made sure she knew I wouldn't be anywhere in the vicinity, but that my blessings would always be with her.

*****

Christmas was a thrill for Terrell, too, with his grandparents lavishing him with gifts. I should have been solely happy for my boy, but looking at all his presents, the elaborate train set stretched across the living room floor, the battery-operated car so big it could've fit me, along with all the rest just made my gifts seem paltry and insignificant. It was all I could do not to turn around and leave. Fortunately, I stayed, but I couldn't help but feel that once again I'd failed.

Terrell, on the other hand, was all Ho-Ho-Ho and wanted me to have fun with him, to be a part of his world of mirth. I suggested we go outside. I had seen a football on the porch, and I wanted to watch him zoom up and down the pavement in his fancy red car. Eager to please, my boy shot out the door.

After zipping around in his new ride, I put him through his paces with the football, tiring him out with some drills until he was more than ready to go back inside where it was warm and dry.

While we'd been enjoying the fun and games, his mother, Gwen, had been watching from the window. I often wondered what she was thinking when I'd see her smile from Terrell's excitement or frown from us nearly having an accident. I supposed two things: that she may have been wishing we were a family instead of us having this division, or that this was her only child and I had him out in the middle of this dangerous street in his plastic car.

Despite these sad times, the saga of my self-destruction continued undeterred. Gwen was just one more good woman that I allowed to fall by the way. Corruption had robbed, and was continuing to rob, me of any semblance of a normal life.

*****

My crack consumption had increased dramatically. And when I wasn't using, I constantly waited for the next hit in turmoil with my stomach twisted and knotted. By this time, any thoughts of abstinence, even those of fantasy, had gone by the wayside.

Along with my downward spiral using the stuff, there was also the growing problem of getting it, of finding the cash and a reliable dealer, and then a safe place to use (like there was such a thing) ... and then the cycle would start all over again.

I began picking up strangers in crack-infested areas in the middle of the night. About four in the morning, out on one of my seemingly impossible crack pursuits, I was driving around depressed that I hadn't scored when I decided to give the hunt one final shot. This led me to drive to the other side of town. Hitting the area, I saw a man with the largest pair of eyes I've ever seen in my life, giant orbs the size of silver dollars. Then the man noticed me and his eyes grew bigger. I knew his look. He was a crack addict. And though I'd yet to reach the depths of his depravity, I knew we were brothers of sort.

This owl-eyed fellow ran up to my passenger door saying, "Let me in! Let me in!" With the rain pounding away outside the car, all I was hoping for was him maybe pointing me in the right direction; I'd give him some pocket change and be on my way. Instead, the man shot to my passenger side and got in, him and the smell. Gawd, the stench, like something dead and flayed open on a pathologist's table, old, rotten, and with a mix of spoiled chicken eggs.

And it was all okay. The man knew where we needed to go. With that kind of information, I'd sit with anyone or anything.

It was just my luck, though, that we had to travel several miles to get where we needed. With the windows down, I tried engaging the man in conversation. But what do you talk about with a 24-hour crack-chasing clucker? Answer's easy. Crack. How good it is, how bad it can be, how much a person's pissed when they end up buying bunk, and of course, from the passenger, whether or not you wanted to buy this piece or that piece of paraphernalia.

Once we arrived, my foul-smelling guest had the audacity to ask for money. My experience in Oakland, however, had taught me a lesson. Rather than just sit there, I handed him $50 and said, "Let's go."

"You can't go with me. They'll think you're a cop."

"Don't worry about it. Let's just do our thing, and then I'll drop you off back at the transit stop."

With a nod, he led off towards what I could see was an afterhours. The thought of going in didn't thrill me, would be too easy to meet people I knew around town, fellow partyers, gamblers, women, the works; the last thing I wanted was for any acquaintances to see me with this guy. The one benefit to the place was a single entry/exit. I was able to stay in the back while my partner made the transaction. The least of my worries was something going wrong.

Going inside, my man quickly surveyed the place looking for his dealer.

Normally, a drug-dealer wouldn't stand for anybody approaching them out in the open, especially when out in public, but business is business. All I could do was hope things finished as quickly as possible. I'd already caught some curious glances from some of the guys I regularly played pool against— not good. No doubt they were wondering why I was acting standoffish and not joining in on the fun, but the reality was my mind wasn't thinking about pool. Moments later, despite whatever damage my reputation took, my partner started making his way back, flashing his yellow-toothed smile.

Good. The deal was done. I was still stuck driving him back to the other side of town, but for only the cost of a piece of dope and a lift, it· was a fair deal. Besides, I didn't know if I'd ever need this freaky-eyed fellow ever again; networking... always gotta be makin' and keepin' one's connections.

Driving away, again with the windows down, my nose started to burn, and my stomach to roil. I was about to wretch. My passenger was putting out massive amounts of gas, if not outright shitting his pants. "Gawd, man, what are you doing? You're killing me."

"I'm sorry, can't help it. I need a hit, gimme a little and it'll stop, all I need is a hit. Just pull over and fire me a puff."

"A puff? What's that gonna do, fix your clothes?"

Maniacal laughter. "Yeah, I know ... ain't changed nothing in, I dunno, two weeks." More laughter.

Oh, Lord, what was I doing?

Finally, we were at the man's stop. I pulled over and wished him a good day as I let the man out. He started to step out into the downpour, but suddenly stopped and leaned back towards me, his face sporting a hideous smile.

"Hey," he said, eyes buggin'. "Ever have a blow job while huffin', yo glass?"

Horrified, I started to yell, "You better get your crazy black a —," but the words got cut off in my throat as the man leaped out and started running down the street laughing like the Mad Hatter.

Networking. Never forget the importance of networking.

(Twenty-two years later, I'd see this same guy again in prison, and incredibly, he'd pretend as if the proposition had never happened: For people such as him, men and women, not remembering such an event is not beyond the realm of possibility, but he knew, and he knew I remembered as well. He tried mixing with the fellows and me until I gave him a blazing stare. Getting the message, he shuffled off with his head hung low.)

A few weeks later I drove down to San Diego to recoup my jewelry from the car dealer; the man was not only surprised to see me, but stunned that I had brought the cash to not only reclaim my gems, but to pay off my car as well. It took a while, what with the man trying to steer me towards some other fantastic deal, but after realizing my frustration and probably getting tired of his own procrastination, he went to the safe and returned my jewelry. The one fatal error made... me not paying off Marline's car at the same time. Deal done, I headed straight back to Seattle before anyone missed me.

*****

The moon beamed brightly one Saturday night, I was stuck at a red light heading to a nightclub out by the "Space Needle" when suddenly, Jasmine pulled alongside me. I was thrown off-guard momentarily, especially seeing that I was the one left behind in San Francisco. And now, what were the odds? Whatever the reason for her being back in town, I figured it was better for us to keep our separate ways. Jasmine, however, being the way-out person that she was, couldn't leave well enough alone. She started to follow me. As I pulled into the parking lot of the nightspot, she came in close behind and started yelling at me as I headed for the front door. Ignoring her, all I could do was hope she'd just go away, and let me enjoy my night out.

A hand gripped my arm. "Terry, wait a minute. We need to talk."

"Would've figured you'd be all talked out after that Dear John."

"Terry, I can explain."

"Really? I wouldn't have guessed. Now, why don't you just head on out and go back to Richie Rich."

"We aren't together anymore, okay ... shit. The bastard was a controlling pig ... treated my kids like crap and me like a piece of furniture. I left him."

"Well, good for you. And I mean that ... I ain't mad. Way we live, disappointment's part of the game."

Silence.

"Look, let's get out of here and talk over a hot meal."

Agreeing to Jasmine's request, I got in her car and we left for a restaurant. On our way, she said, "How's Grandma Bessie? You eat any soul food lately?"

"I've been to Cali twice since. Grandma's fine. Food's the same."

"When can we go back?"

"Say what?"

"I thought we could, you know, start over."

"Sounds brilliant, Jasmine. Couple of players going all Peaches & Herb. Might be better this time out if we just try being friends."

"That's fine, Terry. That's all I want." Her hand reached over and gripped my knee, then rose, kneading my thigh. "But after all this time apart, even friends can know how to have a 'hello' ... at least for one night."

Sitting there, my dark browns boring into her, I couldn't help but be amazed that this gorgeous, unpredictable woman still burned for me.

My mind also turned to Marline and our soured sex life. With crack serving as a kind of a sexual nitrous oxide, I'd become insatiable, coming in off the streets and venting my lust on Marline. There was no love in my insatiable desires, just the constant desire to have at it. Marline knew this and didn't care for just being used ... or just servicing me. No bother. When she wasn't available, I took my needs elsewhere.

After all, after being in prison I was due, right? Man's gotta make up for lost time, and it ain't no bother whose heart was trampled in the process.

With Jasmine's hand on me, and the promise of her luscious, six-feet of purebred female anatomy, I couldn't resist; and with the romp that followed, the throng of pillow-talk lies, and the false promises made, we did our thing; giving me a haunting memory to last a lifetime. This would be the final act between us.

*****

The thing about lust, about addiction, is that it's insatiable — it consumes. I started pawning my jewelry again, and with a monster that continually had to feed, I left it pawned beyond the expiration date. Marline, covering for and supporting me, suffered, too, with car payments several months overdue. I'd never gotten around to paying them as I had promised. Matters worse, Marline got into a car accident that required several repairs.

One rainy Seattle morning, I hurried out to my day's various runs when I found my car missing. Confused, I didn't know what to do, or what had happened. Dumbstruck, I talked to Marline but not having had a clue of what had happened, she wasn't of any help. For a split-second, I could identify with the many car owners that Mark and I had stolen from.

For hours, I racked my brain until Marline suggested I call the dealer. He confirmed that he had repossessed my car, due to not being able to locate Marline's. Who would have thought that a California lot would have connections with a local Washington Dealership? I argued with the dealer:

"Why'd you take my car? I paid for my car. 'Sides, it's worth a hell of a lot more than hers."

But the man stood firm, mumbling a bunch of legal jargon, reminding me of the contract I'd signed, that I had 90-days to handle my financial obligation before my car would be auctioned. What to do, what to do? The lie flowed easily. I promised the man he'd have his balance within the next three months.

Easy peasy.

With me out on the streets more than at home, sharing a car with Marline was a pain. But that kind of minor inconvenience paled to the condemnation and self-loathing felt whenever I did make it home to find my two-year-old welcome me with knowing eyes. Strange the way I would pick him up and he'd wrap his arms around my neck and gaze into my dilated eyes, every part of him seeming to cry out, 'Daddy what's wrong with you?'

*****

During one of my regular visits to my Mom's kitchen, she asked, "Son, you're not on that drug they call crack, are you? Don't be telling me you've been messin' with the stuff."

"Mom, does it look like I'm on drugs?"

"Naw, son, it doesn't."

"Well, good. Now let's talk about something else."

"Like what?"

"Like what you got cookin' that's causing that aroma."

"Boy, that all you do ... come over to eat me out of house and home."

"Don't be saying that, Momma; you know I come by to see about you."

"Kind of hard to tell when all you do is hang out at the dining table."

With Mom having the right of it, all I could do was laugh. At the same time, I had to find a way to get out of this line of conversation and, instead, get my lips greasy (the word, by the way, is pronounced gree-zee) from the homemade batter on her deep-fried chicken, 'fore gobblin down her red beans, dirty rice, and hot water cornbread. And if that got me too full, half of her sweet potato pie was leaving with me, too. No need to worry, either. No need for any denial. Mom already knew the truth... That I was a soul food junkie, and man, did the woman love to feed my jones.

Leaving Mom's pad, the thought occurred that maybe I should do something special for her. Mom loved perfume. With Eternity the hot new fragrance, I decided I'd get her a bottle.

267

About this time, Samuel's sudden death was fast approaching. Samuel and I were not friends, nor did I have any respect for him as a man or as a stepfather; he was just too mean. At the same time, I didn't harbor any contempt towards him, either. Since I was a kid in Louisiana, if I'd seen one, I'd seen a thousand grumpy old men just like him.

With a neck full of metal clamps, and a breathing tube inserted down his throat, Samuel sat confined to his favorite corner of the couch. He had throat cancer. Daily, he'd just sit, waiting for the Grim Reaper to come and make his call.

The results of his cancer medication, along with his diminishing health, had the whole of his and Momma's place smelling like death. A person can take such a sight for only so long. Samuel had been a mean ol' cuss his whole damn life, but I wouldn't have wished such a thing on anybody. Looking at the man wilt away was such an awful sight that my trips to Mom's and her kitchen grew less frequent. And when I think about how my Mom dealt with it all, day in and day out, I stand in awe. Where does a person find such strength?

Samuel even tried making peace best he could, writing short notes, and using friendly hand gestures. He let me know that it had never been personal. He'd just been selfish, wanting Mom all to himself. That he'd never bargained raising a bunch of kids.

By chance, I just happened to call one day to see how Samuel was doing. He'd died. Breaking the news, Mom broke down herself, and I was taken aback. I'd grown used to Mom keeping a trap on her emotions. But with the revelation of Samuel's passing on, Mom was no longer reserved. Rather, her love and grief came pouring out.

I accompanied Mom to the funeral. Unable to tell Mom no, there'd been no way out of the duty. But with the service, my mind couldn't help but go back to similar events in Louisiana, what with all the organ playing, the whooping and hollering, and people saying their peace and telling all the various lies: He was a good man, a God-fearin' man. Loved his family, he did. Gonna miss him, and all he did. May he rest in peace.

Rest in peace?

Why 'n-the-hell should a person be laid to rest buried under a mound of lies?

To this day, still doesn't sit well with me. At the same time, I'm older and there are moments when I think that when my number is called, perhaps it wouldn't be too awful if a lie or two were told about me.

Book Two

CRAACKED! MEMOIRS FROM A PRISON CELL

AS I WALKED TO THE EAST SIDE of the tenth floor, I started to hear a battering noise. Looking up at one of the tanks, it was my son, Terrell, crashing his fist against a window to get my attention. Once again, with one of my children, the mere sight of him was bittersweet, except in this case, the bitterness cut deep into my soul like never before. Barely in his twenties, my son's life was already mirroring mine, and there was no way that the both of us imprisoned was coincidence. The stark truth was that I had laid the brick of this dark path that Terrell was now traveling.

Quickly, I shoved my bedding into my cell, then hit the defective intercom button. The desk officer's voice, low in volume and full of static, came on. "What do you need, Mr. Hill? You just stepped inside."

"Was hoping to come out and have a word."

The guard racked my cell door. "Let's get this done." Over the years, this same guard watched me come and go through the prison's revolving doors, and he knew that whatever prison games I might be involved in, I never bothered the staff with anything frivolous.

Getting to the guard, I laid it out straight. "Just saw my son." I pointed to where Terrell was looking down at us. The guard nodded, told me to wait a moment, then verified that I was telling the truth. In short order, Terrell and I had ten minutes together.

In full view of the general population, my son and I gripped each other in a tight embrace. Then we set about trying to

270

comfort one another, him with a possible 30-year sentence hanging over his head, and me with my three strikes.

After about six or seven days trying to greet each from our respective tanks, I set things in motion to move back to the eighth floor, anything to get me away from the agony of being incarcerated with my son.

Not only were Terrell and I under a heavy amount of stress, but the whole facility, and especially those facing life. Among the three-strike candidates, two were losing their wives while a host of others were doing their best to zone out with medication; anything to distract them from the hell of watching the clock.

'Bama, with whom I'd kept company with before my surgery, was now in confinement. He'd already struck out and was now in the process of appealing his life sentence. When I finally did get to see him again, he seemed fine, and he had even maintained his sense of humor that had proven so invaluable to so many. I asked him how he could handle his days so easily, without a care in the world, filling his time with soap operas, Black Entertainment Television, and his usual display of wisecracks. His answer was simple.

"I ain't got nothing to worry about, no matter what happens."

"How's that?"

"I've already made my decision, and it doesn't matter about my appeal, either. I'm just here temporarily. One way or another, I'm gonna have my freedom. I ain't doin' life for nobody."

While Alabama carried on with his impenetrable sense of stalwart resignation, my attorney, Ramona, hammered out my mitigation proposal, charting how right out of the gate, my life had been derailed; slow start in school, tumultuous years with Inez and John, the various group and foster homes, and lastly, the lifelong alcohol and drug problem that had shackled me throughout most of my life.

Ramona seemed confident that the court would show mercy, but I had my doubts. More times than I cared to remembered, I'd seen men and women, faces full of tears, pouring their hearts out before the bench but rarely receiving any compassion. Not only that, but I sympathized with such a reality more than I wanted to. Why? Because more times than I cared to remember, I'd seen men and women try to play the system, doing their best to deceive those they'd deemed as suckers. Hell, I'd been one of them. Seemed that a man like me, sincere or not, was more-'n-likely gonna be crushed by the wheels of justice--a deserved fate for a life so wasted.

Negativity notwithstanding, I continued to assure Ramona that I was staying positive, and furthermore, that I was grateful beyond words for all she was doing.

Then, not a week before my court appointment, Ramona came bearing news: the prosecutor was offering twenty-some-odd years, plus my I.O.U.'s.

Holy hell! There was no way I could imagine doing that kind of time ... or maybe worse, that maybe I could. "Ramona, that would put me out of here in my 60s."

"It's still a chance at freedom."

"But it's not a chance at a life."

Ramona turned serious. "Listen, Terry, here's the thing. The prosecutor has made it clear, if you take this to trial, he'll amend two more charges, either one of which will strike you out if you're found guilty. Plain and simple."

I stared at the woman, the cold truth of the corner I'd painted myself into wracked my guts. Then I saw Ramona start to tear up. "Listen, I know you've done your best, but continue to fight."

"I'll do my best, Terry, but I can't give you any guarantees."

"Just fight the fight."

And Ramona did, wisely using her time between court dates to bargain with the prosecutor. In short order, she returned with a new deal: fifteen-years plus the two that I owed. Ramona seemed to be happy with the offer, but I was not. I urged her to keep trying.

Not a month later, she returned. The prosecutor had said his deal was set, that I had to take it or leave it. Furthermore, Ramona said that she was all tapped out, that there was nothing more she could do. I had a week to come to a decision. Seven days to weigh it, the balance of the rest of my life.

That first night after getting the news, sleep stayed a stranger. And in the days to follow, I could hardly eat, often skipping meals or otherwise eating alone. I could tell that 'Bama was going through the ringer as well. His joking days had apparently come to a halt, and then I found out why. He'd finally gotten a ruling. They had struck him out. *Damn.*

A few days later, right after breakfast an emergency code came through the loudspeakers. I remember standing against a wall as medics rushed by. And then the word got out, right before my court date, too, that 'Bama had committed suicide.

'Bama's words replayed themselves over and over again through my mind: I ain't doin' life for nobody.

Rumor-mill had it that the man had overdosed on psych-meds and ended up having a heart attack in his sleep. No more would that foot-tall flat top of his bring a smile to my face ... at least not outside of my memories.

Made in the USA
San Bernardino, CA
20 June 2017